ALSO BY CHRISTOPHER M. SCHRADER

Catch of the Day
Don't Rock the Boat
Righteous Anger

Beyond a Whistle and a Prayer

Transforming Lives, Pursuing Excellence,
Honoring Jesus through Coaching

CHRISTOPHER M. SCHRADER, PHD.

Touch of Grace Ministry: "Teaching the Mind, Reaching the Heart, Moving the Feet"

ISBN: 978-1-4834-2669-3 (sc)
ISBN: 978-1-4834-2668-6 (e)

Lulu Publishing Services rev. date: 2/19/2015

Contact the author at: touchofgraceministry@gmail.com

100% of all proceeds for the sale of this book are being donated to the Gazelle Foundation, providing clean water to the nation of Burundi: www.gazellefoundation.org.

DEDICATION

To coaches who have gone on to glory, like Dave Barkley: *Soli Deo Gloria*
To coaches who continue to labor, like Jim Bevan: *Inch-by-Inch*
and Gilbert Tuhabonye: *Run with Joy*
To coaches who will join this mission field, like Bree Schrader: *You Got This*
To Jesus: *The same yesterday, today, and forever!*

"I resigned myself quietly to the will of God and prayed not so much for victory but for the grace to run up to my capabilities."

(John Delaney, 1500 meter Gold Medalist, 1956 Melbourne Olympics)

ACKNOWLEDGEMENTS

With all the research required to write this book, I am more convinced than ever that the author of Ecclesiastes stated it correctly: "…there is nothing new under the sun. Is there a thing of which it is said, 'See, this is new'? It has been already in the ages before us" (1:9-10). Therefore, I am deeply indebted to all those who have gone before me and written bits and pieces about coaching that gave me further insights to write specifically about a practical theology of coaching. Thanks to all the former athletes I have had the opportunity to coach and learn from throughout the years. I am truly sorry I did not understand more of what it meant to build my coaching upon the rock-solid tenets of God's Word. Many of you ended up being guinea pigs. I hope and pray the experiments didn't go too awry. Most of all, I thank my wife, Lea, for her continual dispensing of grace upon my life. Without her, I never would have hit the first stroke on the keyboard and continued on to the finish. Lastly, I am thankful to God for blessing us with our daughters. Maddee is not only a true scholar but a superior editor who corrected mistakes and offered insights throughout this process. Bree is running for the Baylor Lady Bears and pursuing an education that will enable her to one day join the collegiate coaching ranks.

May the Lord bless your reading of this book so that transforming lives, pursuing excellence, and honoring Jesus through coaching becomes more and more of a reality in your circle of influence.

CONTENTS

APPENDICES

1

LET YOUR LIGHT SO SHINE

Forty years ago, I embarked on an adventure while riding in the back seat of the family station wagon. It was a journey that would forever change my life – my first day of high school. For most people that day brings with it an ounce of uncertainty. At 4'10" and 90 pounds, my doubt tipped the scales towards trepidation. My mind reeled, my stomach churned. *Gulp* was the only sound that continually rose from the depths of my throat. I was entering a high school in Southern California that had about three thousand students. It was in a district that, throughout the years, produced a plethora of top-tier high school and Division I athletes, as well as some professional and Olympic competitors. How would I be valued in the midst of such a setting?

The first day gave me a quick indicator. Several times I heard, "Hey, pipsqueak, the junior high school's down the street." My value rating plummeted.

But then a funny thing happened. I learned firsthand how this world values people based upon numbers and letters. The second week of school I ran my first cross-country race. I didn't know much about distance running, but I realized that being small in stature didn't matter. Week after week I was the number one freshman runner for our school. Every Monday morning my name was read over the P.A. system. People began patting me on the back and telling me, "Way to go." My English teacher even let me skip class every time I won a race. Life was good. The number one moniker made me highly valued. I ended the season with an unblemished record. The newspaper sang my praises. I was picked to be a varsity starter the next fall on a team predicted to be one of the top ten in Southern California.

Unfortunately, the sophomore jinx was waiting to pounce on my illustrious career. I had grown to 5'7" and was our second-place finisher the first three races of the season. I kept telling myself it couldn't get much worse. Then it did. As I awaited final instructions on the starting line, my coach walked up to me and said, "If you're not number one, you're nothing."

I was "nothing" through the rest of my high school career and well into my freshman year of college. My times improved, but not as quickly as my competitors'. The longer I stayed out of the top position, the further my identity tanked. I bit into the lie that the world had sold me – "Your value is based on letters and numbers." What was your time? What place did you finish? What was your GPA? What was your SAT score? In August of 1977, the summer after my freshman year of college, I dropped down on my knees out of sheer desperation, repenting of my sins and asking Jesus to be my Lord and Savior. I had been told time and time again that Jesus loved me, not because of something I had done, or could do, but because he created me. I was praying it was true.

Afterwards, God laid on my heart a passion to help other athletes see their value as portrayed on the cross, not on the scoreboard. Three years later, I received my first opportunity as a volunteer assistant at Bethel College, a Christian university in St. Paul, Minnesota. But I was still so immature in my faith and coaching experience that I struggled with trying to help our runners to balance glorifying Christ and seeking to beat the competition. Coaching a team to try to win an athletic contest is part of what it means to compete. But how could I do that in a way that glorified Jesus and brought joy to the lives of my athletes? I had no idea, but it had to involve more than a whistle and a prayer.

Five years later, while coaching high school cross country, track, and soccer, I pursued my M.A. degree in education with an emphasis on psychology. My thesis was *Teachers, Tinkers, or Toymakers: Coaches Must Be Accountable to Educate Today's Youth.* Unfortunately, the majority of what we were taught focused on secular psychology. I couldn't figure out how to make it mesh with Scripture, or whether I should even try. As I went back to the drawing board, I finished my master's in Theology at Fuller Seminary, and then completed my doctoral degree in Biblical Counseling. I finally felt that I had the grounding to pursue my passion. Nevertheless, God led me down a different path in ministry for fifteen years, but I was never far from athletics. I kept my hand in coaching whenever the opportunity arose, especially as our daughters participated.

Watching professing Christians coach in secular and sacred settings left me discouraged. Some were just as frustrated as I was when I started coaching. They desperately wanted to use their coaching to minister to their athletes and others, but they couldn't put the pieces together, whether they were in a 'secular' or 'sacred' setting. For others, their coaching was completely compartmentalized, separated from their faith. Their words and actions looked no different from the self-avowed atheists or agnostics on the other sideline. I saw the wreckage of kids' hearts, minds, souls, and bodies strewn across fields, courts, and tracks from the peewee level through college. Many left the sports world forever. So the seed continued to germinate in my soul, partially because I had been responsible for some of the suffering.

So why do I write this now? I have new motivation. Our younger daughter is in her fourth year as a scholarship distance runner for Baylor University. Her goal is to be a collegiate cross-country and track coach. She is presently working towards her B.S. in Exercise Physiology and then onto her M.S. in Sports Pedagogy. One of my greatest desires in writing this book is to do all I can to help her to pursue that passion in a God-honoring, Christ-exalting, Bible-saturated manner. By God's grace, I will succeed. Lord willing, it will bless the lives of others who already have that whistle around their neck, and those who will be joining the ranks in the future.

This book, however, is not written merely for those who are, or will be coaches. It is also for those parents whose children are, or will be, involved in organized sports. What are you praying for, looking for, and hoping for when it comes to coaches for your children? What training/equipping does the coach have or need? What is the vision/mission of your coach and the organization he/

she coaches under? Do your values mesh with the coach's and/or the sports organization/school? May this book help you to see more clearly as you seek to answer questions such as these. The majority of coaches out there have not been implicitly trained in anything beyond the X's and O's, and all-too-many don't even have that background. Do you know who is coaching your kids?

> I'm convinced that the classic result of what happens when you turn a group of young athletes over to a coach who has not been given any ethical standards or assistance in applying them, is that the win-at-all-costs philosophy takes over… Forget about developing character, forget about providing a model of good sportsmanship, and forget about whether or not the children are actually having fun.[1]

Too often, coaches who profess a love for and allegiance to Jesus are coaching without understanding the biblical purpose underlying what they are doing. Their understanding of sports is not theologically informed; it has been shaped by culture and the influence of prior coaches, but not by Scripture. In this situation, how do coaches seek to live out the admonition of 1 Corinthians 10:31? "So, whether you eat or drink [or coach], or whatever you do, do all to the glory of God."

> If your understanding of sports has been informed by culture and not Scripture, the development and expression of athletic skills will be more important to you than the development and display of godly character… The emphasis in Scripture is clearly on godly character and not athletic ability, personal statistics, or ultimately who wins. This must be our priority as we train our children in sports. Coaches, this must be your priority, as we entrust our children to you.[2]

As you will see, the problem is not limited to one age group, gender, or sport. It is not confined to the secular or the sacred. It is a systemic problem that must be tackled. Christian coaches need biblical truths and practical tools to go forward boldly, seeking to be leaders in the quest to redeem the Sports Nation. What about you? Why do you coach? Is the call of Christ being muted by the siren song of the scoreboard? Do you find yourself relying upon biblical slogans or the Spirit-infused Word to guide your coaching? Sadly, coaching is a ministry that many Christians have decided is not compatible with the Bible's rock-solid foundation:

> [T]he coach whose career best crystallized the tensions between living the Christian life and establishing a reputation as a winning coach was Amos Alonzo Stagg… He was hired in 1892 by the University of Chicago's president, who liked having a man "who could direct athletics and pray" at the same time. Yet Stagg's religion never interfered with his compulsion to win… [H]e established a remarkable reputation, not only as a winning coach, but as one who helped put college athletics on a win at all cost trajectory… In an exhaustive analysis of Stagg's career, Peter Iverson reached the disappointing but probably correct conclusion "that football's 'purity

man,' willingly stretched and broke the rules to win, while defending the game as a builder of good character."[3]

Coaches, do not take your influence lightly. Upon what are you building your ministry? Your words and actions will be remembered long beyond those of most teachers, and even those of many parents. What is the extent of this influence that has been bestowed upon you as coaches? Are you developing it and using it in a biblically-consistent manner? Consider carefully the story of seventeen-year-old high school pitcher, Taylor Hooton who hung himself in his bedroom in 2003. His father, Don Hooton, believes anabolic steroids killed his son, if not directly, then close enough.

> His parents and a doctor familiar with the case said they believe that Taylor's death was related to depression that he felt upon discontinuing the use of anabolic steroids. The sense of euphoria and aggression that accompany the use of steroids can be replaced by lethargy, loss of confidence, melancholy and hopelessness when a person stops using performance-enhancing drugs… After Taylor's death, his parents said they had learned from his psychiatrist that he had low self-esteem, and that to feel as if he measured up, he had to make himself bigger, and drive a big pickup truck. A junior varsity coach had also suggested to Taylor that he get bigger, Don Hooton said. Late last winter and into the spring, Don and Gwen Hooton, who is an elementary school teacher, began to notice changes in Taylor's physique and behavior. Taylor, who was 6 feet 1 1/2 inches, grew to 205 pounds from about 175 pounds.[4]

> Don Hooton remains furious with the coach of his son's high school team for making an offhand remark to Taylor about his physical stature. "What the hell are you telling a kid that big that he needs to get bigger to throw a baseball?"… "We are turning over our sixteen-year-old babies to coaches who are untrained. That really gets to the heart of the matter."… "Ultimately, it is Taylor's fault," he says. Yet, as well as anyone can, he also understands the power of coaches over impressionable eager-to-please young athletes.[5]

The time has come to place our coaching against the silhouette of Scripture in order to comprehend clearly what is the wheat to be kept and what is the chaff that is to be destroyed. My hope and prayer is that my background as an athlete in my forty-second year of competing, a coach of several decades, an ordained pastor for twenty-five years, and a biblical counselor for almost twenty years, will aid in bringing biblical truths and practical tools to you in a compelling and concise manner – simple, yet not simplistic. May the Spirit anoint my writing of these words, your reading of them, and our hearts living out the Lord's kingdom agenda so the Father will be glorified and joy will be brought to the Sport Nation.

Chapters 2 and 3 discuss more in-depth the problems that Christian coaches in the United States are facing today and why we must develop a biblically-informed response if we hope to honor Jesus. Chapters 4 through 10 focus on the development of specific biblical characteristics necessary to run the race well as you seek to hear, "Well done, good and faithful servant" when you lay your head upon the pillow each night. Each of these final seven chapters are broken into four or five bite-sized chunks with practical tools and prayers at the end of each section to aid you in transforming lives, pursuing excellence, and honoring Jesus through your coaching. I encourage you to not be in a hurry. Seek to apply the tools in each section to your own coaching before you move ahead.

"Do you not know that in a race all the runners run, but only one receives the prize? So run that you may obtain it. Every athlete exercises self-control in all things. They do it to receive a perishable wreath, but we an imperishable."[6]

Notes

[1] Fred Engh, *Why Johnny Hates Sports: Why Organized Youth Sports Are Failing Our Children And What We Can Do About It*, (Garden City Park, NY: Garden City, 2002), 84-85.

[2] C.J. Mahaney, "Don't Waste Your Sports" (Sermon, Sovereign Grace Ministries, Gaithersburg, MD, 2008), www.sovereigngraceministries.com.

[3] Shirl James Hoffman, *Good Game: Christianity and the Culture of Sports* (Waco: Baylor University, 2010), 132-133.

[4] Don Hooton, "An Athlete's Dangerous Experiment," *Taylor Hooton Foundation*. 12/18/20011, Accessed 4/23/2014. http://taylorhooton.org/taylor-hooton/.

[5] Mark Hyman, *Until It Hurts: American's Obsession with Youth Sports and How it Harms Our Kids* (Boston: Beacon, 2009), 107-109.

[6] 1 Corinthians 9:24-25.

2

THE SPORTS NATION

BOUNTY HUNTERS

Why did you decide to become a coach, whether as a volunteer or as a career? What were you hoping to accomplish? Perhaps you believe that today's youth who participate in organized sports will reap the benefits of improved health – such as endurance, coordination, cardiovascular fitness, muscle strength, and flexibility. What about building character? Do you believe participation in organized sports helps athletes to learn about self-discipline, teamwork, accountability, respect, humility and honesty? Or, if you are a parent, maybe these oft-stated benefits are reasons you've signed your kids up for a local team. Surely if you start them young they'll develop healthy mental, physical, and social lifestyles that will segue into their adult lives. I wish I could tell you that all this was inherently true, but all is not well in America's Sports Nation. The waters are tainted from the professional level all the way down to the pee wee leagues. Lord willing, however, Bible-saturated coaches armed with practical tools can help turn the tide.

Consider the darkness that was brought to light in New Orleans. Between 2009 and 2011, the New Orleans Saints were running an organized bounty system where players received bonuses for hits that sent opposing players to the sidelines - allegedly $1,500 for a player who was knocked unconscious and $1,000 if they were merely taken off the field on a stretcher. But that was pocket change compared to the $10,000 that was apparently offered to knock quarterback Brett Favre of the Minnesota Vikings out of the 2010 NFC championship game. During its investigation, the NFL discovered that head coach Sean Payton knew about the bounty program, though he was not directly involved. The brains behind the bounty system were defensive coordinator Greg Williams, in league with linebacker Jonathan Vilma. Yet Payton was just as culpable, because he failed to act on his knowledge of the improprieties.

This is not exactly the character development we hope today's youth try to emulate. So what message did the league send to try to stem the fallout from this black-eye affair, including the potential trickle-down effect? Sean Payton and Jonathan Vilma were suspended for the 2012 season. Three other players (Will Smith, Scott Fujita, and Anthony Hargrove) were suspended for varying lengths, from three to eight games. Former defensive coordinator Gregg Williams (since hired by the Tennessee Titans) was suspended indefinitely. But Commissioner Goodell went even further up the food chain and suspended the general manager, Mickey Loomis, for eight games.

After a second round of appeals heard by Former NFL Commissioner Paul Tagliabue, he decided that none of the players' punishments would be enacted. Tagliabue cleared Fujita of any wrongdoing. However, he did not absolve the other three players for their conduct that was detrimental to the league. Why the leniency towards the players? Tagliabue insisted that the crux of the problem lay within the organization as a whole: "My affirmation of Commissioner Goodell's findings could certainly justify the issuance of fines. However, this entire case has been contaminated by the coaches and others in the Saints' organization…coaches and managers led a deliberate, unprecedented and effective effort to obstruct the NFL's investigation."[1]

To sum up Tagliabue's findings, we can turn to that great theologian, defensive end Julius Campbell from the film *Remember the Titans*: "Attitude reflects leadership!" The head coach, and others in leadership positions, chose to do nothing when they discovered the unethical, unsportsmanlike actions of their players – after all, they were winning.

Some may protest. "But that bounty program operated on a professional football team! What does Sean Payton have to do with Christian coaching? Have you ever heard him claim to be a Christian?" Fair enough. If you want me to balance the scales, we'll move on to someone who was a self-professing Christian at the time of his coaching debacle.

On October 6, 1990, the 12th ranked Colorado Buffaloes traveled to Columbia Missouri to play the 2-2 Tigers in a football game that would go down in infamy. The Buffaloes, under Coach Bill McCartney, pulled off a last-second victory thanks to an error by the officials. With thirty seconds left in the game, Colorado was given a 5th down which allowed them to score the game-winning touchdown. The mistake, however, was not discovered until after both teams had left the field. Neither the NCAA nor the Big Eight had any authority to tell Colorado what they should do. Yet, there was a precedence Colorado could follow. In 1940, Cornell trailed Dartmouth 3-0 late in the game. On a 5th down, they, like Colorado, scored the winning touchdown. Later, when films proved that Cornell had been erroneously given a 5th down, they forfeited the win, proclaiming Dartmouth the victor.

It seemed like it should have been an easy decision for Coach McCartney who was the founder of the Christian *Promise Keepers* men's movement that espoused maintaining ethical purity as one of their foundational tenets. But neither history nor McCartney's faith apparently held sway that day. Rather, McCartney pontificated how the poor field conditions were not a fair test for his team. "For us to forfeit under all these circumstances is absurd. If I felt like Missouri had outplayed us under fair circumstances and we were inadvertently given an extra play at the end, I'd have met with my coaches and really searched my heart to consider if we shouldn't forfeit the fame. But I don't feel like that,"[2] McCartney emphatically stated.

> The Colorado coach, joined by university president William Baughn, stood firm, refusing to forfeit the game… Later, in a television interview, McCartney invoked

the Bible when justifying the win. "I have to answer to my team. I can't answer to everybody out there. And there is a verse in Scripture – it's 1 Corinthians 4:4- and it says, 'My conscience is clear, but that does not make me innocent. It is the Lord who judges me.' And, you see, only the Lord can judge a man's innermost thoughts."[3]

Nowhere is the phrase "the ends justify the means" more evident than in the world of sports. Unfortunately, this lack of coaching integrity is not a new phenomenon. It is has merely become normative. Few coach and play for the love of the game anymore – the true meaning of "amateur" has been lost. Too many coaches at every level are adopting the mindset of professionals whom they see doing 'whatever it takes' in order get a competitive advantage. How does all of this filter down into the genesis of sports - the youth sports leagues? The Saints aren't the only bounty hunters in town:

> The 2011 Tustin Red Cobras, in suburban Orange County, one of America's elite youth football teams put bounties on the heads of opposing players. Four players and one assistant coach told the "Orange County Register" that they witnessed payments. They talked of how the head coach, Darren Crawford, described the program at a practice and at a film session along with the defensive coordinator. Players described receiving money for hard hits. When the Orange Empire Conference, the governing body for the team involved, investigated, it conveniently disregarded the evidence and found no wrongdoing occurred.[4]

Attitude reflects leadership. I wonder where the Tustin Red Cobras' coach got this idea. In the midst of this mayhem, Christian coaches must move beyond using the world's philosophies and sprinkling them all with a dose of prayer, all in the futile hope that this will honor Jesus. Biblical truths, and the practical tools founded up them, are the only way to properly navigate these turbulent waters.

For some in the Church, sports are meaningless diversions that keep us from focusing on God, from doing the "important" things in life. They are viewed as dangerous activities, infused with a myriad of opportunities to show how vile we are as human beings, as we seek to conquer and vanquish our opponents, to flaunt our superiority rather than our humility. For some, this is too true. Sports allow them to turn off their brains and forget about the world. Sports have become the golden calf [5] that many bow down to in hopes of finding meaning, a medicating effect, or a functional messiah in their lives.

But nothing we do in this life is meaningless. Not if the words of 1 Corinthians 10:31 are true: "So, whether you eat or drink, or whatever you do [coach or play sports], do all to the glory of God." So how do we coach to the glory of God? That is the question we seek to answer as we take this journey together.

SO OTHERS MAY LIVE

And Jesus came and said to them, "All authority in heaven and on earth has been given to me. Go therefore and make disciples of *all nations*, baptizing them in the name of the Father and of the Son and of the Holy Spirit, teaching them to observe all that I have commanded you. And behold, I am with you always, to the end of the age." (Matthew 28:18-20, italics mine)

Do you believe that this mandate reflects God's heart and mission from the foundation of the world? Consider God's promise to Abraham:

Now the LORD said to Abram, "Go from your country and your kindred and your father's house to the land that I will show you. And I will make of you a great nation, and I will bless you and make your name great, so that you will be a blessing. I will bless those who bless you, and him who dishonors you I will curse, and in you *all the families of the earth* shall be blessed." (Genesis 12:1-3, italics mine)

But God's heart and mission are not revealed only to Abraham. God also graciously chose to remind Isaac, Abraham's son, about the mission to the nations:

"Sojourn in this land, and I will be with you and will bless you, for to you and to your offspring I will give all these lands, and I will establish the oath that I swore to Abraham your father. I will multiply your offspring as the stars of heaven and will give to your offspring all these lands. And in your offspring *all the nations* of the earth shall be blessed, because Abraham obeyed my voice and kept my charge, my commandments, my statutes, and my laws." (Genesis 26:3-5, italics mine)

What about you? Have you been commanded to participate in this proclamation, this Great Commission? Do the words Peter spoke to the men of Israel in Acts 3:25-26 apply to you?

"You are the sons of the prophets and of the covenant that God made with your fathers, saying to Abraham, 'And in your offspring shall *all the families* of the earth be blessed.' God, having raised up his servant, sent him to you first, to bless you by turning every one of you from your wickedness." (italics mine)

Are you an 'offspring' of Abraham? Not sure? I believe Paul's letter to the Galatians will clarify your position.

Does he who supplies the Spirit to you and works miracles among you do so by works of the law, or by hearing with faith — just as Abraham "believed God, and it was counted to him as righteousness"? Know then that it is *those of faith who are the sons of Abraham.* And the Scripture, foreseeing that God would justify the Gentiles by faith, preached the gospel beforehand to Abraham, saying, *"In you shall all the nations be blessed."* So then, *those who are of faith are blessed along with Abraham,* the man of faith... [And] If you are Christ's, then you are Abraham's offspring, heirs according to the promise." (Galatians 3:5-9, 29, italics mine)

Does this describe you? Do you, like Abraham, believe God when he makes a promise? Do you believe in the covenant he offered through the blood-bought death of Christ on the cross, the cross that demonstrates that, "God shows his love for us in that while we were still sinners, Christ died for us"?[6] Did you "confess with your mouth that Jesus is Lord and believe in your heart that God raised him from the dead, you will be saved"?[7] Were you "buried with him in baptism, in which you were also raised with him through faith in the powerful working of God, who raised him from the dead"?[8] If yes, then "by grace you have been saved through faith. And this is not your own doing; it is the gift of God, not a result of works, so that no one may boast. For we are his workmanship, created in Christ Jesus for good works, which God prepared beforehand, that we should walk in them."[9]

So rejoice. You have been chosen to perform good works for Christ's glory. Now may you walk in them by seeking to fulfill your part of the Great Commission through coaching athletes. For you are a descendant of Abraham, the one through whom all nations will be blessed through the proclamation of the gospel. And Jesus promised that he would be with you, as a member of the Church, "always, to the end of the age."[10] So go forth boldly.

Still not convinced that coaching is a legitimate conduit through which your "good works" can be used by God to bring others to Jesus and grow them in Jesus? Are athletes worth reaching with the gospel? If yes, then who is better situated on a daily basis than a coach? Seek to serve your athletes in the culture in which you both operate.

> For though I am free from all, I have made myself a servant to all, that I might win more of them. To the Jews I became as a Jew, in order to win Jews. To those under the law I became as one under the law (though not being myself under the law) that I might win those under the law. To those outside the law I became as one outside the law (not being outside the law of God but under the law of Christ) that I might win those outside the law. To the weak I became weak, that I might win the weak. I have become all things to all people, that by all means I might save some. I do it all for the sake of the gospel, that I may share with them in its blessings. (1 Corinthians 9:19-23)

The Apostle Paul makes it clear that there is not one way to reach individuals, people groups, and the nations. Coaching is one path God has provided. To paraphrase Paul, "To the athletes I became an athlete." The only option we don't have in this scenario is whether or not we seek to reach out to the lost, the unreached, the non-Christian, or whatever other term you prefer. Let me leave you with bold words on reaching the lost from a most unlikely source:

> A few years ago atheist Penn Jillette, of the magician duo, Penn & Teller, expressed indignation at evangelicals who don't share their faith, asking, "How much do you have to hate somebody to believe everlasting life is possible and not tell them that? I've always said that I don't respect people who don't proselytize…. If you believe that there's a heaven and a hell, and people could be going to hell or not getting eternal life, and you think that it's not really worth telling them this because it would make it socially awkward—and atheists who think people shouldn't proselytize and who say just leave me alone and keep your religion to yourself—how much do you have to hate somebody to *not* proselytize? How much do you have to hate somebody to believe everlasting life is possible and not tell them that?"[11]

WINDOW OF OPPORTUNITY

But what does this have to do with coaching athletes? Consider the significance of these three well-known representative passages about the gospel: "…for all have sinned and fall short of the glory of God"[12]; "For the wages of sin is death, but the free gift of God is eternal life in Christ Jesus our Lord"[13]; "Jesus said to him, 'I am the way, and the truth, and the life. No one comes to the Father except through me.'"[14] If you hold these verses to be God-breathed truth, how can you not respond by sowing seeds of salvation and sanctification through your coaching? Many people participating in sports in the United States are perishing daily, forever separated from God. How can you, as an offspring of Abraham, not believe that you are also called to be a blessing to the nations, including the Sports Nation?

At this juncture, the conversation all too often turns its attention towards the nations *over there*. People have erroneously posited that the real work of reaching the nations with the gospel of Jesus Christ primarily entails leaving one's home borders. In that case, saying that coaching athletes in the USA can be a vital part of fulfilling The Great Commission seems foolish. But then how do we explain the fact that the United States received more missionaries in 2010 than any other nation, according to the *Center for the Study of Global Christianity*?

Jesus did not leave us with an either/or proposition. We do not either evangelize at home or go to a foreign land. After his resurrection, Jesus came to his disciples in Jerusalem and told them, "You will receive power when the Holy Spirit has come upon you, and you will be my witnesses in Jerusalem and in all Judea and Samaria, and to the end of the earth."[15] It is a both/and commandment. The disciples were in Jerusalem when Jesus told them they would be his witnesses in Jerusalem *and* to the ends of the earth. Coaching is an opportunity for you to worship God by sharing the gospel in word and deed. In the Old Testament, *Avodah* is translated "work" or "worship". Therefore, whether you are a full-time coach or a volunteer, that position is an opportunity for you to worship God through evangelizing and discipling those in your sphere of influence through your work, which is your coaching.

> "In spite of the fact that every country of the world has been penetrated with the gospel, four out of five non-Christians are still cut off from the gospel because the barriers are cultural and linguistic, not geographic."[16]

> Why is this fact not more widely known? I'm afraid that all our exultation about the fact that every *country* of the world has been penetrated has allowed many to suppose that every *culture* has by now been penetrated. This misunderstanding is a malady so widespread that it deserves a special name. Let us call it "people blindness," that is, blindness to the existence of separate *peoples* within *countries* - a blindness, I might add, which seems more prevalent in the U.S. and among U.S. missionaries than anywhere else. (Ralph Winter at Lausanne Congress on World Evangelism)[17]

By all appearances, this "people blindness" is adversely affecting the ability to gain in-roads for the gospel in the United States. Large numbers of peoples in America have not heard the pure, unadulterated counsel of the Bible in a cultural language that resonates with their hearts and minds.

> Two-thirds of the world's population -- more than 4.4 billion people -- live in the 10/40 Window [the area across Africa and Asia from 10 degrees latitude north of the equator to 40 degrees latitude north of the equator]. 90% of the people living in the 10/40 Window are unevangelized. Many have never heard the Gospel message even once. There are either no Christians or not enough of a Christian movement in many cultures of the 10/40 Window to carry out vibrant near-neighbor evangelism. If those groups are to be evangelized, believers will need to leave their own culture and enter another one where they will seek to plant the gospel, perhaps even learning a new language in order to communicate. Such cross-cultural evangelism is required because there are people groups with no church movements that are understandable or relevant to them.[18]

Just because there are churches on every corner in the United States, does not mean that "vibrant near-neighbor evangelism" is occurring. It is time to rethink what it means to "enter other cultures" and "learn new languages" in order to participate in gospel-centered, cross-cultural evangelism through coaching. If we agree with John Piper that, "Winter's message was a powerful call for the church of Christ to reorient its thinking so that nations would be seen as a task of evangelizing unreached peoples, not the task of merely evangelizing more territories," how do we determine who those unreached peoples are in the United States?

Perhaps you would take the 10/40 Window approach and look for the largest number of unreached people groups located in a geographic region within the continental United States. According to the Minnesota Amateur Sports Commission, there is a group in America that contains 35-45 million youth (ages 6-18) who are participating in organized sports. That number is approximately equivalent to the 41 million souls of Iraq and Israel, two countries located in the 10/40 Window. If these two countries are worth pursuing, so is the Sports Nation.

If that number is too much to wrap your brain around, consider the percentage of boys and girls (ages 6-18) who are involved: Between 52% and 69% of girls and 66% to 75% of boys in the United States participate in organized and team sports, according to the 2008 report titled *Go Out and Play: Participation in Team or Organized Sports* and the 2013 report by the Minnesota Amateur Sports Commission. Significantly, the majority of these participants are actively involved on more than one team, which would garner even more potential time for coaches to reach them with the gospel.

It is important to realize that the above numbers, however, don't even include the seven to eight million youth participating in high school athletics, or the half-million on collegiate athletic teams, or the millions of kids who start before the age of eight. These numbers are not going to drop anytime soon. The days of unstructured play on the neighborhood streets and playgrounds are rapidly diminishing. Organized sports are the wave we will ride for the foreseeable future.

WHY ENGAGE THE SPORTS NATION?

Is it legitimate to look upon these 45 million+ people, this Sports Nation, as a group to evangelize? What determines a 'people group'?

> What we have found, in fact, is that a precise definition is probably not possible to give on the basis of what God has chosen to reveal in the Bible. God probably did not intend for us to use a precise definition of people groups. That way we can never stop doing pioneer missionary work just because we conclude that all the groups with our definition had been reached… as long as the Lord has not returned, there must be more people groups to reach, and we should keep on reaching them.[19]

If these 45 million athletes aren't enough to awaken the need for reaching the lost, and sanctifying the saved, through coaching in this country, consider the ripple effect beyond the players, and beyond our borders. What television failed to spur on in the expansion of sports viewing, the internet and live-streaming combined with laptops, Smartphones, and tablets have taken to a level previously unimaginable. No one knows the exact numbers participating in sports as fans on any given day across the globe, but it is an undeniably huge percentage of humanity.

Still don't think coaching can be an effective tool, a God-honoring ministry, to reach the Sports Nation? Organized sports are here to stay. The Body of Christ is apparently all-on-board with participation at every level, including many self-professing coaches from the kindergarten through the college ranks, and all the way to the pros. The question is whether we are making a dent in helping coaches steer the ship in a Christ-exalting direction.

> "Coaches can be enormously influential in the lives of children. If you ask a random group of adults to recall something of significance that happened in their fourth or fifth grade classroom, many will draw a blank. But ask about a sports memory from childhood and you're likely to hear about a game winning hit, or a dropped pass, that, decades later, can still elicit emotion. The meaning that coaches or parents help young people derive from such moments can shape their lives."[20]

I know this is true in my life. I loved playing baseball as a kid in New York. My first chance playing in the 'majors', I was on a team sponsored by the local *Rexall Drugs* store. One of my older brothers played on the team sponsored by the *Combined Books* store. Playing catch with our dad and talking baseball during this period in my life is permanently locked into my memory and emotions. The next year we moved to Southern California, where I joined the Silver Spur Little League. It was my last year to play organized baseball. I retired at age eleven, thanks to a psychotic coach who yelled at me after every pitch I threw. I can still conjure up the visual of a red-faced madman clutching the chain-link fence, spittle flying as he screamed at every teammate who stood in the batter's box. That put me over the edge. Baseball was not fun anymore; I never picked up a baseball glove again. I became part of the seventy-percenters, leaving the sport never to return.

There is an ever-widening chasm the size of the Grand Canyon separating the tenants of the Christian faith and the operation of organized sports in the USA. Coaches, the task can seem daunting. But we must continue to bore deep and examine the landscape of the canyon in order to better comprehend how desperate the situation is, and the Biblical answers on how to close the gap.

Notes

1. NFL.com Wire Reports, "Paul Tagliabue Vacates Saints Player Bounty Suspensions," *NFL*, 12/11/2012, Accessed 12/24/2013, www.nfl.com/news/story/0ap1000000109646/article/paul-tagliabue-vacates-saints-player-bounty-suspensions.
2. Stuart Whitehair, "Colorado Football: CU vs. Missouri 1990 (The Fifth Down Game)," *Bleacher Report*, 6/23/2008, Accessed 4/20/14. www.bleacherreport/articles/31980-colorado-football-cu-vs-missouri-1990-the-fifth-down.
3. Tom Krattenmaker, *Onward Christian Athletes: Turning Ballparks into Pulpits And Players Into Preachers* (USA: Rowman and Littlefield, 2010), 169.
4. Leigh Steinberg, "Youth Football – Parents Gone Wild," *Forbes*, 11/3/2012, Accessed 12/12/2013. www.forbes.com/stes/leighsteinberg/2012/11/03/youth-football-parents-gone-wild/.
5. Exodus 32.
6. Romans 5:8.
7. Romans 10:9.
8. Colossians 2:12.
9. Ephesians 2:8-10.

[10] Matthew 28:20.

[11] Penn Jillette, "An Atheist Chastises Evangelicals Who Don't Evangelize," *The Gospel Coalition*, 7/21/2013, Accessed 12/31/2013. www.thegospelcoalition.org/blogs/justintaylor/2013/07/21/an-atheist-chastises-evangelicals-who-dont-evangelize.

[12] Romans 3:23.

[13] Romans 6:23.

[14] John 14:6.

[15] Acts 1:8.

[16] John Piper, *Let The Nations Be Glad!* (Third Edition) (Grand Rapids: Baker, 2010), 180.

[17] Ralph Winter in Ibid.

[18] Southern Nazarene University, "10/40 Window: Do You Need To Be Stirred To Action?" *Southern Nazarene University*, Accessed 12/2/2013, www.home.snu.edu/~hculbert/1040.htm.

[19] Piper, op. cit., 212.

[20] David Bornstein, "The Power of Positive Coaching," *New York Times*, 10/20/2011, Accessed 11/5/2013. www.opinionator.blogs.nytimes.com/2011/10/20/the-power-of-positive-coaching/?_r=0.

3

THE CHASM

"Winning isn't everything. It's the only thing!" I'm not sure what Vince Lombardi, the famed coach of the Green Bay Packers had in mind when he uttered these infamous words, but the impact continues reverberating across our sports fields. There is a stress-filled atmosphere where our youth are being taught in word and deed that sports are all about the scoreboard. Even Christian universities have been guilty of joining this campaign, sending the wrong message about the main objective of Christians who participate in sports as coaches and athletes.

"[Jerry] Falwell started an athletic program two years after founding Liberty University in 1971, and a few years later told a writer from *the Washington Post* that he wanted to field a football team that would beat Notre Dame. 'Winning is very important to us,' said Falwell… 'We want to win and we cry when we don't win.'[1] I'm not against the pursuit of winning a game. In fact, isn't that part of what it means to compete against another team or person in sports? But I have trouble with Falwell's apparent angst over losing, "We cry when we don't win."

"Second place means first loser" is the flag that flies over many programs. What about your team – is the Word of God the rudder by which you seek to guide your athletes or does your hand gravitate towards the helm that culture has provided? Higher education in America continues to preach the student-athlete, character-building mantra, but behind closed doors an entirely different agenda is brewing. From high school to college, many athletes are given free passes in the classroom and tutors are writing term papers in order to keep the players eligible for game time. Yet every coach interviewed about these 'possible' infractions appears shocked and dismayed that it 'might' be happening under their watch.

If you think this is overstating his case, then you'll have to explain the news that recently broke at the University of North Carolina regarding a study showing student-athlete reading levels. In 2010, UNC was being investigated by the NCAA for allegations that several athletes were given A's in bogus classes offered through the African and Afro-American Studies department. Now a study has surfaced that claims that 60% of UNC's athletes can only read at the fourth-grade to eighth-grade level, and some even lower than that. We all know this is not an isolated incident with America's collegiate 'student-athletes.' Who's looking the other way?

Coaches, the ripples of your actions or inactions can have temporal and eternal consequences, whether you are employed by a secular or sacred institution. How far are you willing to go to make sure your team is not "first loser", or worse?

> Several years ago, the president of a small Southern Baptist university allegedly ordered a failing grade to be stricken from the transcript of the school's basketball star, thereby preventing him from being dropped from the team. Later that year the young man played a key role in his team's winning a national championship... The school advertised itself as a Christian college ("committed to serving God and humanity"), the president was an ordained minister for whom the school's graduate divinity school is named, the tournament the team won (thanks to the altered transcript) was the National *Christian* College Athletic Association championship, and a failing grade in question had been earned in a religion class.[2]

If the coach was not complicit in this heinous act, then he was guilty for failing to properly shepherd his players in the front-end of the 'student'-athlete paradigm. If you have ever experienced that insurmountable tug between your 'convictions' and saving your career, what guided your actions? Don't get me wrong. I'm not advocating the YMCA "everybody wins and gets equal playing-time" mantra for all sports, at all times. At younger ages, that's a great philosophy to help introduce kids to sports. We all know, however, that the time will come when the better athletes will get more playing time, and trying to win/keeping the score will be part of the competitive equation. But even when that juncture arrives, winning should not be the central purpose, the apex for Christian coaches.

If sports are the wonderful vehicle touted as a prime tool for building the physical, emotional, and social contours of our youth, then why are seventy-percent opting out by the time they are twelve-years-old? Children are quitting youth sports in droves, according to *The Institute for the Study of Youth Sports*, because they are "not having fun, too much pressure, too much emphasis on winning, overbearing coaches and parents, and the coach played favorites." Christian coaches can play a vital role in helping reverse this trend. There's little point in playing if playing isn't fun. To many parents, fun is not part of the equation. The pot of gold at the end of the rainbow, the athletic scholarship, becomes a primary motivator to keep loading up the minivan. Coaches are often complicit in promoting this façade to unsuspecting families.

For the majority of athletes in the USA, an athletic scholarship is a mirage. "[A]ccording to the *National Center for Education Statistics*, only about one percent of 8th graders will end up receiving some financial aid to play NCAA Div. I athletics. That includes partial scholarships. The percentage receiving full athletic scholarships is even smaller."[3] For those fostering the dream of playing professionally, the dream is even bleaker. Despite this, the tactics of bolstering this ill-fated delusion that "all things are possible" continue from the time kids are toilet-trained. Christian coaches must honestly address this issue, as statistics clearly show:

[W]hat most of these athletes don't realize is that less than 2 percent of those athletes who specialize will play sports professionally, according to the American Academy of Pediatrics. This disappointment can often lead to more serious problems like depression, or a loss of identity, as all of the investment went into one part of the child's self image -- this is what actually leads to depression and a loss in self-esteem when a child realizes their dreams of playing professional sports aren't likely to come true, despite their rigorous training.[4] [The concepts of *self-image* and *self-esteem* present a problem for those whose identities are in Christ, not self.[5]]

My first experience coaching came thirty-three years ago as a volunteer assistant at a Christian university. Since that time, I've also coached peewee kids though high school athletes in public, private, and Christian settings. One constant refrain I have heard from too many young athletes after years of participation is, "This is too much like a job. It used to be fun!"

Who will survive and thrive longer in the sports arena, the athlete who feels constant pressure to win, get a scholarship, and make others proud, or the one who loves to play the sport? In the long run, internal motivation will always trump external cajoling, especially when guilt is used as a primary motivator. Consider how many people join gyms each January as New Year's resolutions because they know they need to get in shape. They dread dragging themselves out of bed in order to work out, and by February, they fail to set foot in another Zumba class. "Want to" will always beat "have to" as a long-term, joy-inducing motivator.

Coaches, how does your theology and methodology honor God and show respect to your athletes? Virtually every day in America, there are young athletes who have knots in their stomachs and lumps in their throats as they contemplate the next practice or the next game. These kids fear losing acceptance by a coach and/or parents if they perform poorly. They sense that the 'love' they receive is conditioned on whether they hit the ball, drain the shot, or pin their opponent. Too many are stressed trying to figure out what will make coach and parents happy. It's time to break out of the "Just win, baby" cul-de-sac.

NO PAIN, NO GAIN?

More of our youth are leaving sports at earlier ages because the quest for winning at all costs has driven some coaches to demand more days of practice, longer practice sessions and seasons, and specialization in one sport. This is leading to never-before-seen levels of burnout and excessive injuries in preteens. At one point, no one would have thought that "burnout" would be the reason some of our youth no longer participate in organized sports. Instead of quitting, however, some young athletes are literally destroying their bodies by ignoring the warning signs, all in misguided attempts to cope. Some turn to drugs, prescribed and/or illegal, to manage the physical and spiritual pain. Are Christian coaches complicit in this destruction of bodies that

God himself designed? Even secular psychology understands that coaches can/should have a positive impact in reducing this stress: "Coaches can buffer the stress of sports performance by helping young athletes to develop realistic, specific, and measurable goals. Decreasing unrealistic expectations will lower the risk of a negative sports experience and the likelihood of reduced athletic participation in the future."[6]

How are you guiding your athletes in setting realistic goals, and not allowing them, or forcing them, to drink from the often misinterpreted "I can do all things" Philippians 4:13 Kool-Aid? It is easy to fall prey to the trap of being influenced heavily by the cultural air you breathe, be it secular, or theologically-lite Christian air. For instance, some of today's youth are being encouraged to start specializing as early as age four or five. Call it the Tiger Woods Effect. Ever since parents saw tiny Tiger with a sawed-off driver make his appearance on prime-time television, the specialization race was on. If Tiger can do it in golf, and the Williams sisters in tennis, and Michael Phelps in swimming, then why not *Just Do It*® with little Bobby or Lucy?

Some coaches will argue that when they get kids who specialize at a young age, the athletes' skills are much more advanced when they get to high school and college. Few will disagree with that fact. However, the other side of the equation is daunting. Those same specialized athletes are more likely to develop overuse injuries than in the past when kids played a variety of sports while growing up. Specialization to better equip athletes is leaving many youth with bodies that are breaking down due to a lack of a respite during the year – a Sabbath, if you will. There is no break for the orthopedic surgeons who are operating at a frenetic pace to get these kids back in one piece either. We need to slow down and carefully examine our coaching.

The professionalization of youth teams from kindergarten through college is causing this egregious behavior to become normative. Many youth coaches hear stories about wounded-warrior professionals who play with broken legs, concussions, and other assorted serious injuries, and they think their athletes should have a similar mindset. God has equipped the human body with a myriad of warning signals. We as coaches must seek to heed these signals in a quest to care for those in our charge who are made in the image of God. Here's a sampling of the warrior mentality played out on the youth stage:

> In her book *Little Girls in Pretty Boxes*, author Joan Ryan tells stories almost too bizarre to believe about training that apparently was routine in the world of elite figure skating and gymnastics. Ryan writes about fourteen-year-old Kristie Phillips, destined to be the next Mary Lou Retton, training with a broken wrist while gulping twelve Advil and six prescription anti-inflammatories each day. Then there's Betty Okino, then seventeen, competing for the U.S. women's gymnastics team in the 1992 Olympics with stress fractures in her back and elbow – and a tendon in her shin held in place with a screw.[7]

Some will argue that these are elite athletes, and not the same as kids coming to youth sports leagues. I don't agree that it is acceptable to destroy a young person's body just because he or she is performing at an elite level, but I'll acquiesce. Here's the havoc that the warrior mentality is wreaking upon run-of-the-mill youth baseball players, as just one example:

> In 2000, [orthopedic surgeon James] Andrews and his colleague, Glenn Fleisig, reported performing Tommy John surgery on 17 youth and high school players, making up 18% of all elbow reconstructions they did that year. In 2010…there were 41 surgeries on kids making up 31% of the procedures. And Andrews says the stats have gotten worse. "The largest number of all those different groups, believe it or not, is high school kids… They outnumber the professionals. There was a tenfold increase in Tommy John at the at the high school/youth level in my practice since 2000"… Andrews said that 25% to 30% of kids who have Tommy John surgery aren't playing baseball two years later.[8]

CHILD PROTECTIVE SERVICES

Since my days as a kid, the guarding of children from child neglect/abuse has risen to heights that were unthinkable a few decades ago. We headed out the door for hours at a time, rode bikes, ran, and played war through the local neighborhoods and forest, no adult the wiser to where we were. Nowadays, the local elementary kids in our neighborhood don't even walk down the street by themselves to get to school. Middle school kids stand at the bus stop while minivans sit around the corner with moms watching until the bus arrives. But these same loving, protective parents sign their children up for youth sports teams every year, and most of them have no idea about the person coaching. They don't know what background the coach has in the sport, what the coach's prevailing philosophy on practice and games is, or what sacrifices are expected of the athletes and their parents. Who will hold the coach accountable when the warning signs of athletes' bodies are shouting, "STOP"?

The potential pain young athletes might endure often comes in more forms than physical. Can someone please explain why it's culturally acceptable for coaches to spit, curse, taunt, belittle, and sometimes even physically harm athletes? Imagine a concert recital where the first chair violin player badly misses a note. A squawking sound resounds throughout the room. The conductor jumps off his podium and gets nose-to-nose with the violinist. "I can't believe you missed that note! How many times do I have to teach you how to play that? Why am I wasting my time and efforts on you? You are a sorry symphony member who always lets down his team. Seriously? You're going to start crying? Get out of my orchestra pit, you momma's boy!"

Everyone would be in shock if that happened, yet it is often considered normal in the sporting world, no matter what age is involved. According to the Minnesota Sports Commission, 45.3% of kids participating in sports claim to have been called names, or been insulted.

One of [Coach] McLaughlin's favorite conditioning drills [for his lacrosse club] is running young Sky Walkers up and down flights of stairs at full speed until they are physically spent or feeling so ill that they throw up. This happens so often that McLaughlin has a standard response to a child who staggers off the steps with an unsettled stomach: "If you're going to throw up, throw up. But when you're finished, get up and get back in." The stern approach is necessary for children to get in touch with their inner lacrosse warrior or, as McLaughlin puts it, to master the sport's "mental aspect." Same for the repertoire of insults that McLaughlin has been known to hurl during particularly intense practices and games.[9]

Unfortunately, antics like McLaughlin's are not an anomaly. "Coincident with this spike in participation [of youth in organized sports in the USA] is America's top position in a survey of 22 countries that measured the number of adults who'd witnessed abusive behavior at a child's sporting event."[10] Too many coaches are following the Bobby Knight and Vince Lombardi drill sergeant mindset, verbally abusing in the name of motivation.

Fear certainly motivates, but it is absolutely not a God-honoring, Christ-exalting method to train and equip athletes. All it does is ratchet up the pressure, decrease the fun, cause kids to leave the sports they used to enjoy, and teach kids that their ultimate value is tied to a game, which is a meaningless event, in and of itself - unless it is tethered to Scripture. If we never had organized sports, life would go on. Organized sporting events, though we enjoy participating in them as athletes and coaches, are nonessential. They are not necessary to our survival, nor are they equivalent with love, food, water, air, and shelter. Yet they are being presented to our youth as life or death scenarios, with phrases like "This is our time! This is our house! This is what people will remember!"

Too many of our youth are dying slowly due to their coaches. Are you guilty of playing Russian roulette with your athletes' health in the quest to get that almighty Win? The plight of eating disorders associated with sports like distance running, figure skating, and diving have long been known. Yet the potential danger continues to be accepted, or given a blind-eye to by some coaches, as these athletes ride a razor's edge in the quest to be as lean and light as possible. In a study of Division I college athletes, one-third of women reported attitudes and symptoms placing them at risk for eating disorders. Could your words cause athletes to drift towards unhealthy eating habits? They definitely played a role in Kimiko Hirai Soldati's plunge into the horrifying pit of bulimia.

When Soldati was on the gymnastics and diving teams in high school, one of her coaches jokingly told her she was "getting big." Another time when she asked a college coach what she could do over the summer to improve her diving, he said, "Don't get fat." The pressure to perform and look good is much greater in college than high school," she says. "Your scholarship may be on the line or you may want to get a scholarship. Or you may want to be the starter on your team or be taken to the meets. Being a female in this culture, it's hard to have a normal relationship with food… It's hard to not cross over and become obsessive." …At one point she was "purging pretty much everything I ate. I was so obsessed about calories that I didn't want to chew gum because there are 5 calories in a stick."[11]

The dangerous dance with weight loss is not limited to our high schools and colleges. It trickles all the way down to youth sports. Yes, all the way back to the foundations of a young person's introduction to sports in the USA:

A good friend of mine from Atlanta told me of a mother in the league he was coaching who had gone to her son's football practice to pick him up early for a dentist appointment that she'd forgotten about. When she arrived at the practice, however, she didn't see her son anywhere. And she went up to the coach and asked him where her son was. He told her nonchalantly that he was trying to make the weight limit… "He's over in my car," the coach admitted. "He's just trying to drop a few pounds to make the 98-pound limit. We have weigh-ins tonight."

The mother knew that her son's normal weight was around 105… She immediately ran toward the car in a state of shock. She found her son sitting in the car wrapped in plastic garbage bags with the engine running and the heater on high. The coach's plan was to get her son, who is a good running back, down to weight by sweating it off. The goal had completely eclipsed his concern for the welfare of the player. The fact of the matter is that his ignorance and negligence placed a child's health and potentially his life, at risk. We do not call this child abuse?[12]

TRAIN THEM UP

As parents continue to aid their children in pursuing the 'holy' trinity of athletic fame, scholarships, and future fortunes as professionals, more families are fracturing. Parents who have multiple children involved in sports are seeing less of each other each week. The electronic synching of schedules is the only way all the kids get to the appropriate fields at the predetermined times for practices. Sometimes it means dropping one child off, rushing to field number two, then blitzing back to field number one before that practice is over. Meanwhile the spouse is across town with child number three at the pool for swim team practice. A sit-down meal entails being in the minivan, grabbing dinner at the drive-thru (where they know you by name), then gulping it down before hitting the driveway. Shower, homework, bed, school, practice, repeat. The weekends only bring more chaos. And for some coaches at the high school and collegiate levels, the time demands exponentially increase the drain on the marriage and family. But is that a necessity, or merely a desire to appease the sports gods? Let's dig a little deeper and see why families may need to rethink their present trajectory:

The Rev. Stephen Fichter understood just how dominant a role sports has assumed in the culture when a family told him they would be out of town Good Friday to

Easter Sunday to attend their child's volleyball tournament. "It's truly sports that has become like the religion" for many people, said Fichter, a researcher and the pastor of Sacred Heart Church in Haworth, N.J. From youth travel teams to big-time national festivals such as the Final Four, sports have been making increasing inroads in the busy lives of many Americans. And it is having an impact on religious groups, which report increasing difficulty convincing families that are willing to spend half a day traveling to a 9-year-old's softball or soccer game to make time for worship services.[13]

How many coaches are responsible for adding to this fracturing of families in America, including their own? But there is another group that needs mention - those like you who are reading this book. You desire to honor Jesus with your coaching, but no one has come alongside you to help you see more clearly how to develop the traits of a Biblically-saturated, transformational coach.

Less than ten percent of youth coaches have been trained how to coach their respective sports. From my experience, there are also many high school and small college coaches who are in this category. They may be well-intentioned, but they are ill-equipped to train their athletes. Yet, the coaching ranks continue to tell parents to leave the coaching to them. Would these same parents readily leave their children at the local high school, or pay to send them to a college, if the teachers and professors had the same gaps in their educational and experiential backgrounds? Who wants to be coached by someone who is clueless about the sport? And if this is true about the sport itself, I wager that it is also true for many about what it means to fulfill their ministry as a 'Christian' coach. When I began coaching, I was a Christian living a compartmentalized life. I wish I knew then what I know now. I needed a better way, a holy way, to train up athletes through organized sports. But I was theologically ignorant when it came to coaching. Yet, by the grace of God, not to the degree of some that are out there today.

Consider what some coaches are teaching young people from the following case involving Pop Warner football. They apparently take their youth football way too seriously in South Florida where nine men were arrested in 2012 after a report from *Outside the Lines* aired, and a subsequent 18-month investigation by the Broward Sheriff's Office. The men, some who were coaches and mentors, were betting on the outcome of games involving boys ages 5 to 15. They also bet on individual plays, developing scores, and scads of other side bets. And not all of these were penny-ante type bets. $20,000 was bet on a rivalry game, and up to $100,000 on the league's championship games at the end of the season. And these were no choir boys coaching these kids. Six of the nine arrested were ex-convicts with ties to felony drug, assault, and theft charges.

And apparently some of the fans were not among a host of angels either. The *Outside the Lines* story showed people freely exchanging money in the stands and on the sidelines, coaches with wads of cash getting in on the action, and yet no one stepping in to stop the heinous behavior. "At some of the games, the money is being dealt so wide open a blind man could see the gambling taking place," said the Rev. Wesley Smith, a local pastor who had his son switch leagues a couple of years ago because he was worried that an argument over high-stakes gambling debts would lead to violence at one of the parks. You think it's wrong that colleges make money off the backs of their athletes? What about off of 30,000 kids in the South Florida Youth Football League who are playing a game? But the 'coaches' didn't keep all the money to themselves. Sometimes they would seek to influence the outcome of a game by bribing and paying the kids when they played well. Sports teach virtue? No, that has to come through the coaches, and they failed miserably in this league.

Who was your model, your mentor for coaching? What example are you leaving for the next generation of coaches? As Christian coaches, we must show a different way than what is frequently exhibited in living color, played out through the words and actions of many high profile coaches, and others who are flying below the radar. Do a web search for "coaching scandals." Mine spit out 5,520,000 results in 0.15 seconds. There is no lack of bad coaching examples. Will you help the world see the positive side of coaching, the side that points to the all-satisfying person of Jesus?

According to the 2006 President's Council on Physical Fitness and Sports, "It is the positive relationships and experiences with teammates, coaches, and involved parents that instill life lessons and develop the character of young participants in sports. The adults teach youth how to control emotions and behaviors after winning and losing in sports…The development of good character and morals that sports can foster supports youth in growth socially, emotionally, and mentally (Malina and Cumming, 2006).[14] Sounds good, doesn't it? There's only one catch. In a culture that has dismissed the concept of absolutes and moral truths, who decides what connotes "positive relationships," and "good character and morals"?

Obviously you don't want to be in the camp of someone of whom it was said, *"He treats us all the same – like dogs."* So said Henry Jordan, former Green Bay Packer, about Vince Lombardi. So what are your options?

> Undoubtedly, Lombardi was a successful football coach in terms of wins, losses, and championships. His Green Bay Packers teams are legendary. But were his methods the best way to treat human beings? Can't you be successful on the scoreboard and treat people with respect and dignity? …For every Lombardi or Bobby Knight you give me, I can give you an equally successful -- if not more successful -- humanistic coach. For example, in football, Don Shula (who co-wrote a book about coaching from the *heart*), Bill Walsh, John Gagliardi (the all-time winningest college football coach whose only team rule was *The Golden Rule*), Tony Dungy, and Oregon State's Mike Riley come quickly to mind. In basketball, there's John Wooden, Dean Smith, and today, the Boston Celtics' Brad Stevens, who miraculously took tiny Butler to back-to-back men's Final Fours with a humanistic, people-centered approach to coaching…

> Despite the success of Wooden, Shula, Dungy, Stevens, and others, our society has conditioned us to think that autocratic coaches are better coaches; that they win more often. It's a myth. But it's a vicious cycle. Athletes are conditioned by

autocratic coaches from Little League on. When they grow up and become coaches themselves, they model the behavior of the coaches they remember from their playing days. And on it goes ... unless we individually and collectively decide to stand up and stop it.[15]

HELP WANTED: BIBLICALLY-TRAINED TRANSFORMATIONAL COACHES

Respect and dignity. Success on the scoreboard. What's not to like about emulating these coaches placed in opposition to Lombardi and Knight? Most of these coaches are or were professing Christians. But carefully read the first paragraph of that quote again. Are you, as a Christian, supposed to take a "humanistic, people-centered approach to coaching"? No, and I believe the Christian coaches mentioned would agree, especially in light of the following passages which are representative of the entirety of Scripture:

> The God who made the world and everything in it, being Lord of heaven and earth, does not live in temples made by man, nor is he served by human hands, as though he needed anything, since he himself gives to all mankind life and breath and everything. And he made from one man every nation of mankind to live on all the face of the earth, having determined allotted periods and the boundaries of their dwelling place, that they should seek God, and perhaps feel their way toward him and find him. Yet he is actually not far from each one of us, [28] for *'In him we live and move and have our being.'* (Acts 17:24-28, italics mine)

> Therefore God has highly exalted him and bestowed on him the name that is above every name, so that *at the name of Jesus every knee should bow, in heaven and on earth and under the earth, and every tongue confess that Jesus Christ is Lord*, to the glory of God the Father. (Philippians 2:9-11, italics mine)

How does "coaching from the heart" work when Jeremiah 17:9 tells us that, "The heart is deceitful above all things, and desperately sick; who can understand it?" Everything you do must be put against the silhouette of Scripture to attempt to coach within the parameters set forth by the Word. This is the kind of coach desperately needed today if we are to engage the Sports Nation with the gospel! "If we want our teaching or witness [or coaching] to have power and produce effects, let us stay close to the revealed Word of God."[16]

One of the problems previously discussed is that only ten percent of all the youth coaches in the United States have any kind of training. The numbers improve dramatically for high school and collegiate coaches. But what kind of training is being disseminated? Is anyone going beyond the X's and O's for the few who are being trained?

A handful of non-profit national organizations…have sprung up over the years to educate various constituents in the youth sports boom, including coaches, administrators, and parents, and a part of this work is aimed at teaching grown-ups to act their age. The National Alliance for Youth Sports, founded in 1981, "seeks to make the sports experience safe, fun and healthy for ALL children," according to its mission statement, and includes educating parents as one of its primary purposes. Another, Positive Coaching Alliance, emphasizes the character-building opportunities of youth sports, and helps parents focus on life lessons rather than the scoreboard. David Jacobson, who runs communications there, estimates [however] that their organization affects roughly 1 million kids a year -- or a tiny fraction of the population of kids who play.[17]

"Safe, fun, and healthy for ALL children" is a goal that I believe all Christian coaches can agree with. But is that it? What about excelling in one's chosen sport, and the competition against opponents? Winning should not be the ultimate purpose for participating in sports, but merely one of the goals. Only then can biblically-informed life lessons mesh with the goal of seeking excellence through improved competency in the sport. And the scoreboard, if seen through the lens of Scripture, will then become a valuable tool in helping shape today's youth.

Or perhaps the *Iowa High School Athletic Association* has the key to helping us decide what tools coaches need to develop in order to guide our athletic youth: "[P]articipation in sports must do more than teach skills and encourage students to be physically fit… [P]articipation in youth sports should have an educational focus in order to help develop the total person. A young person's physical, social, emotional, and spiritual health improves as a result from such participation."

Who's going to decide what constitutes improvement in physical, social, and emotional health, and what spiritual realm are we trying to improve? Let's see if Dr. Joseph Luxbacher, head coach of the University of Pittsburgh men's soccer team, and Kevin K. Wong (U.S. Olympian, NBC broadcaster, and founder of the Hawaii Spike and Serve Youth Volleyball League), can bring any clarity to this issue:

A well-structured and organized youth sports program can provide many benefits and positive experiences for young athletes. When done correctly and with the athlete's well-being in mind, organized sports can play an important role in a young person's life.[18]

Sports are faster than life. A three-month season is an epic journey of victories and losses, and ultimately of growth. Through practice and play there are more teaching opportunities per minute in a sporting arena than nearly any other venue. Lessons of cooperation and communication can be celebrated during the best of times. Lessons of resilience, resetting, and regrouping are learned during struggles…If they are properly framed.[19]

The problem with all of these visions on how to coach today's youth is that there is no universal agreement on the foundation or the finish line. What is the tool used to decide if a sports program has been "done correctly" in order to promote the physical, social, emotional, and spiritual health of the participants? What is the measuring stick to decide what constitutes an "athlete's well-being" or if victory and defeat "are properly framed"? There are obviously a myriad of ideas on how to operate any program or team. We must stand firm upon the Bible to seek to answer these questions. Otherwise, we will be afloat in a sea of syncretism, taking whatever parts please us from a multitude of coaching philosophies.

In recent decades, some pundits also have been advocating the meshing of Christianity and 'sport psychology' to produce a new coaching philosophy. For instance, one of the questions being asked is how spirituality and religion can be reconciled into current athlete-centered models. Doesn't the term "athlete-centered" belie an inherent problem as a starting point when placed against the silhouette of Scripture that calls for a Christ-centered life, a life of dying to ourselves? Another question asks how spirituality and religion can be accommodated in sport psychology counseling. Can Christian coaches merely look at their faith as being 'accommodated' into anything – as merely tacking it on to something else? Jesus Christ must be the foundation, and his Word the silhouette against which everything else is placed to see whether it is viable in helping to promote a kingdom agenda.

> Following the recommendations of [Sports Psychologist Gloria] Balague (1999), it is argued that when athletes have curtailed religious practices due to busy sporting schedules or when suffering from anxiety and/or depression, sport psychology consultants should encourage athletes to renew religious practices. It is likely that this would assist the athlete in coping with sport and life issues in a more constructive manner, by helping them to be reflective and learn from the inevitable disappointments of competitive sports. In turn, this would most likely lead to character development and enhanced sporting performance. [20]

It appears from this statement that 'religious practices' are seen merely as a means to an end, not foundational to the very life of the Christian athlete. Gospel-centered faith is not foundationally a tool to improve sports' performance according to the world's standards, scoreboard or otherwise.

What tools are available to help coaches implement Christian principles into the sporting arena, which will flow out into the community-at-large? We must not allow mere Christianese platitudes or coffee mug verses to be hijacked and used as our guides. If we want to be regularly sowing seeds of salvation and sanctification, we must "stay close to the revealed Word of God."

> How can a young man keep his way pure? By guarding it according to your word. With my whole heart I seek you; let me not wander from your commandments! I have stored up your word in my heart, that I might not sin against you. Blessed are you, O LORD; teach me your statutes! (Psalm 119:9-12)

Let's examine the story of Nebraska Assistant Football Coach, Ron Brown, to help us in our quest to be gospel-centered coaches:

> [Nebraska football coach] Ron Brown is fearless... His love of Christ trumps all... This guy is a rare jewel in contemporary evangelicalism. And he is living it out in a media fishbowl. I asked Brown why he is so bold, so outspoken. He responded, Jesus said, "Whoever desires to save his life shall lose it. If you deny me before men then I will deny you before my Father." My greatest burden is not losing my job or what people might say about me. My greatest burden is faithfulness. I want to be faithful. I want to see the body of Christ be faithful. I want to see unbelievers come to Christ.

> Brown is 100 percent Division I football coach and 100 percent preacher. When he talks you want to strap on the spiritual helmet and get in the game... Brown has a reputation for boldly speaking out on moral issues... *Why is this a concern?* Because many, like this columnist, hear a list of "do's" and "don'ts" in his sound bites and statements. This is where we all should be listening to those who listen to us. Are they hearing gospel or moralism? Are we preaching the gospel of what Jesus did or what we need to do/not do?

> D. A. Carson has helpfully said, "It is easy to sound prophetic from the margins, what we need is to be prophetic from the center." That is, preaching against issues that flow out of a rejection of the gospel (sexual sin, abortion, etc) are peripheral and must be addressed by means of the core gospel, that which is of first importance...

> [For I delivered to you as of first importance what I also received: that Christ died for our sins in accordance with the Scriptures, that he was buried, that he was raised on the third day in accordance with the Scriptures, and that he appeared to Cephas, then to the twelve (1 Corinthians 15:3-5).]

> [W]e must be prophetic from the center [as Coach Brown seeks to be]. They will hear what we are passionate about. We have to keep hitting those gospel notes, because it is a strange sound to people who do not yet recognize the tune.[21]

What tune do athletes, parents, and fans hear flowing forth from your life, your words and deeds? Is the clarion call of Christ being crowded out by the siren song of the scoreboard? Whether you coach in a secular or sacred setting, you can honor Jesus and show respect for those you coach, and those you work with and for. But to make this a reality you must be willing to take a different road than has been traveled for the last half-century by Christians in sports.

There has been a deafening silence into which professor Shirl Hoffman has shouted. He does a masterful, soul-searching synopsis of the Christianity and sports marriage that must be meditated upon in order to progress in our desire to be gospel-centered coaches:

> Not being willing to wrestle with the difficult task of understanding sport and its relationship to their faith, evangelicals have lost their influence in the world of big-time sports [and youth sports]… Those who believe that sport will eventually be reclaimed for the Christian worldview when enough of Christian athletes and coaches have invaded sports would do well to reflect on the enormous numbers of evangelicals already involved in sports… Mostly the evangelical-sport machine has chugged along on a set of unexamined assumptions about the Christian approach to competition [and coaching]…[22]

God is calling Christian coaches to fulfill their ministries. The task is overwhelming. In fact, without God's direction and empowering, it is impossible. Don't despair. Forge on and you will find Biblical truths and practical tools to help transform your life and your ministry, as you seek to shine light into the darkness of the Sports Nation.

Notes

[1] Shirl James Hoffman, *Good Game: Christianity and the Culture of Sports* (Waco: Baylor University, 2010), 138-139.

[2] Ibid, 15-16.

[3] Ken Reed, "Let's Put the 'Youth' Back in Youth Sports," *Huffington Post*, 10/1/2013, Accessed 10/26/2013. www.huffingtonpost.com/ken-reed/lets-put-the-youth-back-i_b_4023676.html

[4] Sharon Chirban, Ph.D., "Specialization vs. Sampling in Youth Sports: Which is Healthier?" *Huffington Post*, 3/10/2011, Accessed 10/26/2013. www.huffingtonpost.com/sharon-chirban-phd/specialization-vs-samplin_b_832470.html

[5] Galatians 2:20, for example.

[6] Gilbert, Gilbert, and Morawski (2007), quoted in Jeanine A. Johnson, "Understanding the Thoughts and Attitudes Related to Participation in Youth Sports," PhD Dissertation (Philadelphia: Philadelphia College of Osteopathic Medicine, Department of Psychology, 2012).

[7] Joan Ryan in Mark Hyman, *Until It Hurts: American's Obsession with Youth Sports and How it Harms Our Kids* (Boston: Beacon Press, 2009), 69.

[8] Laken Litman, "Youth Pitchers Feeling the Pinch of Tommy John Surgery Epidemic, *USA Today Sports*, 7/23/2014, Accessed 8/26/2014. www.usatoday.com/2014/07/tommy-john-surgery-youth-sports.

[9] Mark Hyman, *Until It Hurts: American's Obsession with Youth Sports and How it Harms Our Kids* (Boston: Beacon Press, 2009), 58-59.

[10] Laura Hilgers, "Youth Sports Drawing More Than Ever," *CNN*, 7/5/2006, Accessed 1/26/2013. www.cnn.com/2006/US/07/03/rise.kids.sports/

[11] Nanci Hellmich, "Athletes' Hunger to Win Fuels Eating Disorders," *USA Today, Health and Behavior*, 2/5/2006, Accessed 4/25/2013. www.usatoday30.usatoday.com/news/health/2006-02-05-women-health-cover_x.htm.

[12] Fred Engh, *Why Johnny Hates Sports: Why Organized Youth Sports Are Failing Our Children And What We Can Do About It*, (Garden City Park, NY: Garden City Publishers, 2002), 90-91.

13 David Briggs, "The Final Four, Travel Teams and Empty Pews: Who is Winning the Competition Between Sports and Religion?" *Huffington Post*, 4/3/2013, Accessed 10/26/2013. www.huffingtonpost.com/david-briggs/final-four-travel-teams-and-empty-pews-who-is-winning-the-competition-between-sports-and-religion_b_3006988.html

14 Barbara Walker, Ph.D., "The Benefits of Participation in Youth Sports," *Vimeo*, 10/27/2012, Accessed 10/26/2013. www.vimeo.com/57066707

15 Ken Reed, "It's Time To Bench Tyrannical Coaches," *Huffington Post*, 12/14/2012. Accessed 1/2/2014. www.huffingtonpost.com/ken-reed/sports-coaches_b_4195220.html

16 John Piper, *Pierced by the Word* (Sisters, OR: Multnomah, 2003), 22.

17 Laura Hilgers, "Youth Sports Drawing More Than Ever," *CNN*, 7/5/2006, Accessed 1/26/2013. www.cnn.com/2006/US/07/03/rise.kids.sports/

18 Joseph Luxbacher, PhD, "Pros and Cons of Youth Sports Participation," *University of Pittsburgh Medical Center*, Accessed 10/26/2013. www.upmc.com/Services/sports-medicine/newsletter/pages/pros-cons-youth-participation.aspx

19 Kevin K. Wong, "Teaching Positive Life Lessons Through Sports," *Huffington Post*, 9/4/2013, Accessed 10/26/2013. www.huffingtonpost.com/kevin-k-wong/post_5491_b_3825138.html

20 Nick J. Watson and Daniel R. Czech, "The Use of Prayer in Sport: Implications for Sport Psychology Counseling," 2005, *Athletic Insight*, Accessed 12/18/2013. www.athleticinsight.com/Vol7Iss4/PrayerinSports.htm

21 Erik Raymond, "Is This Evangelical Coach Out of Bounds?" *The Gospel Coalition*, 4/29/2012, Accessed 1/2/2014. www.thegospelcoalition.org/blogs/tgc/2012/04/29/is-this-evangelical-coach-out-of-bounds/

22 Hoffman, op. cit., 13, 143.

4

TREASURE JESUS

Stop trying to validate your existence by comparing yourself to others. The world's idea of achievements, accolades, and affirmations are all built on sand. They are appetites that need to be fed increasingly in vain attempts to satisfy the soul. On the cross Jesus proclaimed, "It is finished." That victory affirmed that you are loved; the only accolade your soul truly needs!

"For I delivered to you as of *first importance* what I also received: that Christ died for our sins in accordance with the Scriptures, that he was buried, that he was raised on the third day in accordance with the Scriptures." (1 Corinthians 15:3-4, italics mine)

∞ *What is the primary reason that you coach, whether as a volunteer or as a career?*

Be honest. Take a deep look into the mirror of your soul. What motivates you to coach? Is your reasoning based upon a biblical foundation or the prevailing winds of the world swirling about you? Consider the following as you seek to answer these questions:

> I remember lecturing at Ohio State University, one of the largest universities in this country. I was minutes away from beginning my lecture, and my host was driving me past a new building called the Wexner Center for the Performing Arts.
>
> He said, "This is America's first postmodern building."
>
> I was startled for a moment and I said, "What is a postmodern building?"
>
> He said, "Well, the architect said that he designed this building with no design in mind. When the architect was asked, 'Why?' he said, 'If life itself is capricious, why should our buildings have any design and any meaning?' So he has pillars that have

31

no purpose. He has stairways that go nowhere. He has a senseless building built and somebody has paid for it."

I said, "So his argument was that if life has no purpose and design, why should the building have any design?"

He said, "That is correct."

I said, "Did he do the same with the foundation?"

All of a sudden there was silence.

You see, you and I can fool with the infrastructure as much as we would like, but we dare not fool with the foundation because it will call our bluff in a hurry.[1]

Everyone then who hears these words of mine and does them will be like a wise man who built his house on the rock. And the rain fell, and the floods came, and the winds blew and beat on that house, but it did not fall, because it had been founded on the rock. And everyone who hears these words of mine and does not do them will be like a foolish man who built his house on the sand. And the rain fell, and the floods came, and the winds blew and beat against that house, and it fell, and great was the fall of it."[2]

Following Jesus is not the Christian version of a rabbit's foot that you rub in the hopes that your team will win. Rather, the foundational reason for coaching should be the same as in every other area of your life: "Man's chief end is to glorify God and to enjoy him forever."[3] Coaching should not be a tool used to bolster your standing in society, be it through social acceptance, monetary gain, or the ever-deceitful "self-worth." Coaching is not about you! To quote Max Lucado, "To say 'it's not about you' is not to say you aren't loved; quite the contrary. It's because God loves you that it's not about you."

Each of us must honestly assess whether Jesus Christ is truly the ultimate treasure in our lives. Do you seek to have your coaching centered upon bringing glory to Jesus? Is he the reason that you have that whistle around your neck? If not, it's time to ask yourself who or what is defining you, so that you can destroy those false gods and passionately follow Jesus. Too many coaches love the thought of people honoring them because of their positions. Your life as a coach should be centered upon proclaiming the gospel, living it out in word and deed. What good is winning a game or a championship if your athletes lose their very souls?

For there is one God, and there is one mediator between God and men, the man Christ Jesus, who gave himself as a ransom for all, which is the testimony given at the proper time. (1 Timothy 2:5-6)

And *this gospel of the kingdom will be proclaimed throughout the whole world* as a testimony to all nations, and then the end will come. (Matthew 24:14, italics mine)

The primary objective behind your coaching should be to show the awe-inspiring beauty that Jesus is in your life. By doing so, you will sow seeds of salvation and sanctification in the lives of your athletes, their families, fellow coaches, fans, and opponents.

TOOLS

Ω **Memorize the following from the Westminster Shorter Catechism. Daily ask the Holy Spirit to make it a reality in your coaching, so that the world will see the positive side of coaching, the side that points to the all-satisfying person of Jesus. Consider using it as the home screen for your phone, or screensaver for your computer.**

"Man's chief end is to glorify God and to enjoy him forever." (Westminster Shorter Catechism)

Ω **What is your personal mission statement for coaching? If you do not have one, ask the Holy Spirit to help you to craft a short, biblically-infused statement that will help you to continually seek to keep Jesus as your treasure through your ministry.**

Example: "I coach in order to show the all-satisfying value of Jesus through my pursuit of excellence, the transformation of athletes' lives, and the impact my coaching has on families, fellow coaches, opponents, and fans."

Ω PRAYER

"Gracious and heavenly Father, your Word tells us that, No one can serve two masters, for either he will hate the one and love the other, or he will be devoted to the one and despise the other. Grant me wisdom to see if there are any areas in my coaching where I am trying to serve two masters. Immediately reveal to me when my status, the scoreboard, or some other master subtly creeps into my heart so that I will repent and turn back to you. Forgive me for caring so much about what others think rather than caring most about your ultimate valuation, portrayed through the death of your Son on the cross. Do not allow fear to hamper the calling you have placed on my life to proclaim the Good News. As one of your children, I am the light of the world. A city set on a hill cannot be hidden. Nor do people light a lamp and put it under a basket, but on a stand, and it gives light to all in the house. In the same way, may my light shine before others, so that they may see my good works through coaching and give glory to you, my Father who is in heaven. Empower me to walk in wisdom toward outsiders, making the best use of the time. And let my speech always be gracious… so that I may know how I ought to answer each person" (Matthew 6:24, 5:14-16, Colossians 4:5-6).

GOD-CENTERED, GOD-FOCUSED, GOD-INTOXICATED, GOD-ENTRENCHED[4]

"We exist to spread a passion for the supremacy of God in all things [including coaching] for the joy of all peoples through Jesus Christ." (John Piper)

"You who fear the LORD, praise him! All you offspring of Jacob, glorify him, and stand in awe of him, all you offspring of Israel!" (Psalm 22:23)

∞ *What does it mean to 'glorify' God?*

That word echoes throughout multitudes of corporate worship gatherings around the world. Many, however, are unable to grasp its meaning. It floats away to the heavens like a helium balloon whose string has slipped through grasping fingers. To help us in our journey, consider the actions of the Magi, the Wise Men in Matthew's Gospel, as a starting point.

Ever chasing the sun, they headed west. Days blending together like raindrops descending from a cloudburst – one indistinguishable from the rest. Forging ahead. Never knowing how much longer. "After Jesus was born in Bethlehem in Judea, during the time of King Herod, Magi from the east came to Jerusalem and asked, 'Where is the one who has been born king of the Jews? We saw his star in the east and have come to worship him.'"[5]

That singular question stirred up a wave of anxiety throughout the royal city. "When King Herod heard this he was disturbed, and all Jerusalem with him."[6] "King of the Jews?" He winced at the Magi's question. If the stars were signaling the birth of another "King of the Jews," that led Herod to only one conclusion. The same star signaled his demise. That child must die so that Herod might live.

When he [Herod] had called together all the people's chief priests and teachers of the law, he asked them where the Christ was to be born. "In Bethlehem in Judea," they replied, "for this is what the prophet has written: "'But you, Bethlehem, in the land of Judah, are by no means least among the rulers of Judah; for out of you will come a ruler who will be the shepherd of my people Israel.'"[7]

"Bethlehem, hmm." With that initial inquiry complete, Herod summarily dismissed the religious cadre with a wave of his hand. But without their knowledge, he would have remained coiled, not knowing where to strike.

Then Herod called the Magi secretly and found out from them the exact time the star had appeared. He sent them to Bethlehem and said, "Go and make a careful search for the child. As soon as you find him, report to me, so that I too may go and worship him."[8]

Herod readied his fangs. Naively, the Magi provided the usurper with the first chance to strike. Not content with this knowledge, however, Herod desired to know the exact identity of the child. Dispatching his venom deep into the flesh of this little one would save his throne – at the cost of his soul.

"After they had heard the king, they went on their way, and the star they had seen in the east went ahead of them until it stopped over the place where the child was. When they saw the star, they were overjoyed."[9]

The pagan Magi had traveled hundreds of miles and pressed on in a joyous procession to worship the King of the Jews. Meanwhile, the blind chief priests and teachers of the law, who had always had the location at their fingertips, didn't make the mere five-mile journey when they heard of the King's birth.

"On coming to the house they saw the child with his mother Mary, and they bowed down and worshipped him. Then they opened their treasures and presented him with gifts of gold and of incense and of myrrh."[10]

Are you more like Magi, willing to experience all kinds of inconvenience, traveling untold miles from friends and family to find the King of Kings? Or are you more like the chief priests and teachers of the law, who couldn't be bothered to travel five miles from Jerusalem to Bethlehem to meet the Royal Child, men too busy seeking to protect their positions of power at the possible cost of their own souls? May none of us be in league with Herod, who symbolizes all those who falsely seek after the Lord but never manage to find him! You are either for Jesus or against him in how you coach. There is no middle ground. Just as there was no apparent awe in Jerusalem at the news the Magi brought that day, so it is for many coaches today when it comes to Jesus and his kingdom agenda.

> The word [glory] signals high honor. The Hebrew term for *glory*, descends from a root word meaning heavy, weighty, or important. And God's glory, then, celebrates his significance, his uniqueness, his one-of-a-kindness. As Moses prayed, "Who is like you, O LORD, among the gods? Who is like you, majestic in holiness, awesome in glorious deeds, doing wonders?" (Exodus 15:11)[11]

> Unfortunately, "To most moderns…a sense of awe comes with the greatest difficulty. We have domesticated angels into stuffed toys and Christmas ornaments, made cartoons of St. Peter at the gate of heaven, tamed the phenomenon of Easter with bunny rabbits, and substituted the awe of shepherds and wise men for cute elves and a jolly man dressed in red. Almighty God gets nicknames like 'The Big Guy' and 'The Man Upstairs.'"[12]

> *Glory is what you see and experience and feel when God goes public with his beauty! … God is praised when he is prized!*[13]

In your role as a coach, do you see Jesus as worthy of your worship, the object of your ultimate affection, the Beauty you want others to also experience? If yes, then you will seek ways to make his name known both to those you coach and to the circles ever-widening from that center. If this is your heart's passion and pursuit, then you will glorify God. You will, by the power of the Holy Spirit, show and tell the world that Jesus is your ultimate treasure. "In the Hebrew Old Testament, the primary word for worship means 'to bow down in reverence and submission.' And in the New Testament, the most common Greek word for worship means 'to come forward to kiss.' Between those two – or combining both – lies our best approach to God [fear and friendship]."[14]

Why do the heavens, the earth, and everything in it exist? "The heavens declare the glory of God, and the sky above proclaims his handiwork."[15] We were created to worship. What does your coaching reflect as your ultimate treasure? "... *[E]verything* from quarks to quasars, from butterflies to baseballs, were created and are sustained so that you and I might delight in the display of divine glory."[16] Building on anyone or anything other than Jesus will leave you teetering on a foundation of shifting sand.

TOOLS

Ω **Does your coaching, on a daily basis, more closely resemble the attitude of the Magi, the chief priests and teachers of the law, or Herod?**

Ω **Do you prize Jesus through your coaching? Can you give specific examples? Would others you trust agree with your answer? Go ahead, ask them!**

Ω **Does your daily/weekly pattern in life show the world that you prize Jesus? In other words, what patterns in your life show the world that following Jesus is a priority?**

Ω **PRAYER**

"Heavenly Father, please help me to see how you want me to proclaim the good news today through my coaching. Do not allow me to be mired in comfortable traditions when you are seeking to do a new thing to reach the world around me. Grant me the courage, the desire, and the passion to proceed like the Magi, who traveled far from their homeland to worship you. How much more should I, who have been given the full revelation of Scripture, be willing to point others to Jesus in response to your call upon my life? Help me to avoid the complacency of the religious leaders, who knew where you were, but failed to act upon your revealed knowledge. Forgive me for too often wanting to be in power and in authority, just like King Herod. Grant me eyes to see, ears to hear, and a heart to follow only you. Holy Spirit, help me to hold fast, believing you will guide me how to use my position as a coach to help fulfill The 'Greatest Commandments' and my part of 'The Great Commission.' Empower me in my coaching to keep your ways and not turn aside from your commands. May I treasure your words more than my portion of food." (Mark 12:30-31; Matthew 28:18-20; Job 23:12)

HOLY, HOLY, HOLY

"The debt was so great, that while man alone owed it, only God can pay it." (Anselm)

"There is none like you among the gods, O Lord, nor are there any works like yours. All the nations you have made shall come and worship before you, O Lord, and shall glorify your name. For you are great and do wondrous things; you alone are God… I give thanks to you, O Lord my God, with my whole heart, and I will glorify your name forever. For great is your steadfast love toward me; you have delivered my soul from the depths of Sheol." (Psalm 86:8-10, 12-13)

∞ *Why should God's glory be the primary reason that you coach?*

1.   God is the Creator, and the reason you exist is to continually point others to Jesus.

"In the beginning was the Word, and the Word was with God, and the Word was God. He was in the beginning with God. All things were made through him, and without him was not any thing made that was made."[17] Only God can create something *ex nihilo* - "something from nothing." Man can at best only seek to imitate God's creative acts. At worst, man seeks to usurp God's authority and place himself on the throne.

It all started back in the Garden of Eden when the serpent was tempting Eve to eat the fruit. Do you remember the Serpent's reply when Eve said she and Adam would die if they ate from that forbidden tree? "'You will not surely die,' the serpent said to the woman. 'For God knows that when you eat of it your eyes will be opened, and you will be like God, knowing good and evil.'"[18] What might that temptation look like for coaches? "All eyes will be on you. All will bow down at your coaching acumen, your prowess, your ability to produce champions." You might not put it in these exact words, but you know precisely what I'm talking about. When's the last time you had your heart checked?

Let's consider again how John's Gospel starts, because it gives us a clue toward conquering this twisted thinking: "In the beginning was the Word…." Sound familiar? John knew when he penned those words that his Jewish audience would automatically be drawn back to the very first words of their sacred Scriptures: "In the beginning God…." This phrase means that God existed before everything else came into being. He alone is at the root of the universe. In the beginning, before creation, God existed – and alongside him was Jesus, the Divine Word.

"The Word [Jesus] was with God" means that from everlasting to everlasting the Father and Son are together. "The Word was God" means that Jesus always has been God, and will always will be God. Before any created thing came into being, Jesus existed.

If we, coaches, are to have a proper perspective regarding our roles in this vast universe, we must remember our position. We are the created. God is the Creator. God is not dispensable. We are. It's all about God. It's not about you.

"For by him all things were created, in heaven and on earth, visible and invisible, whether thrones or dominions or rulers or authorities—*all things were created through him and for him.*"[19] The main reason that you have the breath of life, the main reason that you have an opportunity to coach, is so that people will be in awe of the God you serve. It is not about your win-loss record or any other accolades you might accrue during any given season or career. All those trophies will eventually begin to rust or end up in the city dump, and the applause will quickly fade. If the win-loss column is your god, then your name, at best, will be remembered on a plaque that will rust, or, if you were really good, perhaps on a building. That building, too, will eventually end up as a pile of rubble. But not so with Jesus. His name will continually be lifted up and his accolades will be sung about forever![20]

2.   Your salvation showcases God's love, mercy, and grace for his name's sake.

"I, I am he who blots out your transgressions for my own sake, and I will not remember your sins."[21] As a Christian coach, your salvation should keep you constantly seeking the wisdom of the Holy Spirit on how, when, and where to help your athletes and coaches, their families, your opponents, and all the fans understand the reason why you exist: "The people whom I formed for myself that they might declare my praise."[22]

Jesus did not willingly go to the cross to make much of you, but so that his Father would be glorified. The reality that you joyfully bow your knee to Jesus because his death has paid for your sins and removed God's wrath from being poured out upon you is all the more reason that your coaching should reflect Jesus as your ultimate treasure. There will be a point in history where every knee will bow down and confess that Jesus Christ is Lord. For many, it will be a grievous reality that a death sentence has been levied upon their lives: "And being found in human form, he humbled himself by becoming obedient to the point of death, even death on a cross. Therefore God has highly exalted him and bestowed on him the name that is above every name, so that at the name of Jesus every knee should bow, in heaven and on earth and under the earth, and every tongue confess that Jesus Christ is Lord, to the glory of God the Father."[23]

R. C. Sproul wrote that the most perplexing theological question is not why there is suffering in this world, but why God tolerates us in our sinfulness.[24] God redeemed you and saved you by substituting his Son, Jesus, in your place. By taking your sins onto himself, Jesus died the death you should have died. By having his righteousness given to you, the death sentence has been lifted and God's wrath has been averted! How can the win-loss column or the accolades of the world compete with that for your affections?

3.   God commands you to give glory to him alone.

"For my name's sake I defer my anger, for the sake of my praise I restrain it for you, that I may not cut you off. Behold, I have refined you, but not as silver; I have tried you in the furnace of affliction. For my own sake, for my own sake, I do it, for how should my name be profaned? *My glory I will not give to another.*"[25] "So, whether you eat or drink, or whatever you do, do all to the glory of God."[26]

Many people know the beginning of Psalm 46:10, "Be still and know that I am God." But how does the rest of the verse go? What should be the result of being still and knowing who God is? "I will be exalted among the nations, I will be exalted in the earth!" May your coaching exalt the Creator, Redeemer, and Sustainer of the universe. Consider the following two examples of three people who failed to give God his proper due. Two of them were sons of Aaron, the priest. The other was a pagan king. The end result, however, was the same for all parties involved. I'm not sharing these stories to frighten you into thinking this might happen to you. Rather, I want you to see how seriously God is offended when someone fails to honor his glory, or seeks to steal it:

> Now Nadab and Abihu, the sons of Aaron, each took his censer and put fire in it and laid incense on it and offered unauthorized fire before the LORD, which he had not commanded them. And fire came out from before the LORD and consumed them, and they died before the LORD. Then Moses said to Aaron, "This is what the LORD has said: 'Among those who are near me I will be sanctified, and before all the people I will be glorified.'" And Aaron held his peace. (Leviticus 10:1-3)

> On an appointed day Herod put on his royal robes, took his seat upon the throne, and delivered an oration to them. And the people were shouting, "The voice of a god, and not of a man!" Immediately an angel of the Lord struck him down, because he did not give God the glory, and he was eaten by worms and breathed his last. (Acts 12:21-23)

To the King of the ages, immortal, invisible, the only God, be honor and glory forever and ever. Amen.[27]

TOOLS

Ω Meditate upon and memorize Jude 24-25. Ask the Holy Spirit to stir up your affections for Jesus – for who he is, for what he has done, what he is doing, and what he promises to continue doing on your behalf. Are you casting your crown or coveting it?

"Now to him who is able to keep you from stumbling and to present you blameless before the presence of his glory with great joy, to the only God, our Savior, through Jesus Christ our Lord, be glory, majesty, dominion, and authority, before all time and now and forever. Amen."

Ω Meditate upon and memorize 2 Corinthians 5:21. What does it mean that you have "become the righteousness of God"? How should that impact how you interact with your athletes, their families, other coaches, administrators, faculty, and fans?

"For our sake he made him to be sin who knew no sin, so that in him we might become the righteousness of God."

Ω Meditate upon and memorize Romans 8:31-34. How does the reality of Jesus being "for you" and "interceding" for you affect how you coach?

"What then shall we say to these things? If God is for us, who can be against us? He who did not spare his own Son but gave him up for us all, how will he not also with him graciously give us all things? Who shall bring any charge against God's elect? It is God who justifies. Who is to condemn? Christ Jesus is the one who died—more than that, who was raised—who is at the right hand of God, who indeed is interceding for us."

Ω PRAYER

"Heavenly Father, thank you for showing me that Jesus is God. Jesus was there 'in the beginning.' He is not a created being. He has always existed. How much more plainly could you have attested to these truths than, 'the Word was God'? What a glorious truth. And yet, you don't stop there in attesting to the deity of Jesus. Jesus is the Creator: 'Through Him all things were made.' Jesus is the Giver of life: 'In Him was life.' Praise you, heavenly Father, for sending your Son to shine his light in the darkness of this world. What a joy to behold that the Light is triumphant over the darkness. In Jesus I live and move and have my very being. Help me, Father, to defer all attention away from myself and point it upon Jesus. Help me to stand firm upon your promise that was given long ago regarding the identity of the Light. He has come into the world and he is Jesus - the Creator, Redeemer, and Sustainer of all life, both now and forevermore. To him alone belong all glory and honor!" (John 1:1-5)

MIRROR, MIRROR, ON THE WALL...

"The only yardstick for success our society has is being a champion. No one remembers anything else." (John Madden)

"And do not turn aside after empty things that cannot profit or deliver, for they are empty." (1 Samuel 12:21)

∞ *What is the opposite of glorifying God?*

If you have a win-at-all-costs mentality, the end result will leave you gasping for air, flopping on the floor like the proverbial fish out of water. You may have street cred for years on end. People may even hold you up as a hero, but your kingdom will one day come crashing to the ground if God's glory and your enjoyment of him are not the ultimate reasons that you coach. Need a reminder? Look at the life of the once-mighty, seven-time Tour de France winner, Lance Armstrong, the man who once said, "The riskiest thing you can do is get greedy."

Few athletes will ever have the worldwide renown of Lance Armstrong. Who can forget the photos of a spindly, bald-headed Armstrong courageously battling the cancer that had ravaged his body? Yet, in a relatively short time, "after" photos showed him crushing the mountains of Europe and blasting down the other side as he won seven Tours in a row. Yellow Livestrong wrist bands appeared everywhere as he helped raise over $500 million dollars for cancer research. Nike loved him, and named a building after him on their campus. Celebrities and common folk from all walks of life desired to rub shoulders with him.

Yet, not everyone believed his guts-to-glory story. Multiple claims were levied against him regarding illegal methods he was using to win. Lance, an untouchable god in his own mind, called these detractors "trolls." His lack of humility spotlighted his vengeful spirit. You were either for Lance or against him. There was no middle ground in his mind.

Armstrong seemingly did everything within his power to gain a competitive advantage over his fellow cyclists, from testing his Oakley sunglasses in a wind tunnel to aging his tires in cool, dry cellars in order to make them more resistant to flats. Unfortunately, as we now know, Lance seemed to look at his body as just another piece of equipment that needed to be managed, manipulated, and maximized in order to continue his winning ways. No one could prove that he was taking growth hormones or testosterone, or performing blood doping. After winning the 2005 Tour with the fastest recorded average, Armstrong brazenly proclaimed that he was the most tested athlete in history: "I've been tested 500-600 times and not a single positive test."

Retirement ensued, and it looked as if Lance would survive all the attacks from former teammates, competitors, the Cycling Union, and the United States Anti-Doping Agency. But glory is a dangerous drug. Four years later, Armstrong was back in the saddle attempting to win another Tour in 2009 at the age of thirty-eight. Not content to merely ride again, or even place, Armstrong was there to win. His third place finish, a disappointment to him, raised more red flags, given his advanced age.

In October 2012, the testing world finally caught up to the scientific advances of the Armstrong Empire in the long-standing cat-and-mouse game. The United States Anti-Doping Agency released more than a thousand pages proving that Lance and his teammates had been doping. Within a week, his name was removed from one of the buildings at Nike's headquarters. And the dominoes continued to fall from Tour de France Trophies to Bud Light Beer and the rest of his sponsors, until Lance was left with nothing but an Oprah Winfrey opportunity to perform his *mea culpa,* forever remembered as a liar and a cheat. His kingdom had come, his will was not done.

"The tricky thing about idolatry is that it is usually the pursuit of something that is otherwise good... idolatry is enslavement to something we love... it's a good thing that is elevated to a God thing."[28] "No servant can serve two masters, for either he will hate the one and love the other, or he will be devoted to the one and despise the other. You cannot serve God and money [or winning, or accolades]."[29]

Every coach has to deal with the subtle lies of the Serpent, who says, "You can be just like God." So do not think that it is uncommon that the temptation to glorify yourself seems to be waiting to devour you at every turn. Are you prepared to war against it so that it does not get a stranglehold on you and squeeze out every breath of life that should be singularly devoted to God's glory? "Or do you not know that your body is a temple of the Holy Spirit within you, whom you have from God? You are not your own, for you were bought with a price. So glorify God in your body."[30]

Others have no idea that their need for approval drives them to physical, emotional, mental, and spiritual exhaustion. They are just dying (literally) to hear, "We don't know what we'd do without you!"

So is it wrong to pursue winning? Only if it is your ultimate goal for being a coach. Then you are enslaved. Perhaps you 'need' another hit of the glory drug in order to feel valued, or to justify your existence, or to prove you are better than other coaches, or because it's what gives you the juice to jump out of bed in the morning. If you do not seek, by the empowering of the Holy Spirit, to have God's glory at the epicenter of your coaching, you are an idolater, and your coaching is in vain. May you learn from the experiences of King Solomon, the wisest and richest man of his time:

I said in my heart, "Come now, I will test you with pleasure; enjoy yourself." But behold, this also was vanity. I said of laughter, "It is mad," and of pleasure, "What use is it?" I searched with my heart how to cheer my body with wine—my heart still guiding me with wisdom—and how to lay hold on folly, till I might see what was good for the children of man to do under heaven during the few days of their life. I made great works. I built houses and planted vineyards for myself. I made myself gardens and parks, and planted in them all kinds of fruit trees. I made myself pools from which to water the forest of growing trees. I bought male and female slaves, and had slaves who were born in my house. I had also great possessions of herds and flocks, more than any who had been before me in Jerusalem. I also gathered for myself silver and gold and the treasure of kings and provinces. I got singers, both men and women, and many concubines, the delight of the sons of man. So I became great and surpassed all who were before me in Jerusalem. Also my wisdom remained with me. And whatever my eyes desired I did not keep from them. I kept my heart from no pleasure, for my heart found pleasure in all my toil, and this was my reward for all my toil. Then *I considered all that my hands had done and the toil I had expended in doing it, and behold, all was vanity and a striving after wind, and there was nothing to be gained* under the sun. (Ecclesiastes 2:1-11)

This emptiness, this straining for things, experiences, or people to satisfy our souls, has always been part of the curse of the Fall. It is not unique to the world of coaching, the world of sports, America, or the 21st Century. It is a disease enmeshed in the fiber of every man, woman, and child. "In the 1830's, when Alexis de Tocqueville recorded his famous observations on America, he noted a 'strange melancholy that haunts the inhabitants…in the midst of abundance.' Americans believed that prosperity could quench their yearning for happiness, but such a hope was illusory, because, de Tocqueville added, 'the incomplete joys of this world will never satisfy [the human] heart.'"[31] Like any addict, you'll always need a little more, and true satisfaction, true happiness will always be a win away, because you're only as good as the outcome of your next game or season. Is winning what you look to in your search for significance, security, and fulfillment? If yes, then you have replaced God with an idol of your own making.

> You cannot desire pleasure too much. You *can* desire the *wrong kind* of pleasure. You can rely on the wrong things to satisfy your soul…[32] C.S. Lewis [said] "*the books or the music [or paintings] [or sporting performance] in which we thought the beauty was located will betray us if we trust to them; it was not in them, it only came through them, and what came through them was longing. These things…are good images of what we really desire; but if they are mistaken for the thing itself, they turn into dumb idols, breaking the hearts of their worshippers. For they are not the thing itself; they are only the scent of a flower we have not found, the echo of a tune we have not heard, news from a country we have never visited.*"[33]

"For some, sport is experienced as a kind of 'ecstasy,' a diversion from the humdrum of daily life. For others, sport has acquired an importance that goes beyond that of mere amusement or entertainment and has become a way of life itself, or a surrogate for religious experience."[34] Is your coaching pointing others to the all-satisfying treasure of the Rock or helping to raise another generation of addicts?

TOOLS

Ω Spend a week meditating upon Matthew 6:19-21, memorizing it, and asking the Holy Spirit where you are laying up your treasures – heaven or earth.

"Do not lay up for yourselves treasures on earth, where moth and rust destroy and where thieves break in and steal, but lay up for yourselves treasures in heaven, where neither moth nor rust destroys and where thieves do not break in and steal. For where your treasure is, there your heart will be also.

Ω Find your idols, then repent and trust in the empowering of the Holy Spirit for lasting change in your life.

In order to help you find your potential idols, begin asking yourself questions like these: Who are you trying to please through your coaching? What accolades are you hoping to accrue through your coaching? How do you react when your athletes don't perform as you hoped, or when you are not appreciated by those you are trying to please? Why?

Ω Do an emotional check-up. Ask others you trust to help you to clearly see your emotional barometer and what causes the pressure changes in your life.

"In this paradigm, we can locate idols by looking at our most unyielding emotions. What makes us uncontrollably angry, anxious, or despondent? What racks us with a guilt we can't shake? Idols control us, since we feel we must have them or life is meaningless."[35]

Ω Can you relate to Harold Abrahams, an Olympic sprinter portrayed in the movie *Chariots of Fire*? Do you find contentment in your coaching on a regular basis?

When asked why he runs, he says, he does not do it because he loves it. "I'm more of an addict…" he replies. Later, before running the hundred-meter Olympic event, he sighs: "Contentment! I'm twenty-four and I've never known it. I'm forever in pursuit and I don't even know what it is I'm chasing…I'll raise my eyes and look down that corridor, four feet wide, with ten lonely seconds to justify my whole existence…but will I?"[36]

Ω What battle plan can you learn from Jesus' temptation in the wilderness – as he was tempted with making idols of power, approval, comfort, and security?

> Then Jesus was led up by the Spirit into the wilderness to be tempted by the devil. And after fasting forty days and forty nights, he was hungry. And the tempter came and said to him, "If you are the Son of God, command these stones to become loaves of bread." But he answered, "It is written, 'Man shall not live by bread alone, but by every word that comes from the mouth of God.' " Then the devil took him to the holy city and set him on the pinnacle of the temple and said to him, "If you are the Son of God, throw yourself down, for it is written, 'He will command his angels concerning you,' and 'On their hands they will bear you up, lest you strike your foot against a stone.' " Jesus said to him, "Again it is written, 'you shall not put the Lord your God to the test.' " Again, the devil took him to a very high mountain

and showed him all the kingdoms of the world and their glory. And he said to him, "All these I will give you, if you will fall down and worship me." Then Jesus said to him, "Be gone, Satan! For it is written, 'You shall worship the Lord your God and him only shall you serve.' " Then the devil left him, and behold, angels came and were ministering to him. (Matthew 4:1-11)

Ω PRAYER

"Gracious and heavenly Father, Open my eyes that I may see wondrous things out of your law… Turn my eyes from looking at worthless things; and give me life in your ways…that my ways may be steadfast in keeping with your statutes…so I will bear fruit in keeping with repentance. When the snare of self-glorification is set about my feet, when the siren song of winning at all costs calls out to me, or when I rationalize not wholly following your ways, protect me from Satan's lies. Remind me that, No temptation has overtaken me that is not common to man. You, Lord God, are faithful, and you will not let me be tempted beyond my ability, but with the temptation you will also provide the way of escape, that I may be able to endure it. Therefore, empower me to flee from idolatry. I beg of you, 'Grant me the desire and ability to dig deep and lay a foundation on the rock so when the floods of temptations arise and the stream of lies my idols spew forth pound against my house, it will not be shaken. To you alone, belong all glory and honor and power!" (Psalm 119:18, 37, 5; Matthew 3:8; 1 Corinthians 10:13-14; Luke 6:48)

THE SILHOUETTE OF SCRIPTURE

"The Cross is the blazing fire at which the flame of our love is kindled, but we have to get near enough for its sparks to fall on us." (John Stott)

"And we all, with unveiled face, beholding the glory of the Lord, are being transformed into the same image from one degree of glory to another. For this comes from the Lord who is the Spirit." (2 Corinthians 3:18)

∞ *Why should we "study" the Bible?*

Provision

All Scripture is breathed out by God and profitable for teaching, for reproof, for correction, and for training in righteousness, that the man of God may be complete, equipped for every good work. (2 Timothy 3:16-17)

And beginning with Moses and all the Prophets, he [Jesus] interpreted to them in all the Scriptures the things concerning himself. (Luke 24:27)

Protection

See to it that no one takes you captive by philosophy and empty deceit, according to human tradition, according to the elemental spirits of the world, and not according to Christ. (Colossians 2:8)

… that their hearts may be encouraged, being knit together in love, to reach all the riches of full assurance of understanding and the knowledge of God's mystery, which is Christ, in whom are hidden all the treasures of wisdom and knowledge. I say this in order that no one may delude you with plausible arguments. (Colossians 2:2-4)

Prescription

You have commanded your precepts to be kept diligently. Oh that my ways may be steadfast in keeping your statutes! Then I shall not be put to shame, having my eyes fixed on all your commandments. I will praise you with an upright heart, when I learn your righteous rules. (Psalm 119:4-7)

This Book of the Law shall not depart from your mouth, but you shall meditate on it day and night, so that you may be careful to do according to all that is written in it. For then you will make your way prosperous, and then you will have good success. (Joshua 1:8)

∞ *How close are you willing to get to Jesus? What price are you willing to pay to sit and learn from him?*

Do you remember the story of Mary and Martha?

Now as they went on their way, Jesus entered a village. And a woman named Martha welcomed him into her house. And she had a sister called Mary, who sat at the Lord's feet and listened to his teaching. But Martha was distracted with much serving. And she went up to him and said, "Lord, do you not care that my sister has left me to serve alone? Tell her then to help me." But the Lord answered her, "Martha, Martha, you are anxious and troubled about many things, but one thing is necessary. Mary has chosen the good portion, which will not be taken away from her." (Luke 10:38-42)

Martha had good intentions, but wrong priorities at that moment. The preparations took priority over the Person. The work of the Lord was more important than the Lord of the work. Are you taking time to daily sit at the feet of Jesus, or are you distracted, worried, or upset about so many things that you don't choose what is better? If coaching is your profession, perhaps you feel that the time spent preparing workouts, game strategies, reviewing game film, checking on travel arrangements, and a myriad of other necessary tasks have kept you from sitting at the feet of the Rabbi. What story does your calendar disclose? Mary or Martha?

Watch and learn from Jesus' interaction with Zacchaeus. The Savior didn't have a day planner that mastered his every movement:

> He [Jesus] entered Jericho and was passing through. And behold, there was a man named Zacchaeus. He was a chief tax collector and was rich. And he was seeking to see who Jesus was, but on account of the crowd he could not, because he was small in stature. So he ran on ahead and climbed up into a sycamore tree to see him, for he was about to pass that way. And when Jesus came to the place, he looked up and said to him, "Zacchaeus, hurry and come down, for I must stay at your house today." So he hurried and came down and received him joyfully. And when they saw it, they all grumbled, "He has gone in to be the guest of a man who is a sinner." And Zacchaeus stood and said to the Lord, "Behold, Lord, the half of my goods I give to the poor. And if I have defrauded anyone of anything, I restore it fourfold." And Jesus said to him, "Today salvation has come to this house, since he also is a son of Abraham. For the Son of Man came to seek and to save the lost." (Luke 19:1-10)

Jesus was *passing through* Jericho. But He wasn't in such a hurry to keep on schedule that he forgot his true destination. He came to seek and save what was lost. What is your ultimate reason for coaching?

Do you spend your time worrying about getting from place to place in order to check off each task as it is completed? Or is your focus more on Jesus, his mission, and his glory? "Therefore, since we are surrounded by so great a cloud of witnesses, let us also lay aside every weight, and sin which clings so closely, and let us run with endurance the race that is set before us, looking to Jesus, the founder and perfecter of our faith, who for the joy that was set before him endured the cross, despising the shame, and is seated at the right hand of the throne of God.[37]

There are times when Christ and the calendar do not peacefully coexist. At those times, who will be your Master? Zacchaeus made his decision when he relinquished over half of his possessions in a heartbeat. When he saw Jesus, awe and love, reverent fear and rejoicing friendship flooded his heart. The same held true for Jonathan Edwards when he sat at the feet of Jesus.

> He [Edwards] wanted to experience and enjoy God through as many God ordained channels as possible. He didn't just read a chapter or two from the Bible and whisper a brief prayer of thanks, engaging in as few of the disciplines as possible

without feeling guilty. Edwards viewed all the biblical spiritual disciplines as the divinely appointed means of experiencing the holy God he found so addictive to the soul.[38]

∞ *Do you desire this same type of intimacy? What are some of the reasons that might be keeping you from meditating upon the Bible, soaking it in, studying it more in-depth?*

Priorities

- You have to plan time in the day to read Scripture. The pressing needs of the day are continually screaming at us, so we hurry through Scripture in the hopes something will stick. The thought of finding undistracted time in the Scriptures seems daunting.
- We ultimately might not have a conviction as to its true value in our lives.

My son, if you receive my words and treasure up my commandments with you, making your ear attentive to wisdom and inclining your heart to understanding; yes, if you call out for insight and raise your voice for understanding, if you seek it like silver and search for it as for hidden treasures, then you will understand the fear of the LORD and find the knowledge of God. (Proverbs 2:1-5)

Perspiration

- We live in a sound bite culture. More than 140 characters causes overload for some of us. That reality means activities like meditation upon Scripture are avoided, because it takes undistracted time being still. But what joy would flow forth if we had experiences like Edwards?

I seem too often to see so much light exhibited by every sentence, and such a refreshing food communicated, that I could not get along in reading; often dwelling on one sentence to see the wonders contained in it, and yet almost every sentence seemed to be full of wonders.[39]

- The word *study* implies "zeal", "earnest endeavor", "diligence", "to examine closely." Too many churches have imitated secular educational systems where memorization and regurgitation are the norm. The result is that meditation and thinking are not developed.

Work hard so you can present yourself to God and receive his approval. Be a good worker, one who does not need to be ashamed and who correctly explains the word of truth. (2 Timothy 2:15)

Preparation

- "I don't know how to meditate upon Scripture."

The tendency of most Christians in hurried, overburdened times is to close the Bible as soon as they've read it and turn to the next thing on the to-do list. If pressed, we'd usually have to admit – immediately after closing the Bible – that we don't remember a thing we read. Reading alone will seldom give us the encounter with God, the spiritual nourishment that our souls need. Reading is the exposure to Scripture – and that's the starting place – but meditation is the absorption of Scripture. And it is the absorption of Scripture that causes the water of the Word of God to percolate deeply into the parched soil of the soul and refresh it.[40]

- "I don't know how to study Scripture. I've never been taught." It is difficult to find even a basic class in most churches on 'how-to' study Scripture.

We have too often bitten into the lie that the pastors are the professionals, and we should leave the thinking to them. An undo amount of pressure and expectations is placed upon pastors to do the work and then feed the rest of us. It needs to be a partnership with pastors and people participating in the blessing of delving into the Word!

And all the people gathered as one man into the square before the Water Gate. And they told Ezra the scribe to bring the Book of the Law of Moses that the LORD had commanded Israel. *So Ezra the priest brought the Law before the assembly... And he read from it facing the square before the Water Gate from early morning until midday, in the presence of the men and the women and those who could understand. And the ears of all the people were attentive to the Book of the Law.* And Ezra the scribe stood on a wooden platform that they had made for the purpose... And Ezra opened the book in the sight of all the people, for he was above all the people, and as he opened it all the people stood... And Ezra blessed the LORD, the great God, and all the people answered, "Amen, Amen," lifting up their hands. And *they* bowed their heads and worshiped the LORD with their faces to the ground... Also...*the Levites, helped the people to understand the Law*, while the people remained in their places. They read from the book, from the Law of God, clearly, and they gave the sense, so that the people understood the reading. (Nehemiah 8:1-8, italics mine)

∞ *What Does it Take to Begin this Journey?*

* Must depend on the Holy Spirit to guide and direct.

> The natural person does not accept the things of the Spirit of God, for they are folly to him, and he is not able to understand them because they are spiritually discerned. (1 Corinthians 2:14)

* Must have a desire to understand God's Word.

> I will study your commandments and reflect on your ways. I will delight in your decrees and not forget your word. (Psalm 119:15-16)

* Must have a desire to see, understand, and tell others about the majesty of God.

> …just as men spontaneously praise whatever they value, so they spontaneously urge us to join them in praising it: 'Isn't she lovely? Wasn't it glorious? Don't you think that magnificent?' The Psalmists in telling everyone to praise God are doing what all men do when they speak of what they care about. (C.S. Lewis)

> If we were not allowed to speak of what we value and celebrate what we love and praise and what we admire, our joy would not be full… [God] loves us and seeks the fullness of our joy that can be found only in knowing and praising Him, the most magnificent of all Beings. [41] (John Piper)

* Must realize you are valuable in God's eyes.

> So *God created human beings in his own image.* In the image of God he created them; male and female he created them…Then *God looked over all he had made,* and he saw that it was *very good*! (Genesis 1:27, 31, italics mine)

> God alone can awaken in our souls the marvel and wonders of which he is worthy... That alone will break the power of sin, deliver us from spiritual mediocrity, and bring us into the depths of delight for which he created us.[42]

TOOLS

Ω **Plan a specific time and place where there are no distractions so you can read, meditate, study, and feast upon God's Word - no texts, no social media, no phone ringing, no interruptions.**

Have someone be praying for your desire to build this pattern into your life. Also, grant them permission to keep you accountable by asking, in love, how the process is going.

> All Scripture is breathed out by God and profitable for teaching, for reproof, for correction, and for training in righteousness, that the man of God may be complete, equipped for every good work. (2 Timothy 3:16-17)

> We must get into the Word and the Word must get into us. We get into the Word by hearing it preached, reading it, studying it, and memorizing. We get the Word into us through meditation. By meditating on it, we assimilate the Word of God into our spiritual lives.[43]

Ω Find a Bible reading plan that helps you work through the entire Bible so that you are continually immersing yourself in the big picture. Learn to study the Word at a deeper level.

Reading through the Bible "in a year" is not the ultimate goal – the goal is reading the entire Bible. (See the appendices for the *Basic Inductive Bible Study Steps* & *Three Tips for Better Bible Reading*).

- Various Bible Reading Plans can be found on the Bible Study Tools website.
- Several *One Year Bibles* are available through vendors like Amazon.
- ***Read The Bible For Life: Your Guide to Understanding & Living God's Word*** by George H. Guthrie.
- ***Dig Deeper: Tools for Understanding God's Word*** by Nigel Benyon & Andrew Sach.

Ω Study the gospel message that centers on the atoning work of Christ on the cross as you read through Scripture.

To grow in your *passion* for what Jesus has done, increase your *understanding* of what He has done. Never be content with your current grasp of the gospel.

- Romans, Galatians, atonement, substitution, propitiation, justification, reconciliation, salvation. *The Gospel for Real Life* by Jerry Bridges explains each of these words in detail.
- Listen to Cross-centered recordings on the daily commute.
- Read your whole Bible with your eyes peeled for the Gospel. It has been noted that every passage of Scripture - in both the Old and the New Testaments - either predicts, prepares for, reflects, or results from the work of Christ. For discovering the storyline of the gospel throughout Scripture, there is no better guide than the two volumes *For the Love of God* by D.A. Carson; and *According to Plan: The Unfolding Revelation of God in the Bible* by Graeme Goldsworthy.

- Make it an annual goal to read or reread at least one book on the cross: *The Cross of Christ* by John Stott; *The Discipline of Grace* by Jerry Bridges; *The Power of the Cross of Christ* by Charles Spurgeon; *The Cross and Christian Ministry* by D. A. Carson.[44]
- I'd also recommend *Living the Cross Centered Life* by C. J. Mahaney.

Ω Meditate upon and memorize these passages of Scripture as a starting point to help you remember how the gospel has changed you.

He was despised and rejected by men; a man of sorrows, and acquainted with grief; and as one from whom men hide their faces he was despised, and we esteemed him not. Surely he has borne our griefs and carried our sorrows; yet we esteemed him stricken, smitten by God, and afflicted. But he was pierced for our transgressions; he was crushed for our iniquities; upon him was the chastisement that brought us peace, and with his wounds we are healed. All we like sheep have gone astray; we have turned—every one—to his own way; and the LORD has laid on him the iniquity of us all. (Isaiah 53:3–6)

…for all have sinned and fall short of the glory of God, and are justified by his grace as a gift, through the redemption that is in Christ Jesus, whom God put forward as a propitiation by his blood, to be received by faith. This was to show God's righteousness, because in his divine forbearance he had passed over former sins. It was to show his righteousness at the present time, so that he might be just and the justifier of the one who has faith in Jesus. (Romans 3:23–26)

So admit it: you're the worst sinner, you know. Admit you're unworthy and deserve to be condemned. *But don't stop there!* Move on to rejoicing in the Savior who came to save the worst of sinners. Lay down the luggage of condemnation and kneel and worship at the feet of him who bore your sins. Cry tears of amazement. And confess with Paul: "But I received mercy for this reason, that in me, as the foremost, Jesus Christ might display his perfect patience as an example to those who were to believe in him for eternal life."[45] [1 Timothy 1:16]

Ω PRAYER

"Heavenly Father, your hands have made me and fashioned me; give me understanding that I may learn your commandments…so my heart will be blameless in your statutes, so that I will not be put to shame…for your word is in my mouth and in my heart, so that I can do it. Empower me, therefore, to lay aside every weight and sin that clings so closely so that I may run with endurance the race that is set before me, looking to Jesus, the founder and perfecter of my faith, who for the joy that was set before him endured the cross, despising the shame, and is now seated at your right hand. Daily grant me a passion to behold the glory of Jesus so that I will be continually transformed into his image from one degree of glory to another. Empower me to hunger and thirst after righteousness, for then I will be satisfied. Let me never forget your precepts, for by them you have given me life… for whatever was written in former days was written for our instruction, that through endurance and through the encouragement of the Scriptures we might have hope. So may I daily search the Scriptures because in them is eternal life because they bear witness about Jesus." (Psalm 119:73, 80; Hebrews 12:1-2; Deuteronomy 30:14; Matthew 5:6; Psalm 119:93; Romans 15:4; John 5:39)

Notes

[1] Justin Taylor, "Ravi Zacharias on Postmodern Architecture at Ohio State," *The Gospel Coalition*, 1/13/14, Accessed 6/9/14. http://thegospelcoalition.org/blogs/justintaylor/2014/01/13/ravi-zacharias-on-postmodern-architecture-at-ohio-state/.

[2] Matthew 7:24-27.

[3] Westminster Shorter Catechism.

[4] John Piper & Justin Taylor, General Editors, *A God Entranced Vision of All Things: The Legacy of Jonathan Edwards* (Wheaton: Crossway, 2004), 86.

[5] Matthew 2:1-2.

[6] Matthew 2:3.

[7] Matthew 2:4-6.

[8] Matthew 2:7-8.

[9] Matthew 2:9-10.

[10] Matthew 2:11.

[11] Max Lucado, *It's Not About Me* (Brentwood: Integrity, 2004), 38.

[12] Philip Yancey, *A Bow and a Kiss*, Christianity Today, (May, 2005).

[13] Sam Storms, *One Thing: Developing a Passion for the Beauty of God* (Scotland: Christian Focus, 2004), 34-35.

[14] Yancey, op. cit.

[15] Psalm 19:1.

[16] Storms, op. cit., 20.

[17] John 1:1-3.

[18] Genesis 3:4-5.

[19] Colossians 1:16, italics mine.

[20] i.e., Romans 4:8-11.

[21] Isaiah 43:25.

[22] Isaiah 43:21.

[23] Philippians 2:8-11.

[24] R.C. Sproul in C.J. Mahaney, *Living the Cross Centered Life: Keeping the Gospel the Main Thing* (Colorado Springs: Multnomah, 2006), 60-61.

[25] Isaiah 48:9-11, italics mine.

[26] 1 Corinthians 10:31, italics mine.

[27] 1 Timothy 1:17.

[28] Mark Driscoll, *Have No Other Gods*, Sermon – 12/15/2013. Mars Hill Church, Seattle, WA.

[29] Luke 16:13-15.

[30] 1 Corinthians 6:19-20.

[31] Alexis de Tocqueville in Timothy Keller, *Counterfeit Gods: The Empty Promises of Money, Sex, and Power, and the Only Hope that Matters* (New York: Dutton, 2009), x.

32 Storms, op. cit., 28.

33 C.S. Lewis in Ibid., 54-55.

34 Edited by Kevin Lixey, L.C., Christoph Hubenthal, Dietmar Mieth, and Norbert Muller, *Sport & Christianity: A Sign of the Times in the Light of Faith* (Washington, D.C.: The Catholic University of America Press, 2012), 2.

35 Keller, op. cit., xxii.

36 Harold Abrahams in Ibid, 73.

37 Hebrews 12:1-2.

38 Piper & Taylor, op. cit., 125.

39 Jonathan Edwards in Ibid., 113.

40 Ibid., 49.

41 John Piper, *Desiring God: Meditations of a Christian Hedonist* (Colorado Springs: Multnomah, 2011), 49.

42 Storms, op. cit., 149.

43 LeRoy Eims, *Be The Leader You Were Meant To Be* (Wheaton: Victor, 1996), 21.

44 Mahaney, op. cit., 141-144.

45 Ibid., 130.

5

UNCEASING PRAY-ER

THE GREAT OMISSION

"Make it easy on your soul by exposing your senses to those things that awaken spiritual desire and deepen holy longings. God has appointed specific activities that are designed to ignite passion for his Son and elicit insatiable hunger for his presence…prayer and Scripture."[1]

"Rejoice always, pray without ceasing, give thanks in all circumstances; for this is the will of God in Christ Jesus for you." (1 Thessalonians 5:16-18)

By all accounts, these quotes sum up the regular rhythms of Jonathan Edward's life. "Prayer, then, for Edwards was both planned and informal, scheduled and spontaneous, on a daily basis… it was as though Edwards could not think long of God without speaking or singing to him."[2] Is this the longing of your heart for your prayer life? If you are not quite in the same league as Edwards, don't be discouraged. Few are. But that doesn't mean that you can't progress in your journey, by the power of the Holy Spirit.

"[T]he most advanced leader is conscious of the possibility of endless developing in his prayer life… But, strange paradox, most of us find it hard to pray… We call it indispensable; we know the Scriptures call for it. Yet we often fail to pray."[3] It truly is the Great Omission in many of our personal and corporate lives in America. Why is that so frequently the case? "In the early days of the church, the founding members spent hours in prayer. Today the church is large, well-attended, well-funded. Who needs to pray? Success begets amnesia."[4]

The total amount of time the average professing Christian spends in daily prayer is less than five minutes. The most common type of prayer is a brief "grace" before a meal. Can you imagine having a spouse, good friend (not just the Facebook variety), boyfriend or girlfriend with whom you communicated for less than five minutes per day? What would be the end result of such a relationship?

God has chosen prayer as a primary means for his interaction with his people. Even for Jesus, prayer was a life-giving source in every circumstance. He prayed to know the Father's will, to have power to do that will, and to have perseverance to finish his course. How can we do any less and expect to follow the narrow path? But maybe amnesia is not your problem. Perhaps your reason is like many who I've heard from over the years: "No one ever taught me how to pray."

Towards the end of his life, Samuel Chadwick mused, "I wish I had prayed more, even if I had worked less; and from the bottom of my heart I wish I had prayed better."[5] May those words warn and encourage you.

∞ *How is your prayer life?*

Do your knees weaken when prayer time is announced? Find yourself licking parched lips while desperately searching for an escape, afraid that someone will call on you to pray? Maybe you're not afraid to pray, but you're still not sure if you're doing it "right." Have you ever wondered what Jesus' brother James meant when he said, "When you ask, you do not receive because you ask with wrong motives, that you may spend what you get on your pleasures"?[6] Do you know how to pray with right motives?

Early on in life, the traditional method of praying via the Presbyterian Church became my staple diet. Head bowed, eyes closed, fingers clasped so tightly that knuckles turned white. Any peep other than from the responsive reading met with scolding glares. Never mind the fact that I couldn't understand half of the responses – "Wither thou goest, I will beith with theeith for evereth." Opening one eye in my best *Popeye* imitation during prayer time caused further me confusion during my early years. All the white knuckles around the sanctuary reminded me of being on a flight experiencing serious turbulence. This scene repeated itself wherever I visited friends and relatives in Methodist, Lutheran, and Baptist congregations. I'd heard the Catholics did things differently than Protestants – including praying. Something about Hail Marys and grocery beads. But I also confess that paying close attention was not one of my strong suits as a child.

Since I was of some Irish descent, a visit to my Catholic kin in Pennsylvania gave me a chance at a first-hand education in this style of prayer. During my first Mass, we solemnly paraded down the center aisle, each person dipping his or her finger in water, kneeling and making the sign of the cross before entering the pew – except for me. It didn't get any better as the service progressed. Have you ever seen the person in the marching band who is a step behind, his gaze flashing side-to-side in an attempt to figure out which direction to head next? That was me. Like parts in a fully automated factory, every other person rose in synch, sat in synch, prayed in synch, genuflected in synch, and flipped the kneeling pads down and back up in synch.

Frantically flipping pages through the Catholic order of worship, I'd just get to the right place when they finished their prayers – which everyone else had memorized. "...Died under Pontius Pilate, buried, rose three days later..." I only thought I was lost – then the priest broke out in Latin.

After becoming a disciple of Jesus, I figured that praying would be a snap. Open mouth, prayers flow forth, done deal. Wrong. I searched everywhere I could think of to get a grasp on prayer. Talk about chasing after the wind. Healing services plopped me in a pew next to a person praying out loud in 'tongues', which I had most definitely not been introduced to in the Presbyterian Church! Charismatic prayer times seemed like a spiritual aerobics class.

Certainly graduating from a Christian university and two seminaries would bring fluidity to my prayers. Unfortunately, all that formal training didn't include one class on prayer. So the words of James continued to haunt me. Were my prayers self-centered, seeking to squander what I received on myself? Did I have evil motives or pure ones? How could I possibly know with certainty that I was praying God's will?

Then one day it hit me. If I pray God's Word back to him, I know those prayers will be in harmony with his will. To that end, we will start by examining what is commonly known as the "The Lord's Prayer" – a prayer that has been said so many times that I fear we have become numb to its implications for our lives.

TOOLS

Ω **Spend a few days asking the Holy Spirit to daily give you peace about where you are in your prayer journey. Ask him to release you from any fears or frustrations so that you have a clear pathway as you seek to grow in your prayer life.**

Prayer is his idea. God commands you to "pray without ceasing," and he will empower you as you progress towards that goal. He wants you to be successful!

Ω **Search your own coaching background for how you help your athletes learn new ideas about their sport, or how you help them to improve upon areas where they already have knowledge and experience.**

Understand that God's patience towards you in this process and desire for you to learn how to communicate with him is exponentially greater than your most patient and passionate coaching day.

Ω PRAYER

"I praise you, Lord Jesus, for coming in the flesh so I might see and understand you more clearly. Help me to fall at your feet and worship you, whom I see throughout Scripture. And Holy Spirit, help me to perceive when the Great Deceiver is in my midst. I never want to doubt the reality and identity of my resurrected Lord, and fail to properly worship you. What a joy to know that you, Lord Jesus, constantly pursue me because of your great love. I do believe that you have all authority in heaven and on earth. So 'I bow my knee before your throne, I know this life is not my own.' Grant me the eyes to see where you want me to go to make disciples, the wisdom to know when to baptize them, the ability to teach them your commands, and the heart to believe that truly you are with me always. You alone can empower me to love you with all of my heart, all of my soul, all of my mind, and all of my strength, and to love my neighbor as myself. May your will be done on earth as it is in heaven!"

OUR FATHER

"Surely if anyone could have sustained life without prayer, it would be the very Son of God himself… [But] to Jesus, prayer was not a hasty add-on, but a joyous necessity."[7]

"Beware of practicing your righteousness before other people in order to be seen by them, for then you will have no reward from your Father who is in heaven… And when you pray, you must not be like the hypocrites. For they love to stand and pray in the synagogues and at the street corners, that they may be seen by others. Truly, I say to you, they have received their reward. But when you pray, go into your room and shut the door and pray to your Father who is in secret. And your Father who sees in secret will reward you. And when you pray, do not heap up empty phrases as the Gentiles do, for they think that they will be heard for their many words. Do not be like them, for your Father knows what you need before you ask him." (Matthew 6:1, 5-8)

∞ *How did Jesus teach his disciples, (including those in the 21ˢᵗ century), to pray?*

Before we jump straight into what is commonly known as The Lord's Prayer, it is important to see what Jesus said immediately preceding his well-known petition. In Matthew 6:1-8, Jesus warns his disciples about "practicing their righteousness before men in order to be seen by them." It is a strong rebuke about playing the role of the holy person merely so that others will think highly of you. What might this look like in someone's prayer life? Verses 5-6 warn against big production pray-ers, the kind of people who perform and put themselves in good positions in order to be seen and heard by others. The focus is upon the pray-er, not the Savior. In verses 7-8, Jesus warns against thoughtless prayers that are mere repetitive babblings. The mouth is engaged, but not the heart. These people hope that many words will garner God's attention. So what will safeguard you from these errors?

> Pray then like this: "Our Father in heaven, hallowed be your name. Your kingdom come, your will be done, on earth as it is in heaven. Give us this day our daily bread, and forgive us our debts, as we also have forgiven our debtors. And lead us not into temptation, but deliver us from evil. (Matthew 6:9–13)

Pray Then Like This

The first thing to notice is that "pray" is in the present imperative, which simply means that it is supposed to be an ongoing practice in your life. It should be as consistent as the ocean waves lapping up on the shore. That is the natural, God-designed rhythm of the ocean. Yes, there are times when the waves come more frequently or with greater force, but they always keep coming. This should be the ultimate goal of your prayer life – praying without ceasing.

Second, Jesus gives his disciples a framework to follow, a guide to help them pray in a God-honoring way. It is critical to understand that Jesus said to pray "like" this, not necessarily with these exact words. Yes, The Lord's Prayer is obviously great to pray as is, but that's not all it is meant to be. This is a model to also help guide you in all your other prayers. So let's turn to some of the key phrases in this prayer that will aid you in praying with right motives.

Our Father In Heaven

"Our" implies a corporate mindset, a team, the Body of Christ unified in bringing our requests before the Lord in a manner that puts his glory and our dependence on display. This means that you are not alone in this journey. You have brothers and sisters who are running the race alongside you. We need each other! It is imperative that your athletes know this is true for their lives also. Even if they are not Christians, or maybe even more so, they need to know that they are part of a corporate entity that truly wants the best for them, and also helps them to understand that they cannot achieve that potential on their own. The ultimate hope is that your team will be a springboard to help all your athletes desire to be part of the Body of Christ. "Two are better than one, because they have a good reward for their toil. For if they fall, one will lift up his fellow. But woe to him who is alone when he falls and has not another to lift him up!"[8]

> I wonder if we should expect our private prayer life to advance in maturity and depth and intensity if we never pray with others who can lift us higher and take us deeper. Wouldn't that be like expecting a young person to become a gifted conversationalist, but always sending him away to play by himself whenever there was a serious conversation? Praying together is not for the sake of exalting our individual strengths but for the sake of becoming one with the family and helping each other mature in the life of prayer.[9]

Be honest. Do you have trouble envisioning God as your Father, your Abba Daddy[10]? You're not alone. The idea never seemingly crossed the minds of any Jewish person before Jesus arrived on the scene. They rarely addressed God as "Father." When the term is used in the Old Testament, it is as an example, not as a child calling out to his dad. For instance, "As a father shows compassion to his children, so the LORD shows compassion to those who fear him."[11] Jesus, however, addressed God as his Father in every prayer but one.[12]

The early church followed the pattern Jesus taught in this prayer and the pattern he taught through his life, and so should you. "For you did not receive the spirit of slavery to fall back into fear, but you have received the Spirit of adoption as sons, by whom we cry, 'Abba! Father!' "[13] "And because you are sons, God has sent the Spirit of his Son into our hearts, crying, 'Abba! Father!' "[14]

Come and talk to your loving heavenly Father. He is waiting with open arms, regardless of how he may have been portrayed to you in your past.

Staring out the windows of the fellowship hall, I watched the whitecaps dance atop the ocean. Birds darting back and forth, with occasional dive-bombs to the water's surface, captivated the mind of this eleven-year-old transplant to Southern California. The sermon held no sway compared to God's orchestration of creation's movements. Turning my metal folding chair ninety-degrees in order to get a better view was probably not the best idea. "Mister, turn that chair around and pay attention!" I obeyed, reluctantly. An ensuing crick arose in my neck from straining to see the majesty of the poetry unfolding outside.

The situation disintegrated further after the sermon ended. "Come on Chris. Hurry up. We're going to see the new sanctuary being built." Once I was inside, my eyes zeroed in on the stairs. Like a shot, I bolted up, ran across the balcony and back down the other side. On my fourth lap I was stopped abruptly by a hand jerking on the back of my shirt.

"Young man, do you know where you are?" said the pastor.

"Yah," I said, with head tilted and one eyebrow raised.

"This is God's house! We do not run in God's house. If I ever see you running in here again I will put the fear of God in you!"

With that, his bony fingers released my shirt and he summarily dismissed me, furrowed brow and beady eyes following me as I slinked out the door.

So my dark journey into religion continued. The fear of God meant the same thing as the hammer of God to me. Follow the rules and God will be happy – "Sit still, don't talk, close your eyes when you pray, don't even think about doodling on the collection envelope, and never-ever run!" Fear wracked my mind. I was constantly on the alert that God was watching and waiting for me to fail. And I was supposed to go and talk to him?[15]

But I praise God that the truths in his Word have been the reliable weapon for me to slay the serpent as he hisses lies into my ears about my Father:

Ask, and it will be given to you; seek, and you will find; knock, and it will be opened to you. For everyone who asks receives, and the one who seeks finds, and to the one who knocks it will be opened. Or which one of you, if his son asks him for bread, will give him a stone? Or if he asks for a fish, will give him a serpent? If you then, who are evil, know how to give good gifts to your children, how much more will your Father who is in heaven give good things to those who ask him! (Matthew 7:7-11)

Yet as much as I desire that you know that intimacy with God, and seek that it gets passed on to your athletes, I am compelled to issue a warning. In our day when "Relaxed, Relevant, and Real" seems to be the overarching mantra in many churches, the awe and reverence of a holy God is lost. "In heaven" is a reminder that God is not just your Father to whom you can run. He is also the Creator, Redeemer, and Sustainer of the entire universe before whom you should tremble. "Be not rash with your mouth, nor let your heart be hasty to utter a word before God, for God is in heaven and you are on earth."[16] May the Spirit enable you to live out the balance between running to God and falling on your knees in his holy presence.

Hallowed Be Your Name

This is one of those churchy words that many people are in the dark about. "The word 'hallow' means sanctify, which can mean *make* holy or *treat as* holy. When God sanctifies us, it means that he makes us holy. But when we sanctify God, it means that we treat him as holy."[17] When we sin, we do the opposite and profane his name. "You recently repented and did what was right in my eyes by proclaiming liberty, each to his neighbor, and you made a covenant before me in the house that is called by my name, but then you turned around and profaned my name when each of you took back his male and female slaves, whom you had set free according to their desire, and you brought them into subjection to be your slaves."[18]

The name of God refers to his identity, character, and authority. It represents all that God is – holy and perfect, loving and merciful, with no equal. Therefore, his name is hallowed, treated as holy, when his people show that he is their greatest treasure by obeying his commands through the empowering of the Holy Spirit, because this is God's passion for his name.

Therefore say to the house of Israel, Thus says the Lord GOD: "It is not for your sake, O house of Israel, that I am about to act, but for the sake of my holy name, which you have profaned among the nations to which you came. And I will vindicate the holiness of my great name, which has been profaned among the nations, and which you have profaned among them. And the nations will know that I am the LORD, declares the Lord GOD, when through you I vindicate my holiness before their eyes. I will take you from the nations and gather you from all the countries and bring you into your own land. I will sprinkle clean water on you, and you shall be clean from all your uncleannesses, and from all your idols I will cleanse you. And I will give you a new heart, and a new spirit I will put within you. And I will remove the heart of stone from your flesh and give you a heart of flesh. And I will put my Spirit within you, and cause you to walk in my statutes and be careful to obey my rules."[19]

John Piper gives a succinct summary of this concept for us: "'Hallowed be your name' = cause your word to be *believed*, cause your displeasure to be *feared*, cause your commandments to be *obeyed*, and cause yourself to be *glorified*.[20] Consider the following:

Believe God's Word: And the LORD said to Moses and Aaron, "Because you did not believe in me, to uphold me as holy in the eyes of the people of Israel, therefore you shall not bring this assembly into the land that I have given them."[21]

Fear Displeasing God, not Man: "For am I now seeking the approval of man, or of God? Or am I trying to please man? If I were still trying to please man, I would not be a servant of Christ."[22]

Obey God's Word: "So you shall keep my commandments and do them: I am the LORD. And you shall not profane my holy name, that I may be sanctified among the people of Israel. I am the LORD who sanctifies you, who brought you out of the land of Egypt to be your God: I am the LORD."[23]

Hallowed = Glorified: Then Moses said to Aaron, This is what the LORD has said: "Among those who are near me I will be sanctified, and before all the people I will be glorified."[24]

Your Kingdom Come, Your Will Be Done, On Earth As It Is In Heaven

This part of the prayer will help you to keep an eternal perspective in your coaching. "What is your life? For you are a mist that appears for a little time and then vanishes."[25] Life is a vapor. All that you think, say, and do as a coach should ultimately be focused on the fulfillment of God's kingdom purposes here on earth. Seasons will come and go in the blink of an eye, but God's sovereign reign is forever.

The Lord's Prayer asks for God's perfect will to be done here on earth, just like it is in heaven. There is no middle ground. Your focus will either be "My will be done" or "Thy will be done." Do you believe in God's sovereign, loving will? I hope so. For it is the only way that you can handle the highs and lows that come with every season, every athlete, and every career (even if it is as a part-time volunteer). This clings closely to the reality in the often-quoted Romans 8:28-30:

And we know that for those who love God all things work together for good, for those who are called according to his purpose. For those whom he foreknew he also predestined to be conformed to the image of his Son, in order that he might be the firstborn among many brothers. And those whom he predestined he also called, and those whom he called he also justified, and those whom he justified he also glorified.

Do you anticipate a day when you will be glorified? For "our citizenship is in heaven, and from it we await a Savior, the Lord Jesus Christ, who will transform our lowly body to be like his glorious body, by the power that enables him even to subject all things to himself."[26] Do you anticipate a day when there will be no more evil, no more tears, no more pain, no more suffering? "And I heard a loud voice from the throne saying, 'Behold, the dwelling place of God is with man. He will dwell with them, and they will be his people, and God himself will be with them as their God. He will wipe away every tear from their eyes, and death shall be no more, neither shall there be mourning, nor crying, nor pain anymore, for the former things have passed away.'"[27]

Now think about what that day will be like for the athletes under your care who are not Christians. "Then the kings of the earth and the great ones and the generals and the rich and the powerful, and everyone, slave and free, hid themselves in the caves and among the rocks of the mountains, calling to the mountains and rocks, 'Fall on us and hide us from the face of him who is seated on the throne, and from the wrath of the Lamb, for the great day of their wrath has come, and who can stand?'"[28] Your coaching has significance way beyond athletic performances and preparation for life here and now. Every athlete you coach has an eternal destination in front of them. Will you lead them in the right direction?

Give Us This Day Our Daily Bread

This petition acknowledges that you are dependent on God in order to survive and thrive. The necessity to ask for daily bread represents the reality that you come before God with nothing but open hands for all your needs to be met. As I remember hearing once, "This prayer is for all our needs, not our greeds." It is only pride or delusion that allows anyone to believe he can accomplish anything apart from God. "I am the vine; you are the branches. Whoever abides in me and I in him, he it is that bears much fruit, for apart from me you can do nothing."[29]Does your prayer life in regards to each facet of your coaching reveal a continual dependence upon him? That type of heart-attitude glorifies God and shows him to be holy, because he alone is the Sustainer of all things. For "in him we live and move and have our being."[30] Or do you rely too heavily on your past experiences, education, and intuition as your guide apart from God?

And Forgive Us Our Debts, As We Also Have Forgiven Our Debtors

This petition reflects a humble awareness of our ongoing need for God's forgiveness. How are you doing in this arena? Are the words of the Psalmist a recurring theme in your prayers? "Search me, O God, and know my heart! Try me and know my thoughts! And see if there be any grievous way in me, and lead me in the way everlasting!"[31] This may be the best starting point for you in dealing with the sins, failures, and affronts of those you deal with regularly as a coach. Players, parents, administrators, and other coaches are all human, which means that you will be sinned against. How do you respond in those situations?

> The point is that true prayer is motivated by a humble spirit ever cognizant of personal failures and inadequacies. Expectation of God's forgiveness is predicated upon a forgiving spirit extended to those who have sinned against us. Erecting barriers and continually harboring resentment toward others will have a corresponding negative impact on our relationship to God (cf. vv. 14–15; 18:21–35).

In fact it is a betrayal of our identity as God's children to maintain a spirit of animosity and bitterness toward others.[32]

May God open your eyes to the depth of your sins against the holy and righteous God of the universe so that the sins of others against you are seen in proper perspective. I'm not saying to pretend they don't exist. I'm saying you need to deal with them with the focus upon God's glory and not your own. If the offending party has already been forgiven through Christ's atoning work on the cross, you can add nothing to that majestic work. Conversely, if that person is doomed to hell, you can add nothing that will make that sentence of eternal damnation any worse.

> Then Peter came up and said to him, "Lord, how often will my brother sin against me, and I forgive him? As many as seven times?" Jesus said to him, "I do not say to you seven times, but seventy-seven times. (Matthew 18:21-22)

> Repay no one evil for evil, but give thought to do what is honorable in the sight of all. If possible, so far as it depends on you, live peaceably with all. Beloved, never avenge yourselves, but leave it to the wrath of God, for it is written, "Vengeance is mine, I will repay, says the Lord." To the contrary, "if your enemy is hungry, feed him; if he is thirsty, give him something to drink; for by so doing you will heap burning coals on his head." Do not be overcome by evil, but overcome evil with good. (Romans 12:17-21)

And Lead Us Not Into Temptation, But Deliver Us From Evil (or Evil One)

Did you notice that the final three petitions were linked by the word "and"? Many commentators believe that this is a way to show that life is not sustained by food alone. Our dependence on God's intervening and sustaining includes the forgiveness of sins and the deliverance from temptation. Matthew Henry illustrates it this way, "Our daily bread doth but fatten us as lambs for the slaughter if our sins be not pardoned."[33]Without deliverance from temptation, we are stuck in a downward spiral of sin upon sin. But God has provided us with a way out. Satan is looking to devour you. Do you regularly pray for protection from temptation and deliverance from him? Consider all the opportunities that arise to bend the rules, cut corners, flat-out cheat, or treat your athletes as commodities in the quest to win. How will you battle against those temptations when they come?

> Be sober-minded; be watchful. Your adversary the devil prowls around like a roaring lion, seeking someone to devour. Resist him, firm in your faith, knowing that the same kinds of suffering are being experienced by your brotherhood throughout the world. (1 Peter 5:8-9)

It is important to note that this petition is not asking God to keep us from being confronted with temptations. That would be odd considering the fact that the Holy Spirit led Jesus into the wilderness to be tempted by Satan.[34] And Jesus himself said, "…it is necessary that temptations come, but woe to the one by whom the temptation comes!"[35] What this petition means is, "don't let us fall to Satan's temptations" and "empower us to keep from sinning as a result of giving into temptations." Daily calling upon the Lord's protection from temptation and the evil one should be the starting point. But you must follow through with seeking further wisdom from his Word on how to resist the devil, and the Holy Spirit's empowering to follow through.

> Therefore let anyone who thinks that he stands take heed lest he fall. No temptation has overtaken you that is not common to man. God is faithful, and he will not let you be tempted beyond your ability, but with the temptation he will also provide the way of escape, that you may be able to endure it. Therefore, my beloved, flee from idolatry. (1 Corinthians 10:12-14)

TOOLS

Ω Do you have a regular set time and place for prayer? Do you pray spontaneously throughout the day as different circumstances or promptings arise?

Find a set time and place each day where you can and will pray without being interrupted. As soon as possible, begin developing a habit of daily prayer time. Ask someone to pray for the Spirit to empower you to develop this habit, and to increase your delight in Jesus during these times of prayer.

Ω Do you have regular set times of prayer with others?

If you are married, this should be your starting point, if it is not already a habit in your lives. Outside of this, prayerfully seek out other coaches, friends, teachers, or administrators based on where you are coaching. If you do not have these corporate times of prayer on a regular basis, ask the Holy Spirit to specifically reveal who you should ask.

Ω Do a study of God's names in order to go deeper in your understanding, appreciation, and awe of his holiness and his loving sovereignty operating in your life.

Two resources you may want to consider are *The Names of God* by Ann Spangler, and *Praying the Names of God* by Ann Spangler.

Ω Carefully study Jesus' prayers in Matthew 11:25-30, Mark 14:36, and John 17:1-26.

See what themes you can find that are similar to what we have learned together from the Lord's Prayer.

Ω PRAYER

"Our Father in heaven, hallowed be your name. Your kingdom come, your will be done, on earth as it is in heaven. Give us this day our daily bread, and forgive us our debts, as we also have forgiven our debtors. And lead us not into temptation, but deliver us from evil."

PRAYING THE SCRIPTURES

"The Word of God is the fulcrum upon which the lever of prayer is placed, and by which things are mightily moved."[36]

"Man shall not live by bread alone, but by every word that comes from the mouth of God." (Matthew 4:4)

Several years ago our family flew into Charlotte, North Carolina for the Footlocker Regional Cross Country Championships. After gathering up our suitcases at the baggage claim, we headed to the elevators that would take us to the rental cars. On board the elevator with us was an elderly woman who was apparently traveling by herself. Our 'hello' was met with a 'Guten Tag' and a nervous smile. Now if I had been traveling by myself, I could understand a nervous smile. But I was with my wife and two daughters. Something didn't seem right.

Exiting the elevator we proceeded towards our rental car company. Glancing over my shoulder, I could tell our German companion was obviously on the wrong floor. She looked left, then right, and then turned back towards the elevator. "Chris," my wife said, "you'd better see if you can help her. She's obviously lost." My four years of high school German, twenty-five years in the past, was about to be mightily tested. I hoofed it back to the elevator and hit the down button, hoping to find the Frau. Three stops later I spied her wandering about in a serpentine pattern at the curbside pick-up area.

When I caught up to her, the look on her face had gone from befuddled to anxious. I tried every phrase I could think of to find out where she belonged. She apparently understood me, but her rapid fire *Deutsch* left my head spinning trying to translate. Without a smart phone to help, I was on my own, and my linguistic skills were seriously lacking. Finally, I pulled out my wallet and showed photos of my family and pointed to my wife and said, "Frau," and then to our daughters and said, "Tochter." She pulled out her wallet, pointed to one man and said, "Bruder." Game on!

I knew "Telefonapparat," or something like that, was German for "telephone", and I knew how to play charades. Between my rudimentary German and pantomimed motions like dialing a phone, we were suddenly communicating. She pulled a telephone number out of her wallet, handed it to me, and said, "Bruder." I dialed the number and was delighted to have an English-speaking individual on the other end. A scant ten minutes later the German family was reunited. I received a smile, a "Danke," and the satisfaction that those four years of a foreign language hadn't been a total waste.

What does this have to do with praying the Scriptures? Everything! That woman reminded me of the confused and anxious look I've seen multitudes of times over the years when it comes to prayer. It is a foreign language to many, if not most Christians. Ask people why they don't feel comfortable praying, and you'll hear a constant refrain ringing forth: "I don't know what to say." But that's not all I learned in my encounter in Charlotte. It was a stark reminder that studying four years of German a quarter-of-a-century in the past did me little good in the present. "Use it or lose it" applies to Scripture and prayer also. The more you do it, the more fluent you will become. The more you put it on your shelf, the more you will realize that it has become impossible for you to carry on a conversation. So whenever possible, pray with your Bible open.

TOOLS

Ω I offer you the *Praying G.R.A.C.E.* model as a primer, a beginning tool to learn how to pray God's Word back to him.

It can be used with any passage of Scripture you're studying, reading, or hearing proclaimed through a sermon. For practice, meditate upon the Great Commission below, and ask the Holy Spirit to help you look for the following five elements. But don't get bogged down trying to figure out which category something fits in because there is usually a bit of overlapping. The idea is to give you basic categories to help you learn to pray Scripture.

G - God's Attributes to Praise ["Hallowed by your name]
"Let them praise the name of the LORD! For he commanded and they were created." (Psalm 148:5)

R –Riches to Receive (Promises) ["Daily Bread"]
"Your promises have been thoroughly tested, and your servant loves them." (Psalm 119:140) (NIV)

A – Actions to Imitate ["Your Kingdom Come"]
"Beloved, do not imitate evil but imitate good. Whoever does good is from God; whoever does evil has not seen God." (3 John 1:11)

C – Commands to Obey ["Your Will Be Done"]
"With my whole heart I seek you; let me not wander from your commandments!" (Psalm 119:10)

E – Error or Evil to Avoid ["Deliver Us From Evil]
"Do not be overcome by evil, but overcome evil with good." (Romans 12:21)

Practicing Praying G.R.A.C.E.

Then the **(A)**<u>eleven disciples went</u> to Galilee, to the mountain <u>where Jesus had told them to go</u>. When **(G)**<u>they saw him</u>, **(A)**<u>they worshipped him</u>, but **(E)**<u>some doubted</u>. Then **(G)**<u>Jesus came to them</u> and said, **(G)**<u>"All authority in heaven and on earth has been given to me</u>. Therefore **(C)**<u>go and make disciples</u> of all nations, **(C)**<u>baptizing</u> them in the name of the Father and of the Son and of the Holy Spirit, and **(C)**<u>teaching them to obey everything I have commanded you</u>. And surely **(R)** <u>I am with you always</u> to the very end of the age. (Matthew 28:16-20)

> **A** – eleven disciples went…where Jesus had told them to go
> **G** – God came in the flesh so mankind could *see* him
> **A** – they worshipped him
> **E** – some doubted the Jesus that they saw/they didn't worship
> **G** – Jesus is the Pursuer! He came to them.
> **G** – Jesus has all authority
> **C** – go and make disciples of all nations
> **C** – baptizing
> **C** – teaching them to obey everything I have commanded you
> **R** – Promise to cling to: "I am with you always"

G.R.A.C.E. Prayer

"Lord Jesus, as I look upon the actions of your eleven disciples going to Galilee, I desire to imitate them. Grant me the passion to go where you tell me because you know what is best for me. I praise you, Lord Jesus, for coming in the flesh so I might see and understand you more clearly. Help me, also, to fall at your feet and worship you, whom I see throughout Scripture. And Holy Spirit, help me to perceive when the Great Deceiver is in my midst. I never want to doubt the reality of who my resurrected Lord is and fail to properly worship you. What a joy to know that you, Lord Jesus, constantly pursue me because of your great love. I do believe that you have all authority in heaven and on earth. So 'I bow my knee before your throne, I know this life is not my own.' Grant me the eyes to see where you want me to go to make disciples, the wisdom to know when to baptize them, the ability to teach them your commands, and the heart to believe that truly you are with me always. Make my life a prayer to you!"

Ω Do you know any Bible stories? Have you ever thought of using them to help you in your prayer life?

Even if you don't have your Bible handy, or at this juncture in your life you feel that you lack a depth of biblical knowledge, you can still pray the stories.

Example: Imagine you've been dealing lately with some parents who are extremely vocal about their son getting more playing time. Phone calls are getting lengthier, emails nastier, threats more constant. What biblical story could you pray as you seek God's wisdom in how to deal with this situation in a way that will honor him? Let's try Solomon's wisdom with the baby and the two moms.

"Lord, I remember that time when two women came to Solomon because they were in a disagreement over the identity of a baby.[37] They both had children born at the same time but one of them died. Now they were arguing over the baby that was still alive. Solomon had no way of knowing who was telling the truth until you revealed a brilliant idea to him. He asked for a sword and said he was going to divide the child in two and give half the baby to each woman. It then became readily apparent who the mother of the child was because she pleaded with Solomon to not use the sword. I need that same kind of wisdom from you in how to deal with these parents whose actions are threatening to divide our team rather than unify it."

Example: What story might you pray if you're having trouble remembering that the Great Commission and the Greatest Commandments are supposed to be your priority, especially when everyone around you is expecting a winning team? Let's use the shepherd going after the one sheep and leaving the ninety-nine behind.

"Father, there's a lot of pressure on me to win. Everyone expects it and demands it. If I don't produce, I'll lose my job. Help me to remember that you came to save people, not help us to put points on the scoreboard. Help me to have the heart of the shepherd who owned one hundred sheep.[38] When one of them strayed off, he pursued that sheep until he found it. Help me to do the same for my athletes who don't know you, and for those who do know you but I find out are straying away from your flock, because you said there is great rejoicing in heaven when someone repents and turns back to you. Change my heart to be more like that shepherd!"

Ω **During this next week, ask the Holy Spirit to call to your mind a biblical story that you can pray regarding a situation you presently find yourself.**

Ω **When you come across prayers in the Bible, how can you use them to pray for your athletes or others associated with your team?**

Make the prayers personal by inserting someone's name in them. Take Philippians 1:3-11 as an example:

"I thank my God in all my remembrance of you [Cathy], always in every prayer of mine for you all [her] making my prayer with joy, because of your [her] partnership in the gospel from the first day until now. And I am sure of this, that he who began a good work in you [Cathy] will bring it to completion at the day of Jesus Christ. It is right for me to feel this way about you all [Cathy], because I hold you [her] in my heart, for you are all partakers [she is a partaker] with me of grace, both in my imprisonment and in the defense and confirmation of the gospel. For God is my witness, how I yearn for you all [Cathy] with the affection of Christ Jesus. And it is my prayer that your [her] love may abound more and more, with knowledge and all discernment, so that you [she] may approve what is excellent, and so be pure and blameless for the day of Christ, filled with the fruit of righteousness that comes through Jesus Christ, to the glory and praise of God."

PREYED ON OR PRAYED FOR?[39]

"A person never does a nobler act than when he becomes a priest to others and makes intercession for them." (Clarence Edward Noble Macartney)

"Moreover, as for me, far be it from me that I should sin against the LORD by ceasing to pray for you, and I will instruct you in the good and the right way." (1 Sam. 12:23)

∞ *Do you regularly pray for your athletes?*

In the quest to field competitive teams, sometimes Christian coaches fall into the same trap that ensnares many of their non-Christian counterparts. They treat their athletes as commodities, parts of the machine they are building. If one part doesn't work as well as they want, they toss it aside and replace it with a model that they hope will be new and improved. Why does this happen? Spiritual amnesia sets in, and the words of Genesis 1:27 are forgotten: "So God created man *in his own image*, in the image of God he created him; male and female he created them." Every athlete you work with is made in the image of God, the *imago dei*. If you find yourself treating your athletes like commodities, ask the Holy Spirit to change your heart through Genesis 1:27, and be in awe through this description of Jesus: "He is the *image of the invisible God*, the firstborn of all creation. For by him all things were created, in heaven and on earth, visible and invisible, whether thrones or dominions or rulers or authorities—all things were created through him and for him. And he is before all things, and in him all things hold together.[40]

Furthermore, carefully consider the identity of those athletes on your team who are Christians. They have been given new names and even more intimate identities than merely being made in God's image. They are sons and daughters of God! "See what great love the Father has lavished on us, that we should be called children of God! And that is what we are!"[41]

What's in a name? Have you ever named a child? How much thought and wrestling went into it? You didn't casually toss any old name on your child, did you? Why not? Because names matter – oftentimes they knit and bind children together with their ancestors, and sometimes also give children a sense of destiny and purpose.

For instance, before my brother Dann was born, my dad wanted to name him 'Patrick.' Mom was opposed to it, so 'Patrick' became Dann's middle name – except to Dad. From Dann's birth to Dad's death, our father always called Dann 'Patrick'. That naming aided in a bond that caused them to be closer than Dad and any of his other five children, as witnessed by the fact that Patrick chose to be dad's primary caretaker throughout his battle with Parkinson's. Patrick saw Dad through his daily suffering and helped him cross the great chasm from death to eternal life, because he was called by God.

You received a similar calling upon your life when you, as a son or daughter of the living God, became a coach. And this destiny, this purpose, is the reason that you should be passionately interceding for your athletes before the throne of our heavenly Father, sowing seeds of salvation and sanctification, restoration and reconciliation, through prayer:

> For the love of Christ controls us, because we have concluded this: that one has died for all, therefore all have died; and he died for all, that those who live might no longer live for themselves but for him who for their sake died and was raised. From now on, therefore, we regard no one according to the flesh. Even though we once regarded Christ according to the flesh, we regard him thus no longer. Therefore, if anyone is in Christ, he is a new creation. The old has passed away; behold, the new has come. All this is from God, who through Christ reconciled us to himself and gave us the ministry of reconciliation; that is, in Christ God was reconciling the world to himself, not counting their trespasses against them, and entrusting to us the message of reconciliation. Therefore, we are ambassadors for Christ, God making his appeal through us. We implore you on behalf of Christ, be reconciled to God. For our sake he made him to be sin who knew no sin, so that in him we might become the righteousness of God. (2 Corinthians 5:14-21)

What about you? Do you tend to talk to others about your athletes rather than bringing them before the Lord? As a coach, you are in a key position to be lifting your athletes' battle-weary hands and helping to keep them protected. Not a day should go by when you don't pray for your athletes.

> First, the leaders' [coaches'] prayers should concentrate on the growth and development of each of the people [athletes] whom they lead.[42]

> And so, from the day we heard, we have not ceased to pray for you, asking that you may be filled with the knowledge of his will in all spiritual wisdom and understanding, so as to walk in a manner worthy of the Lord, fully pleasing to him, bearing fruit in every good work and increasing in the knowledge of God. (Colossians 1:9-10)

Second, leaders [coaches] should pray for the spiritual maturity of their people [athletes] and that God might raise up from their midst laborers to go into the harvest fields of the world. [You should also have compassion on your athletes.] "When he saw the crowds, he had compassion for them, because they were harassed and helpless, like sheep without a shepherd.[43]

Then he said to his disciples, "The harvest is plentiful, but the laborers are few; therefore pray earnestly to the Lord of the harvest to send out laborers into his harvest." (Matthew 9:36-38)

Do you have compassion towards your athletes? If yes, how do you exhibit it? To what extent are you willing to bring your athletes before Jesus in order to seek that his grace and mercy, his empowering and equipping, his hope and healing, and his joy and delight might be infused into their lives? Consider the lengths the friends of a paralytic went to bring him into the presence of Jesus:

And when he returned to Capernaum after some days, it was reported that he was at home. And many were gathered together, so that there was no more room, not even at the door. And he was preaching the word to them. And they came, bringing to him a paralytic carried by four men. And when they could not get near him because of the crowd, they removed the roof above him, and when they had made an opening, they let down the bed on which the paralytic lay. And when Jesus saw their faith, he said to the paralytic, "Son, your sins are forgiven." Now some of the scribes were sitting there, questioning in their hearts, "Why does this man speak like that? He is blaspheming! Who can forgive sins but God alone?" And immediately Jesus, perceiving in his spirit that they thus questioned within themselves, said to them, "Why do you question these things in your hearts? Which is easier, to say to the paralytic, 'Your sins are forgiven,' or to say, 'Rise, take up your bed and walk'? But that you may know that the Son of Man has authority on earth to forgive sins"—he said to the paralytic – "I say to you, rise, pick up your bed, and go home." And he rose and immediately picked up his bed and went out before them all, so that they were all amazed and glorified God, saying, "We never saw anything like this!" (Mark 2:1-12)

TOOLS

Ω What are some of the things you can be praying for your athletes, no matter what their age?

Below are seven areas to use as starting points. I am confident that the Holy Spirit will reveal more areas to you as you delve into his Word, practice praying the Scriptures, and spend concerted effort seeking to know your athletes better.

1. *That Jesus will call them and no one will hinder them from coming.*

   Then children were brought to him that he might lay his hands on them and pray. The disciples rebuked the people, but Jesus said, "Let the little children come to me and do not hinder them, for to such belongs the kingdom of heaven." And he laid his hands on them and went away. (Matthew 19:13-15)

2. *That they will respond in faith to Jesus' faithful, persistent call.*

   The Lord is not slow to fulfill his promise as some count slowness, but is patient toward you, not wishing that any should perish, but that all should reach repentance. (2 Peter 3:9)

3. *That they will experience sanctification through the transforming work of the Holy Spirit and increasingly desire to fulfill the greatest commandments.*

   And you shall love the Lord your God with all your heart and with all your soul and with all your mind and with all your strength.' The second is this: 'You shall love your neighbor as yourself.' There is no other commandment greater than these." (Mark 12:30-31)

4. *That once they have responded in faith to Jesus' call, they will not be unequally yoked in intimate relationships.*

   Do not be unequally yoked with unbelievers. For what partnership has righteousness with lawlessness? Or what fellowship has light with darkness? (2 Corinthians 6:14)

5. *That their thoughts will be pure.*

   Finally, brothers, whatever is true, whatever is honorable, whatever is just, whatever is pure, whatever is lovely, whatever is commendable, if there is any excellence, if there is anything worthy of praise, think about these things. (Philippians 4:8)

6. *That their hearts will be stirred to give generously to the Lord's work.*

   All the men and women, the people of Israel, whose heart moved them to bring anything for the work that the LORD had commanded by Moses to be done brought it as a freewill offering to the LORD. (Exodus 35:29)

7. That when the time is right, they will go!

> And Jesus came and said to them, "All authority in heaven and on earth has been given to me. Go therefore and make disciples of all nations, baptizing them in the name of the Father and of the Son and of the Holy Spirit, teaching them to observe all that I have commanded you. And behold, I am with you always, to the end of the age." (Matthew 28:18-20)

Ω Further examples of how you can be praying specifically for your athletes can be found in the appendices.

The *Fall Lady Bear Prayers* are prayers that I wrote for the Baylor University women's cross country team. They contain fifteen weeks of prayers that focus on setting priorities for collegiate freshmen. These can be adapted to other groups.

Ω What are some practical ways you can find out what your athletes' prayer requests are?

Consider having a specific email address and/or a number for texting where they (or others associated with the team) can send you their prayer requests. If you want to have an "anonymous" method to receive prayer requests, consider having a 'prayer box' along with pens and paper at practice, or some other easily accessible place. In conjunction with this, keep the Golden Rule inscribed upon your heart and mind, and you will never be at a loss how to pray for your athletes: "So whatever you wish that others would do to you, do also to them."[44] If you were in their shoes, what would your prayer requests be?

∞ How can you evangelize in lives of those athletes (and others impacted by your program) who are not Christians without proselytizing or pressuring? What is the primary means you can use that no one will complain about?

"It is possible to move men, through God, by prayer alone." (Hudson Taylor)[45]

If you were to rank life's experiences in descending order of the pleasure they bring us, evangelism might appear down near a root canal. Intimidated and insecure, we often keep our hooks and nets out of the water. Some denominations have been historically famous for this mindset. Once a Presbyterian leader serving on a panel was asked the question from the floor, "What would you say has been the greatest contribution by Presbyterians in the area of evangelism?" The man thought for a moment and said, "Restraint." Conversely, what can you learn from the life of Jesus that will help propel you forward to evangelize your athletes?

> You yourselves know what happened throughout all Judea, beginning from Galilee after the baptism that John proclaimed: how God *anointed Jesus of Nazareth with*

the Holy Spirit and with power. He went about doing good and healing all who were oppressed by the devil, *for God was with him.* (Acts 10:37-38)

I know it is a mystery how it all works, but Jesus was fully God and fully man. His human side needed the anointing and empowering of the Holy Spirit before his ministry began. His humanity needed the Holy Spirit for a successful restoration and reconciliation ministry. If Jesus' humanity needed the Holy Spirit to guide him, doesn't it make sense that you need to tap into that same source? You, too, are filled with the Spirit. "Or do you not know that your body is a temple of the Holy Spirit within you, whom you have from God?"[46] And equipping by the Spirit is promised through study and application of God's Word. When God sends a person into a place, he sends them with power:

> Take the helmet of salvation, and the sword of the Spirit, which is the word of God, praying at all times in the Spirit, with all prayer and supplication. To that end keep alert with all perseverance, making supplication for all the saints, and also for me, that words may be given to me in opening my mouth boldly to proclaim the mystery of the gospel. (Ephesians 6:17-19)

Are you plugged into that power source? Let's further examine how Jesus made sure that he was always near to that conduit of power:

> And rising very early in the morning, while it was still dark, he departed and went out to a desolate place, and there he prayed. And Simon and those who were with him searched for him, and they found him and said to him, "Everyone is looking for you." And he said to them, "Let us go on to the next towns, that I may preach there also, for that is why I came out." And he went throughout all Galilee, preaching in their synagogues and casting out demons. (Mark 1:35-39)

First, notice when Jesus arises to begin preparing for the day's ministry - "Very early in the morning, while it was still dark..." Jesus is up before the break of dawn, before anyone else is stirring in the house where he is staying. Based upon the same Greek expression denoting time that is used in Mark 13:35, scholars tell us that Jesus was up somewhere between three and six o'clock in the morning.

Now I'm not telling you when you should arise to prepare for the day ahead. I'm simply sharing with you how Jesus prepared himself to sow seeds of salvation. And, I can guarantee you that the fully human side of Jesus was more tired than we can fathom. Just look at his schedule the night before this pre-dawn rising:

> That evening at sundown they brought to him all who were sick or oppressed by demons. And the whole city was gathered together at the door. And he healed many

who were sick with various diseases, and cast out many demons. And he would not permit the demons to speak, because they knew him. (Mark 1:32-34)

Second, notice *where* Jesus went to prepare. "Very early in the morning, while it was still dark, he departed and went out *to a desolate place...*" Jesus leaves the house, leaves the city, and finds a place where he can be alone with his Father. Third, we need to understand *why* Jesus arose so early and chose to go to a site where he would be alone. Jesus needed uninterrupted time with his Father. Regardless of how busy and exhausting the previous day in Capernaum must have been, Jesus needed time with his Father much more than sleep. He needed guidance to know when and where to fish for men. "For I have come down from heaven, not to do my own will but the will of him who sent me."[47] Jesus only desired to do his Father's will.

That was Jeremiah Lanphier's desire also. Let's see what we can learn from a mere mortal about how God empowered him to evangelize New York City in the 1850's, a time when America was teetering perilously on the brink of economic and spiritual meltdowns:

On July 1, 1857, a quiet and zealous businessman named Jeremiah Lanphier took up an appointment as a City Missionary in down-town New York. Lanphier was appointed by the North Church of the Dutch Reformed denomination. This church was suffering from depletion of membership due to the removal of the population from the down-town to the better residential quarters…

Burdened by the need, Jeremiah Lanphier decided to invite others to join him in a noonday prayer-meeting, to be held on Wednesday once a week. He therefore distributed a handbill:

HOW OFTEN SHALL I PRAY?

…A day Prayer Meeting is held every Wednesday, from 12 to 1 o'clock…This meeting is intended to give merchants, mechanics, clerks, strangers, and business men generally an opportunity to stop and call upon God amid the perplexities incident to their respective avocations. It will continue for one hour; but it is also designed for those who may find it inconvenient to remain more than five or ten minutes, as well as for those who can spare the whole hour.

Accordingly at twelve noon, September 23, 1857, the door was opened and the faithful Lanphier took his seat to await the response to his invitation. Five minutes went by. No one appeared. The missionary paced the room in a conflict of fear and faith. Ten minutes elapsed. Still no one came. Fifteen minutes passes. Lanphier was yet alone. Twenty minutes; twenty-five; thirty, and then at 12:30 p.m., a step was heard on the stair, and the first person appeared, the another, and another, and another, until six people were present, and the prayer meeting began. On the following Wednesday, October 7th, there were forty intercessors.

Thus in the first week of October 1857, it was decided to hold a meeting daily instead of weekly. Within six months, ten thousand business men were gathering daily for prayer in New York, and within two years, a million converts were added to American churches.[48]

Prayer evangelism is a key way to begin the evangelization process without any pressure. Allow God to move hearts so your athletes will be given eyes to see and ears to hear when you have opportunities to proclaim the gospel in word and deed.

TOOLS

Ω Do you have a regular time when you prayerfully listen for the Lord's leading on the *who, how, when, and where* of sowing seeds of salvation among your athletes?

Find at least one other person who will covenant with you to do prayer evangelism at a set time each week.

Ω Read and meditate on Acts 16. What can you learn from the conversions that occurred in this chapter? How will you seek to apply it to your own life?

Ω Below is a model to help you begin prayer evangelism for your athletes and others impacted by your program.

1. *Ask God to give you a burden for 'lost' people.*

    "Dear Lord Jesus, let my heart be filled with bitter sorrow and unending grief for _____. Let my heart break, just as yours did when people failed to repent of their sins and come to you. Help me to have a burden to daily pray for _____ that he might come to a saving relationship with you. Let this truly be the longing of my heart and my daily prayer to you that _____ would be saved." (Romans 9:2-3; Romans 10:1)

2. *Ask God to prepare more leaders for the harvest.*

    "Dear Lord Jesus, there are many athletes, coaches, and fans that do not know you as Lord and Savior. I pray that you, the Lord of the harvest, would please send out more workers like

_____ to join me in praying for our team. Bring workers who will labor alongside me to see a harvest of souls." (Matthew 9:38)

3. *Ask the Holy Spirit for opportunities to share the gospel with your athletes and others.*

"Dear Lord Jesus, help me to be devoted to praying with an alert mind and a thankful heart for _____. Help me to daily remember to pray for _____ that you would give me many opportunities to reach her – and that she would understand that she has rebelled against you, yet you love her and died for her. Help me to proclaim your message in a way that is clear and easy to understand. Holy Spirit, help me to live wisely among those who are not Christians, like _____, and make the most of every opportunity you give me. Let my conversation be gracious, kind, and effective so that I will have the right answer for _____ and others you prepare to hear the gospel from my lips and my actions." (Colossians 4:2-6)

4. *Praise God in advance for the fruit that will be produced.*

"Heavenly Father, praise you that it is not your desire that even one person should perish. Praise you for drawing me to you when I was going the wrong direction. Because you have appointed me to go and produce fruit that will last, I call upon your power through your Holy Spirit to help me with this task. Lord Jesus, when it comes to this everlasting fruit, you said that your Father would give me whatever I ask for, in your name. Because of this promise, I ask for the salvation of _____." (John 15:16; 2 Peter 3:9)

5. *Pray for wisdom and boldness in evangelizing/witnessing.*

"Dear Lord Jesus, help me to be united with other laborers and lift our voices in prayer for our athletes who do not have you as their Lord and Savior. Help us to have the same boldness and wisdom that Peter and John had when they were released from prison. We know that boldness did not come from themselves, but came from the empowering of your Holy Spirit. Do it again, Lord! Heavenly Father, send your healing power for our athletes that are hurting; let miraculous signs and wonders be done through the name of Jesus. And may the arenas and fields where we meet tremble as they are filled with your Holy Spirit. And let us share your message in faith and love, and with great boldness and discernment." (Acts 4:23-24, 29-31)

∞ *But what about you? Is prayer just for the benefit of your athletes? Is anyone praying for you and your role as a coach?*

If this is not your very first time picking up the whistle, then you are fully aware that the "Preyed on or Prayed For" moniker is just as applicable to coaches as to their athletes. In other words, plenty of people are more than willing to look at you as just a commodity to be preyed upon, not as a person who needs assistance through prayer. Just as pastors have a flock to care for, God has placed you over a group of sheep to provide guidance and nurture, not just focus on athletic skill development. But what comes to mind when you think of sheep? Soft, white, fluffy, ambling up to nudge against your leg seeking to get a pat on the head? One problem – if you pet the ram on the head, he may think that you're challenging him to prove dominance, and the head-butting is on. Moses understood what it was like to be a head coach of sheep who weren't averse to going on attack mode.

> In Exodus 17, Pastor [Coach] Moses is having a hard time. At Rephidim, the Israelites are short on water and they blame Moses, the one who is seeking to teach them God's ways. The people call a meeting of the B.T.E. Committee (Back to Egypt) to grumble against Moses and demand him to supply them with water. "Why did you bring us up out of Egypt to make us and our children and livestock die of thirst?" When he hears about their meeting, Moses is frustrated, and asks the Lord, "What am I to do with these people? They are almost ready to stone me." So the Lord comes to his rescue, provides water, and the B.T.E. Committee adjourns.[49]

Have you ever felt like this? All you're trying to do is lead your team to be a cohesive unit, developing their individual and corporate abilities so they can compete on the highest level possible, and they nip and bite at you. If that weren't enough, sometimes the extended family and local community of sheep get in on the act. And sometimes they try to trample you and drag you off into the bushes to die.

Before Moses has a chance to rest from the recent sheep attack from his own team, warriors from another community assault the Israelites:

> Then Amalek came and fought with Israel at Rephidim. So Moses said to Joshua, "Choose for us men, and go out and fight with Amalek. Tomorrow I will stand on the top of the hill with the staff of God in my hand." So Joshua did as Moses told him, and fought with Amalek, while Moses, Aaron, and Hur went up to the top of the hill. Whenever Moses held up his hand, Israel prevailed, and whenever he lowered his hand, Amalek prevailed. But Moses' hands grew weary, so they took a stone and put it under him, and he sat on it, while Aaron and Hur held up his hands, one on one side, and the other on the other side. So his hands were steady until the going down of the sun. And Joshua overwhelmed Amalek and his people with the sword. (Exodus 17:8-13)

Whether you coach at the peewee level or the collegiate level is not the issue. Because you coach, conflict and sheep bites will occur. What will you do to prepare ahead of time for the encounters?

TOOLS

Ω Who is holding up your weary hands? Do you have an Aaron and Hur in your life?

This is critical if you hope to thrive as a coach. You can do everything else 'right.' But if you don't have prayer support, you will eventually become road kill. But take hope! "Satan dreads nothing but prayer. His one concern is to keep the saints from praying. He fears nothing from prayerless studies, prayerless work, and prayerless religion. He laughs at our toil, mocks at our wisdom, but trembles when we pray."[50] "For we do not wrestle against flesh and blood, but against the rulers, against the authorities, against the cosmic powers over this present darkness, against the spiritual forces of evil in the heavenly places."[51]

Ω Examples of how others can be praying specifically for you can be found in the appendices.

Intercessory Prayer on Behalf of Coaches: Fifteen prayers are included that cover numerous topics that we have studied together to this point.

Ω PRAYER

"Heavenly Father, we praise your Name. You are the eternal Promise Keeper from age-to-age. Great is your faithfulness. Morning by morning, new mercies we see. Fill me to overflowing with your Spirit so that I desire to passionately pray for my athletes. Let me be like Epaphras, who was always struggling in prayer on behalf of his brothers and sisters at the church in Colossae, asking that they stand mature and fully assured in all the will of God. Empower me to pray earnestly day and night for each athlete that you have placed under my care so that I will help to bear their burdens, and so fulfill the law of Christ. For I want them to know how greatly I struggle for them so that their hearts may be encouraged, being knit together in love, to reach all the riches of full assurance of understanding and the knowledge of God's mystery, which is Christ. Help me to give people around our program the knowledge of salvation through the forgiveness of their sins. Use me to shine your light into the darkness and the shadow of death in order to guide their feet into the path of peace. For you are the Way, and the Truth, and the Life." (Colossians 4:12; 1 Thessalonians 3:10; Galatians 6:2; Colossians 2:1-2; John 14:6)

THE HUMBLE POSITION

Before we close this chapter on prayer, it's important to check our attitudes again. How we view God is the critical foundation to all prayer. God is not a celestial Santa Claus to whom we give our wish list in hopes that we'll find everything under the tree. Nor is he a piñata, and prayer the stick we use to beat him into submission in order to get all the goodies he has inside. He is the Creator, Redeemer, and Sustainer of the universe. Our heart attitude should be shaped by passages like Jude 24-25: "Now to him who is able to keep you from stumbling and to present you blameless before the presence of his glory with great joy, to the only God, our Savior, through Jesus Christ our Lord, be glory, majesty, dominion, and authority, before all time and now and forever."

True growth in prayer is realizing how dependent you are upon God alone for your creation, daily sustenance, direction, empowering, identity, and eternity. It's a matter of desperation, a humbling of yourself before the throne of grace. "So Jesus said to them, "Truly, truly, I say to you, the Son can do nothing of his own accord, but only what he sees the Father doing. For whatever the Father does, that the Son does likewise."[52] While Jesus walked the earth, he was completely dependent on his heavenly Father's directions and empowering. The Father's grace flowed freely upon his Son. It is critical to understand that grace is not just about forgiveness, but also God's empowering to do what you are commanded to do – like pray!

God will act on behalf of those who wait for him. Stay on your knees. "From of old no one has heard or perceived by the ear, no eye has seen a God besides you, who acts for those who wait for him."[53] "And this is the confidence that we have toward him, that if we ask anything according to his will he hears us."[54]

Furthermore, it is imperative that you realize that God's acting on your behalf is not based upon your merits, but upon what Christ procured on the cross. "When we pray to God for His blessing, He does not examine our performance to see if we are worthy. Rather, He looks to see if we are trusting in the merit of His Son as our only hope for securing His blessing."[55] May you be like the tax collector who comprehended this as he came before God in prayer:

> He also told this parable to some who trusted in themselves that they were righteous, and treated others with contempt: "Two men went up into the temple to pray, one a Pharisee and the other a tax collector. The Pharisee, standing by himself, prayed thus: 'God, I thank you that I am not like other men, extortioners, unjust, adulterers, or even like this tax collector. I fast twice a week; I give tithes of all that I get.' But the tax collector, standing far off, would not even lift up his eyes to heaven, but beat his breast, saying, 'God, be merciful to me, a sinner!' I tell you, this man went down to his house justified, rather than the other. For everyone who exalts himself will be humbled, but the one who humbles himself will be exalted." (Mt. 18:1-14)

And may you not have the false 'thankfulness' of the Pharisee. But be warned. Even if you have the humility of the tax collector, you can still unknowingly treat God as a vending machine. Prayer is not just about bringing requests before God. It's just as much about thanking him for his unchanging character, his rock solid promises, for all that he has done, all he is doing, and all he will do to show his glory and bring his children into eternal fellowship with him. Offering thanksgiving on those levels is also a blessing in that it will help you coach with an eternal perspective. May the Lord transform your heart and mind so that you daily desire to join in the praises of the people of Israel who were taught by David to *sing* God's praises like this:

> Then on that day David first appointed that thanksgiving be sung to the LORD by Asaph and his brothers. Oh give thanks to the LORD; call upon his name; make known his deeds among the peoples! Sing to him, sing praises to him; tell of all his wondrous works! Glory in his holy name; let the hearts of those who seek the LORD rejoice! Seek the LORD and his strength; seek his presence continually! Remember the wondrous works that he has done, his miracles and the judgments he uttered, O offspring of Israel his servant, children of Jacob, his chosen ones! He is the LORD our God; his judgments are in all the earth. Remember his covenant forever, the word that he commanded, for a thousand generations, the covenant that he made with Abraham, his sworn promise to Isaac, which he confirmed to Jacob as a statute, to Israel as an everlasting covenant, saying, "To you I will give the land of Canaan, as your portion for an inheritance." When you were few in number, of little account, and sojourners in it, wandering from nation to nation, from one kingdom to another people, he allowed no one to oppress them; he rebuked kings on their account, saying, "Touch not my anointed ones, do my prophets no harm!" Sing to the LORD, all the earth! Tell of his salvation from day to day. Declare his glory among the nations, his marvelous works among all the peoples! For great is the LORD, and greatly to be praised, and he is to be feared above all gods. For all the gods of the peoples are worthless idols, but the LORD made the heavens. Splendor and majesty are before him; strength and joy are in his place. Ascribe to the LORD, O families of the peoples, ascribe to the LORD glory and strength! Ascribe to the LORD the glory due his name; bring an offering and come before him! Worship the LORD in the splendor of holiness; tremble before him, all the earth; yes, the world is established; it shall never be moved. Let the heavens be glad, and let the earth rejoice, and let them say among the nations, "The LORD reigns!" Let the sea roar, and all that fills it; let the field exult, and everything in it! Then shall the trees of the forest sing for joy before the LORD, for he comes to judge the earth. Oh give thanks to the LORD, for he is good; for his steadfast love endures forever! Say also: "Save us, O God of our salvation, and gather and deliver us from among the nations, that we may give thanks to your holy name and glory in your praise. Blessed be the LORD, the God of Israel, from everlasting to everlasting!" Then all the people said, "Amen!" and praised the LORD. (1 Ch 16:7–36)

And realize that every song of thanksgiving you lift up to the Lord your God, every spoken prayer of thanks, whether whispered or shouted from the rooftops, will be preparing you for eternity, and, Lord willing, others who will be impacted through your coaching.

And all the angels were standing around the throne and around the elders and the four living creatures, and they fell on their faces before the throne and worshiped God, saying, "Amen! Blessing and glory and wisdom and thanksgiving and honor and power and might be to our God forever and ever! Amen. (Revelation 7:11-12)

∞ *Do you seek to search out and savor the myriad of blessings God bestows upon your life through your coaching? When you discover God's blessings do you thank him?*

If we fail to give thanks to God, we do not glorify God. Instead, we cultivate a God-ignoring, man-centered, idolatrous heart and attitude. Then sports become ugly. But…When we give thanks to God, we are acknowledging, "From him, and through him, and to him are all things. To him be the glory forever."[56]

An interesting study by Dr. Robert Emmons, a psychology professor at UC Davis, revealed that there is also a great benefit to those who diligently seek to be thankful for all the blessings in their lives (even if he doesn't use the word 'blessing', or mention the Giver of those blessings.) His research is dedicated to showing that "gratitude heals, energizes, and transforms lives." He had two groups of student volunteers participate in his study. One group kept a gratitude journal for two months. In it they kept track of everything they were grateful for on a daily basis. The second group kept tabs on all the negative events that happened to them over that same two month period.

In an experimental comparison, those who kept gratitude journals on a weekly basis exercised more regularly, reported fewer physical symptoms, felt better about their lives as a whole, and were more optimistic about the upcoming week compared to those who recorded hassles or neutral life events (Emmons & McCullough, 2003). A related benefit was observed in the realm of personal goal attainment: Participants who kept gratitude lists were more likely to have made progress toward important personal goals (academic, interpersonal and health-based) over a two-month period compared to subjects in the other experimental conditions.[57]

Can you see how this might apply to your coaching? But it should not surprise you that being grateful has potential side benefits. "A joyful heart is good medicine, but a crushed spirit dries up the bones."[58]A glad heart makes a cheerful face, but by sorrow of heart the spirit is crushed…All the days of the afflicted are evil, but the cheerful of heart has a continual feast.[59]

TOOLS

Ω Have you ever heard of a blessing jar? It is another simple tool, like a gratitude journal, to help you and your athletes keep track of what you are thankful for…and it has the added potential for a strong visual impact as well.

Do not be deceived, my beloved brothers. Every good gift and every perfect gift is from above, coming down from the Father of lights with whom there is no variation or shadow due to change. (James 1:16-17)

I will praise the name of God with a song; I will magnify him with thanksgiving. (Psalm 69:30)

Praise the LORD! Praise God in his sanctuary; praise him in his mighty heavens! Praise him for his mighty deeds; praise him according to his excellent greatness!… Let everything that has breath praise the LORD! Praise the LORD! (Psalm 150:1-3, 5)

In order to help you stay centered on the glory of God and the multitude of blessings in your life and the life of your team, find a clear jar with a lid. If you're dealing with younger kids, find a plastic jar that you can bring to practices and not have to worry about breakage. If you have an office, keep the jar on your desk where it is visible to everyone. This serves the purpose of being a discussion piece for those who visit your office, and a reminder to those who are "in the know," to be on the lookout for blessings in their lives and the team as a whole.

Every time the Holy Spirit reveals a blessing in your life, your athletes, or the team as a whole, write it on a strip of paper and toss it in the jar. Take a moment to thank God for who he is and/or what he has done/is doing. At different pre-determined intervals, dump out the strips as a team and read them. For those on your team who are Christians, it will remind them who the Lord is and how his blessings have flowed upon your team. For those who aren't Christians, it begins developing in them a posture of thankfulness. Afterwards, if you are in a Christian environment, take time as a team to verbally thank the Lord for his character and blessings. If not, encourage those who are on your team who are Christians to pray silently for the myriad of blessings as they are read.

Pass the blessing on – take time to pray for those who were instruments of God's blessings. Teach your team to drop those people a note, an e-mail, or tell them in person how God blessed them through their lives. Or if you are in a 'mixed' setting, teach your athletes to sow seeds of thankfulness to the individual. Lord willing, this will aid in opening up future discussions.

Ω Consider the following reasons that the Psalmist offers up his thanks to the Lord. How can you use these as a template for offering up your own thanks and teaching your athletes to do likewise?

Highlight or underline the words or phrases that give reasons for thanks. Prayerfully keep your eyes open as you daily read the Word for further reasons to give thanks to God…and then do it.

> Make a joyful noise to the LORD, all the earth! Serve the LORD with gladness! Come into his presence with singing! Know that the LORD, he is God! It is he who made us, and we are his; we are his people, and the sheep of his pasture. Enter his gates with thanksgiving, and his courts with praise! Give thanks to him; bless his name! For the LORD is good; his steadfast love endures forever, and his faithfulness to all generations. (Psalm 100:1-5)

> Then they cried to the LORD in their trouble, and he delivered them from their distress. He sent out his word and healed them, and delivered them from their destruction. Let them thank the LORD for his steadfast love, for his wondrous works to the children of man! And let them offer sacrifices of thanksgiving, and tell of his deeds in songs of joy! (Psalm 107:19-22)

> Sing to the LORD with thanksgiving; make melody to our God on the lyre! He covers the heavens with clouds; he prepares rain for the earth; he makes grass grow on the hills. He gives to the beasts their food, and to the young ravens that cry. His delight is not in the strength of the horse, nor his pleasure in the legs of a man, but the LORD takes pleasure in those who fear him, in those who hope in his steadfast love. (Psalm 147:7-11)

Ω To live a life of continual thanksgiving, learn to daily pray the Gospel.

"To pray the gospel, simply begin by thanking God for the forgiveness of sins, purchased through the death of His Son. Acknowledge that Christ's work on the cross is what makes prayer possible. Thank Him that you'll never be separated from God's love, because Jesus bore God's wrath for sin. Thank Him that because of the cross you're reconciled to God and have been given the Holy Spirit to dwell in you, lead you, guide you, and empower you to resist sin and serve God. Then ask God to bless you graciously with everything you need to obey and glorify Him."[60] Ultimately, all effective prayer is rooted in the cross. Without Christ's blood, you couldn't even approach God. Only in Jesus' righteousness are you invited to enter his presence.

Ω PRAYER

"Heavenly Father, I will praise your name with a song; I will magnify you with thanksgiving. Daily remind me, Holy Spirit, that the one who offers thanksgiving as his sacrifice glorifies you; to the one who orders his way rightly, you will show him your salvation. I pray that your grace extends to more and more people on our team, and those impacted by them, so that an ever-increasing number of people will be offering up thanksgiving to the name of Jesus, so he will be glorified. Therefore, as I received Christ Jesus the Lord, empower me to walk in him, rooted and built up in him and established in the faith, just as I was taught, abounding in thanksgiving. May I continue steadfastly in prayer, being watchful in it with thanksgiving, not anxious about anything, but in everything by prayer and supplication with thanksgiving letting my requests be made known to you. And your peace, which surpasses all understand will guard my heart and my mind in Christ Jesus." (Psalm 69:30/ Psalm 50:23, 2 Corinthians 4:15, Colossians 2:6-7, Colossians 4:2, Philippians 4:5-7)

Notes

[1] Sam Storms, *One Thing: Developing a Passion for the Beauty of God* (Scotland: Christian Focus, 2004), 41.

[2] John Piper & Justin Taylor, General Editors, *A God Entranced Vision of All Things: The Legacy of Jonathan Edwards* (Wheaton: Crossway, 2004), 115.

[3] J. Oswald Sanders, *Spiritual Leadership: Principles of Excellence for Every Believer* (Chicago, Moody, 2007), 83.

[4] Max Lucado, *It's Not About Me* (Nashville: Integrity, 2004), 135.

[5] Samuel Chadwick in Sanders, op. cit., 84.

[6] James 4:3.

[7] Sanders, op. cit., 85.

[8] Ecclesiastes 4:9-10.

[9] John Piper, Sermon – *Our Father* (Minneapolis: Bethlehem Baptist Church).

[10] Elwell, W. A., & Comfort, P. W., *Tyndale Bible dictionary*. Tyndale reference library (2) (Wheaton, IL: Tyndale House Publishers), 2001. Aramaic word for "father," which is applied to God in Mark 14:36; Romans 8:15; and Galatians 4:6. The name expresses a very intimate and inseparable relationship between Christ and the Father and between believers (children) and God (Father). [Hence, 'Daddy'].

[11] Psalm 103:13.

[12] Mark 15:34.

[13] Romans 8:15.

[14] Galatians 4:6.

[15] Chris Schrader, "The Fear of God," *The Ultimate Substitute Blog*, 3/24/2013.

[16] Ecclesiastes 5:2.

[17] Piper, op. cit. Sermon.

[18] Jeremiah 34:15-16.

[19] Ezekiel 36:22-27.

[20] Piper, op. cit., Sermon.

[21] Numbers 20:12.

[22] Galatians 1:10.

[23] Leviticus 22:31-32.

[24] Leviticus 10:3.

[25] James 4:14.

[26] Philippians 3:20-21.

[27] Revelation 21:3-4.

[28] Revelation 6:15-17.

[29] John 15:5.

[30] Acts 17:28.

[31] Psalm 139:23-24.

32 L. Chouinard, *Matthew*. The College Press NIV Commentary (Mt 6:12). (Joplin: College Press, 1997).

33 Pink, A. W. (2005). *The Lord's Prayer* (Mt 6:12). Bellingham, WA: Logos Research Systems, Inc.

34 Matthew 4:1.

35 Matthew 18:7.

36 www.goodreads.com/quotes/333743-the-word-of-god-is-the-fulcrum-upon-which-the. Accessed 7/18/2014.

37 1 Kings 3:16-20.

38 Luke 15:4-7.

39 Terry Teykl, *Your Pastor: Preyed on or Prayed For* (Muncie: Prayer Point Press, 1998).

40 Colossians 1:15-17, italics mine.

41 1 John 3:1.

42 LeRoy Eims, *Be The Leader You Were Meant To Be* (Wheaton: Victor, 1996) 26.

43 Ibid., 26.

44 Matthew 7:12.

45 J. Hudson Taylor in Sanders, op. cit., 89.

46 1 Corinthians 6:19.

47 John 6:38.

48 John Piper, "Jeremiah Lanphier," *Pietist Blogspot*, 5/2007, Accessed 7/10/2014. www.pietist.blogspot.com/2007/05/john-piper-on-jeremiah-lanphier.html.

49 Teykl, op. cit., 32.

50 Samuel Chadwick, GoodReads, www.goodreads.com/quotes/323811-satan-dreads-nothing-but-prayer-his-one -concern-it-to. Accessed 7/14/2014.

51 Ephesians 6:12.

52 John 5:19.

53 Isaiah 64:4.

54 1 John 5:14.

55 Jerry Bridges, *Discipline of Grace* (Colorado Springs: NavPress, 1994), 45.

56 C.J. Mahaney, *Don't Waste Your Sports* Sermon, (Gaithersburg: Sovereign Grace Ministries, 2008), www.sovereigngraceministries.com.

57 Robert Emmons, "Gratitude and Well-Being," *Emmons Lab*, Accessed 7/14/2014, http://emmons.faculty.ucdavis.edu/gratitude-and-well-being/.

58 Proverbs 17:22.

59 Proverbs 15:13, 15.

60 C.J. Mahaney, *Living the Cross Centered Life: Keeping the Gospel the Main Thing* (Colorado Springs: Multnomah, 2006), 137-138.

6

HUMBLE SERVANT

THE GREATEST

"Everybody can be great. Because anybody can serve. You don't have to have a college degree to serve. You don't have to make your subject and your verb agree to serve…You don't have to know the second theory of thermodynamics in physics to serve. You only need a heart full of grace. A soul generated by love." (Martin Luther King, Jr.)

"But whoever would be great among you must be your servant, and whoever would be first among you must be your slave, even as the Son of Man came not to be served but to serve, and to give his life as a ransom for many."(Matthew 20:27-28)

How many of you know anyone that likes to serve?

…Let's take Starbucks as an example. Think about the baristas who work behind the counters… Think about Genesis 3. The lie that the serpent told Eve was what? You can be God. And at Starbucks people act like that. They walk in and treat the baristas as part of their little kingdom. The king is here and needs a mocha, whipp-a, whatever the picka it is. And I want it at 127 degrees, and you need to do a cartwheel and sprinkle some cinnamon on it. Just weird stuff, you know. And I want it in two cups and I want it in my left hand. What they're saying is, "The king is here, and you little minions back there, need to obey the orders of the king. Do you know who is here? The Lord has arrived – the Mocha Lord."

It's weird because people love to give orders and they love to be served. "You did not do it right." Seriously, how many people are there who come to you and say, "How can I serve you?" "How can I make your life better?" "How can I encourage you?" "How can I give mercy to you?" "How can I give grace to you?" Jesus is the Servant we are to imitate. You want to freak a barista out at Starbucks? Just walk up and say, "I'm a Christian. Should I pick up the trash? Do you need a break? Can I wash your car? They'll call 911 [or think they're being punk'd]. We're not in a world where people care, where people help, where people love, where people give, where people are gracious, and merciful and kind.[1]

∞ *What might a humble servant look like in sports?*

Humble = Power to Perform. A humble coach understands that apart from Christ, she and her athletes are powerless to perform. This is reality, whether your athletes are Christians or not. An athlete's relationship to Jesus does not change the fact that the Lord is the Giver, and all humans the recipients. "I am the vine; you are the branches. Whoever abides in me and I in him, he it is that bears much fruit, for apart from me you can do nothing."[2] Zero, nada, zip. Or consider the words of the prophet Jeremiah, which give us an enhanced visual of this Giver and recipient interaction:

> Thus says the LORD: "Cursed is the man who trusts in man and makes flesh his strength, whose heart turns away from the LORD. He is like a shrub in the desert, and shall not see any good come. He shall dwell in the parched places of the wilderness, in an uninhabited salt land. Blessed is the man who trusts in the LORD, whose trust is the LORD. He is like a tree planted by water, that sends out its roots by the stream, and does not fear when heat comes, for its leaves remain green, and is not anxious in the year of drought, for it does not cease to bear fruit." (Jeremiah 17:5-8)

Not a whole lot of wiggle room there. Do you want to be a spindly shrub in the parched wilderness or a green-leafed tree with roots nourished by nearby water? The only way for you to be successful as a coach in God's eyes is to find your strength in him, to trust in him, and not fear or be anxious, especially when athletes' performances don't go as planned. It will happen to every coach, every season at some juncture. Just ask Nick Saban, who was riding high towards the 2013-2014 BCS National Championship until he decided it was a good idea to try a 62-yard field goal against Auburn with one second left on the clock. Oops.

Humble =Proper Perspective. Ultimately, winning or losing according to the world's standards will not determine whether you are successful in God's eyes. Do you want a joy-filled coaching experience? If yes, than consider the advice of Albert Schweitzer: "The only ones among you who will be really happy are those who will have sought and found how to serve." It's not about you. In and of yourself, you bring nothing to the table. Is that tough to swallow? Perhaps you need to check your pride at the door. For Jeremiah further reveals, "Let not the wise man boast in his wisdom, let not the mighty man boast in his might, let not the rich man boast in his riches, but let him who boasts boast in this, that he understands and knows me, that I am the LORD who practices steadfast love, justice, and righteousness in the earth. For in these things I delight, declares the LORD."[3]

Christian Hedonism [The teaching that, "God is most glorified in us when we are most satisfied in him"] combats pride because it puts man in the category of an empty vessel beneath the fountain of God. Philanthropists can boast. Welfare recipients can't. The primary experience of the Christian Hedonist is one of helplessness and desperation and longing.[4]

Servant = Other Person Oriented. This refers back to our discussion of whether you treat your athletes as being made in the image of God or commodities to help you achieve your goals. "For you were called to freedom, brothers. Only do not use your freedom as an opportunity for the flesh, but through love serve one another. For the whole law is fulfilled in one word: 'You shall love your neighbor as yourself.'"[5] What are you doing to help develop your athletes to pursue excellence in their sport and in life – to point them towards true Kingdom greatness?

The term *coach* originally referred to a horse-drawn carriage, something that was designed for the purpose of transporting people and mail. These horse-drawn carriages were originally manufactured in a small Hungarian town of Kocs (pronounced "kotch.") beginning in the 15th century. The word became used in a symbolic sense, around 1830 to refer to an instructor or trainer. It appears in some of the publications of Oxford University as a slang term for a tutor who "carries" a student through an exam. Later, this metaphorical use of the word as someone who "carries" another was used in the realm of athletic competition, beginning in 1861.[6]

Greatness is shown through humble service:

And they came to Capernaum. And when he was in the house he asked them, "What were you discussing on the way?" But they kept silent, for on the way they had argued with one another about who was the greatest. And he sat down and called the twelve. And he said to them, "If anyone would be first, he must be last of all and servant of all." (Mark 9:33–35)

Notice that Jesus does not rebuke his disciples for pursuing greatness. Rather, he redefines what it means to be great. Therefore, if you desire to be great in the eyes of Jesus, you must be a humble servant. But don't let that be an excuse for not pursuing excellence. In other words, being a humble-servant coach does not mean that you are against competition or against winning.

[Because,] "Deliberate mediocrity is a sin" (Elton Trueblood)…I had bought into the prevailing notion that aspiring to greatness was somehow unbecoming to a Christian. I had grown up in a spiritual culture that viewed the desire to be great as pitted against the virtue of humility…greatness in the kingdom of God is a journey toward humility. Being obscure does not render a leader humble. Nor does being famous automatically rule out being humble. Humility and celebrity can coexist. Jesus proves this point. Humility derives from the leader's awareness of where his or her source of strength lies.[7]

Is it even possible to serve without being humble? Absolutely! Service without love can be seen on a daily basis – most likely in our own lives, if we dare seek the Spirit's discernment to understand our heart's motives clearly. Here are two passages of Scripture that we've looked at previously that illustrate a heartless/loveless servant attitude. By outward appearance they were 'servants,' but by inward motives they were 'self-serving':

> The Pharisee, standing by himself, prayed thus: 'God, I thank you that I am not like other men, extortioners, unjust, adulterers, or even like this tax collector. I fast twice a week; *I give tithes of all that I get.*' (Luke 18:11-12, italics mine)

> Thus, *when you give to the needy*, sound no trumpet before you, as the hypocrites do in the synagogues and in the streets, that they may be praised by others. Truly, I say to you, they have received their reward. (Matthew 6:2, italics mine)

Let's see what a humble servant in sports looks like. Now I'm not saying the young man in the following story was doing this as a servant of Jesus Christ, because I don't know his spiritual condition. However, witness a young man serving his fellow competitor with absolutely nothing to gain for himself:

> David Caldwell is a senior at South Charleston High School which abuts St. Albans High School in Kanawha County, W. Va. Caldwell is the only distance runner on the track team… Caldwell's coach brings him to St. Alban's practices so that he can have the benefits of running alongside other boys… Tonight, Caldwell is paying the St. Albans coach and team back… Caldwell is coming for the purpose…of pacing Caleb Ellis in the 3200 meters… Ellis has never gone under 10:00 in the 3200. Caldwell [recently ran] 9:29… When I hear that Caldwell is coming to the meet for some reason other than to blow everybody else away, I think to myself, "I'll believe it when I see it."

> …The gun fires and before they are out of the first turn, it's already a two-man race… They pass the halfway point and are still side by side… [B]ut when they enter the sixth lap, Ellis begins to fade. In the far turn I see Caldwell do something I've never seen him do… [H]e turns his head and faces backward to Ellis, and yells at Ellis to *push it, keep it up, to not give in*… The plan had been for Caldwell to drop out in the sixth lap. But, with Ellis lagging, Caldwell stays in the race, and through the seventh lap turns time and again to Ellis and motions him with his

arm. Ellis seems to find something and closes the gap… Midway into the first straightaway on the eighth and final lap… Caldwell quietly runs off the track and onto the infield. Ellis wins the race in 9:48… Because of [Caldwell], the Ellis kid has done something significant that he quite possibly would never have otherwise achieved… And there was nothing in it for Caldwell.[8]

∞ *What does a humble-servant coach look like? How can you develop this characteristic in your own role as a coach?*

Success and failure are two great impostors. One does not bring life. The other does not bring death. Being at peace on both ends of the spectrum is critical for the humble-servant coach. Humility can be difficult on both sides of the equation. For, "Pride goes before destruction, and a haughty spirit before a fall."[9] Here's picture of pride at work in the coaching arena. Does it look familiar?

> I think coaches scream at kids in games when they make a mistake because they are embarrassed. When a player screws up or a team plays badly, coaches blow up to make it clear that the players aren't doing what they were taught to do. Coaches yell at players because they want to be sure that everyone in the gym knows that they understand the game, and it isn't their fault that their players aren't getting it. (Debbie Colberg, Former Head Women's Volleyball Coach, Sacramento State University).[10]

And here's a great method to keep that pride-fueled destruction from landing on your doorstep:

> When I perceive the glory of God and my relationship to him, I am less vulnerable to self-effort and self-sufficiency. I walk onto the field of play trusting on God, dependent on God… This knowledge of God prepares me and positions me to glorify God and not myself as I play sports. This will keep us from wasting our sports [coaching].[11]

Regularly ask yourself, "Would you want to play for you?" or "Would you want your kids to play for someone who coaches like you do?" You must be willing to stop looking at how your athletes can benefit you, and start asking how you can be a blessing to them. "A servant leader must be willing to get down and dirty with his troops in the implementation of his objectives… most often my day is spent laying aside my own priorities to help others fulfill theirs… servant leadership is about caring for others more than for ourselves. It is about compassion for everyone who serves the group."[12]

> More than any other idols, personal success and achievements lead to a sense that we ourselves are god, that our security and value rest in our own wisdom, strength,

and performance. To be the very best at what you do, to be at the top of the heap, means no one is like you. You are supreme.[13]

Your goal as a humble-servant coach is to serve your athletes – you are seeking downward mobility, not upward self-aggrandizement. The welfare of your athletes takes priority over your prestige. You must continually ask God for wisdom and empowering on the best way to coach each individual athlete, and the team as a whole, in a manner that helps all to pursue excellence in their sport and in their service. Those two should be intertwined, not two separate isolated facets.

TOOLS

Ω **Are you more like The Good Samaritan or The Mocha Lord in your relationships with your athletes?**

What can you do to develop more of a humble servant attitude? Be bold and ask those you trust who watch you coach.

Ω **Take time before every practice and game to be still in God's Word and be in awe of Jesus. Pray for the gospel to be in the forefront of your mind and heart, for your ministry as a humble servant ambassador of Jesus, and for the reality that each athlete you work with is made in God's image.**

"When I behold the glory of God prior to playing [coaching] sports, my heart is affected, my heart is transformed. If I walk onto the field aware of the glory of God, I am less susceptible to self-exaltation. Only an ignorant, arrogant fool would draw attention to himself and exalt himself in light of the greatness of God."[14]

Ω **Meditate upon this passage of Scripture and ask the Holy Spirit to give you an honest picture of who you were before he redeemed you, in order to help weed out the wickedness of pride that seeks to usurp the glory of God.**

"For consider your calling, brothers: not many of you were wise according to worldly standards, not many were powerful, not many were of noble birth. But God chose what is foolish in the world to shame the wise; God chose what is weak in the world to shame the strong; God chose what is low and despised in the world, even things that are not, to bring to nothing things that are, so that no human being might boast in the presence of God. And because of him you are in Christ Jesus, who became to us wisdom from God, righteousness and sanctification and redemption, so that, as it is written, 'Let the one who boasts, boast in the Lord.'" (1 Corinthians 1:26-31)

Ω Meditate upon this passage of Scripture and ask the Holy Spirit how it can translate to your coaching from a humble servant position.

Now before the Feast of the Passover, when Jesus knew that his hour had come to depart out of this world to the Father, having loved his own who were in the world, he loved them to the end. During supper, when the devil had already put it into the heart of Judas Iscariot, Simon's son, to betray him, Jesus, knowing that the Father had given all things into his hands, and that he had come from God and was going back to God, rose from supper. He laid aside his outer garments, and taking a towel, tied it around his waist. Then he poured water into a basin and began to wash the disciples' feet and to wipe them with the towel that was wrapped around him. He came to Simon Peter, who said to him, "Lord, do you wash my feet?" Jesus answered him, "What I am doing you do not understand now, but afterward you will understand." Peter said to him, "You shall never wash my feet." Jesus answered him, "If I do not wash you, you have no share with me." Simon Peter said to him, "Lord, not my feet only but also my hands and my head!" Jesus said to him, "The one who has bathed does not need to wash, except for his feet, but is completely clean. And you are clean, but not every one of you." For he knew who was to betray him; that was why he said, "Not all of you are clean." When he had washed their feet and put on his outer garments and resumed his place, he said to them, "Do you understand what I have done to you? You call me Teacher and Lord, and you are right, for so I am. If I then, your Lord and Teacher, have washed your feet, you also ought to wash one another's feet. For I have given you an example, that you also should do just as I have done to you. Truly, truly, I say to you, a servant is not greater than his master, nor is a messenger greater than the one who sent him. If you know these things, blessed are you if you do them." (John 13:1-17)

Ω PRAYER

"Heavenly Father, I cannot love my athletes as I love myself if I rely on my own self-sufficiency. So clothe me with humility toward each of my athletes and others associated with our program, because you oppose the proud and give grace to the humble. I desire that grace. I desperately need that grace if I am going to be successful at working heartily for your glory and not for the praises of men. I can only coach by the strength that you supply – in order that in everything you may be glorified through Jesus Christ. So continue to build a humble servant mindset in me that seeks the increase of Jesus' glory and the decrease of any empty praises towards me. Far be it from me to boast except in the cross of my Lord Jesus Christ. For to him belong glory and dominion forever and ever." (Mark 12:31, 1 Peter 5:5-6, Colossians 3:23-24, 1 Peter 4:11, John 3:30, Galatians 6:14)

THE CALL

"What's my purpose?" (If most people could ask God one question, from a *USA Today* poll)[15]

"Jesus said to him, 'No one who puts his hand to the plow and looks back is fit for the kingdom of God.' " (John 9:62)

∞ *Have you received a call/opportunity to serve through coaching?*

If you are in a coaching position, then you have one of two options. You either treat it as a calling/opportunity to serve your athletes and honor Jesus through coaching, or you dishonor God by serving yourself. Coaching, like all other calls to serve, can only be fully realized when you are in right relationship with the Creator, Redeemer, and Sustainer of the universe.

So what can you learn about coaching from John the Baptizer's response to the call placed upon his life?

> The beginning of the gospel of Jesus Christ, the Son of God. As it is written in Isaiah the prophet, "Behold, I send my messenger before your face, who will prepare your way, the voice of one crying in the wilderness: 'Prepare the way of the Lord, make his paths straight,'" John appeared, baptizing in the wilderness and proclaiming a baptism of repentance for the forgiveness of sins. And all the country of Judea and all Jerusalem were going out to him and were being baptized by him in the river Jordan, confessing their sins. Now John was clothed with camel's hair and wore a leather belt around his waist and ate locusts and wild honey. And he preached, saying, "After me comes he who is mightier than I, the strap of whose sandals I am not worthy to stoop down and untie. I have baptized you with water, but he will baptize you with the Holy Spirit."[16]

John's main calling was to prepare the way for the Messiah. But he could have just as easily positioned himself to be the marquee player in the eyes of the people. People were curious - was John the Messiah, the one they had been so desperately waiting for? "As the people were in expectation, and all were questioning in their hearts concerning John, whether he might be the Christ."[17] All John had to do was answer one question affirmatively and he would have been #1 in many people's eyes. He had an opening, a straight shot to the top.

What was John's response to this attention? "And this is the testimony of John, when the Jews sent priests and Levites from Jerusalem to ask him, 'Who are you?' He confessed, and did not deny, but confessed, 'I am not the Christ.'"[18] "I am the voice of one crying out in the wilderness, 'Make straight the way of the Lord,' as the prophet Isaiah said."[19]

John's entire life was a sermon based upon the proclamation, "He must increase, but I must decrease."[20] John's success rested on the fact that he understood his role.

We've seen how John responded to his call to serve. But was it just a matter of John's willpower that helped him to reach the finish line? What will you rely on to coach in a manner that honors the calling upon your life? John is not the only prophet you can learn from in this matter. Let's see what we can learn from Elisha's interaction with Elijah:

> So Elijah went and found Elisha son of Shaphat plowing a field. There were twelve teams of oxen in the field, and Elisha was plowing with the twelfth team. Elijah went over to him and threw his cloak across his shoulders and then walked away. Elisha left the oxen standing there, ran after Elijah, and said to him, "First let me go and kiss my father and mother good-bye, and then I will go with you!" Elijah replied, "Go on back, but think about what I have done to you." So Elisha returned to his oxen and slaughtered them. He used the wood from the plow to build a fire to roast their flesh. He passed around the meat to the townspeople, and they all ate. Then he went with Elijah as his assistant. (1 Kings 19:19-21)

Concerning the call of Elisha, observe:[21]

1. **The call to serve is not based upon a person's occupation or training.**

Did you catch the importance of that first line in that passage? Elijah found Elisha plowing a field. Not exactly the kind of training you would expect for the next prophet of Israel. Elisha was performing manual labor. He was not reading the Word or praying. He was plowing. The initial call upon your life to coach may not be based upon your present education or your experience, but on your devoted availability. That said, understand that a calling on your life does not mean that you are now miraculously equipped to go forth and coach. It is your responsibility to find the best training and equipping available to you at the start of your journey, and throughout it. Elisha did not just stay behind the plow after the call came. He took definitive actions to prepare to be a prophet.

2. **The call to serve is an effectual call/a powerful call.**

When Elijah threw his cloak across Elisha's shoulders, it symbolized the passing of power and authority of the prophetical office. Elisha obviously understood the meaning behind the cloak placed upon his shoulders, because he left his oxen standing in the field and ran after Elijah. He then told Elijah that he would follow him immediately after saying goodbye to his parents. The desire to say goodbye is not a wavering on Elisha's part to follow his call to serve, but merely a desire to honor his parents.

"An invisible hand touched his heart [new identity = changed heart], and unaccountably inclined him, without any external persuasions, to quit his occupation and give himself to the ministry."[22] Now I'm not saying that you should quit your present job to devote yourself full-time to volunteer coaching. But, if you feel called to pursue coaching as an occupation, it may be time to consider whether you need to leave other pursuits behind.

Before you begin coaching at any level, however, you need to consider carefully what Elijah says next: "Go on back, but think about what I have done for you." Elijah gives Elisha permission to kiss his parents goodbye, but he also wants Elisha to realize that he is not being forced to follow. "What I have done to you" means, "Do as you please" or "What have I done to stop you?" It is also a challenge to contemplate what it will mean to follow in his footsteps. You, too, should not take the call lightly, whether it's as a volunteer or as a career coach. Count the cost.

3. The call to serve is a call to an undivided allegiance.

"If anyone would come after me, let him deny himself and take up his cross and follow me. For whoever would save his life will lose it, but whoever loses his life for my sake will find it. For what will it profit a man if he gains the whole world and forfeits his soul? Or what shall a man give in return for his soul?"[23] Elisha is not just begging off on a down-and-out existence in the hopes that following Elijah will bring him some better life. He obviously came from a prosperous family. Twelve teams of oxen in the field means that he was walking away from twenty-four oxen. And there's no sense that family dynamics were dysfunctional, because he goes back to kiss his parents and show them they are valued, but not more cherished than the call to serve that Elijah has just placed upon his shoulders.

But what does that look like for your coaching? Are you supposed to walk away from something? Perhaps, if there is something that is keeping you from focusing on your call. If coaching is your vocation, then the time commitment and the call to walk away from other time drains will be greater than if you are just a volunteer. But even in that case, are you able to focus your attention and manage your time well in order to do what needs to get done to honor Christ through your calling?

4. The call to serve is a pleasant and acceptable call.

How do we know this was a pleasant call for Elisha? Not only is he willing to leave the comforts of his family, but he also leaves his wealth behind. He takes the twenty-four oxen and has a massive barbecue for family, friends, and neighbors. He has a sweet time of fellowship with all these people as a celebratory sign of the journey upon which he is about to embark, even though his face would soon be put on a 'Wanted' poster by Queen Jezebel, who sought to kill all of Israel's true prophets. Coaching for the glory of God and the joy of your athletes should be a sweet call to you - even if the Jezebels of the world come after you to keep you from speaking God's truth in love. Coach Dabo Swinney can attest to this.

> The Wisconsin-based Freedom from Religion Foundation…contends that "Christian Worship seems interwoven into Clemson's football program. We are concerned that this commingling of religious and athletic results, not from student

initiative, but from the attitudes and unconstitutional behaviors of the coaching staff." In the complaint, the group contends: Coach Dabo Swinney invited James Trapp to be the team's chaplain. Trapp was given access to the entire team in between drills for bible study. Trapp has an office at the athletic center and displays bible quotes on a whiteboard and organized and led sessions on "being baptized" in the athletic building. The FFRF also contends that Swinney schedules team devotionals… [even though all "religious activities are purely voluntary and there are no repercussions for students who decline to do so.]24

5. The call to serve is a humbling call.

If you want to coach, you must be willing to serve your athletes. Even though Elijah was a wealthy man with land, oxen, servant, and a family, he gave up everything in order to serve Elijah as his assistant. Everywhere that Elijah went, Elisha followed, seeking to minister to his needs. "Elisha's goal was not just to study from Elijah, but to *become like* Elijah – to be transformed into his likeness. A disciple [does] 'not grasp the full significance of his teacher's learning in all its nuances except through prolonged intimacy with his teacher.'"25

TOOLS

Ω. Are you content in preparing the way for Jesus in your coaching or do you want to be the destination, all attention riveted upon you?

As a coach, you, like John, are not in the *glory* position. Accolades are not for you.

Ω If you find yourself dreading service through coaching, seek the Holy Spirit's wisdom on why the call is not pleasant. Learn from Elijah.

Every coach will go through peaks and valleys regarding the call. The key is seeking to find out what is causing the displeasure and then combating it. Even Elijah had to contend with down days.

> Ahab told Jezebel all that Elijah had done, and how he had killed all the prophets with the sword. Then Jezebel sent a messenger to Elijah, saying, "So may the gods do to me and more also, if I do not make your life as the life of one of them by this time tomorrow." Then he was afraid, and he arose and ran for his life and came to Beersheba, which belongs to Judah, and left his servant there. But he himself went a day's journey into the wilderness and came and sat down under a broom tree. And he asked that he might die, saying, "It is enough; now, O LORD, take away my life, for I am no better than my fathers." And behold, there came a voice to him

and said, "What are you doing here, Elijah?" He said, "I have been very jealous for the LORD, the God of hosts. For the people of Israel have forsaken your covenant, thrown down your altars, and killed your prophets with the sword, and I, even I only, am left, and they seek my life, to take it away." And the LORD said to him, "Go, return on your way to the wilderness of Damascus. And when you arrive, you shall anoint Hazael to be king over Syria. And Jehu the son of Nimshi you shall anoint to be king over Israel, and Elisha the son of Shaphat of Abel-meholah you shall anoint to be prophet in your place. And the one who escapes from the sword of Hazael shall Jehu put to death, and the one who escapes from the sword of Jehu shall Elisha put to death. Yet I will leave seven thousand in Israel, all the knees that have not bowed to Baal, and every mouth that has not kissed him." (1 Kings 19:1-4, 13-18)

Ω Whose footsteps are you following in?

Do you have another coach that you can learn from? Someone who will mentor you? Or if you've been coaching for many years, do you have other coaches/peers who might be willing to meet on a regular basis so you can all learn from each other?

Ω PRAYER

"Heavenly Father, open my mind and my heart to truly comprehend that coaching is a humbling call to serve. However, it's not just about serving athletes through teaching them the intricacies of the sport, because the mission of coaches is the same as the mission of Jesus, to seek and to save the lost. Empower me to follow the pattern of the Apostle Paul, who became all things to all people, so that by all means I might save some. Let me do it all for the sake of the gospel, that I may share with others in its blessings. In a race all the runners run, but only one receives the prize. So help me to run that I may obtain it. Every athlete exercises self-control in all things. They do it to receive a perishable wreath, but we an imperishable one. So I do not want to run aimlessly; I do not want to box as one beating the air. But I desire to discipline my body and keep it under control, lest after preaching to others I myself should be disqualified. Grant me wisdom each day to know what I have to leave behind in order to better fulfill my calling. I do not want to have a divided allegiance. I want all of my life, including coaching, to be an offering unto you." (Luke 19:10; 1 Corinthians 9:20-27)

THE QUESTION

"And they came to Jericho. And as he [Jesus] was leaving Jericho with his disciples and a great crowd, Bartimaeus, a blind beggar, the son of Timaeus, was sitting by the roadside. And when he heard that it was Jesus of Nazareth, he began to cry out and say, 'Jesus, Son of David, have mercy on me!'

And many rebuked him, telling him to be silent. But he cried out all the more, 'Son of David, have mercy on me!' And Jesus stopped and said, 'Call him.' And they called the blind man, saying to him, 'Take heart. Get up; he is calling you.' And throwing off his cloak, he sprang up and came to Jesus. And Jesus said to him, '*What do you want me to do for you?*' And the blind man said to him, 'Rabbi, let me recover my sight.' And Jesus said to him, 'Go your way; your faith has made you well.' And immediately he recovered his sight and followed him on the way." (Mark 10:46-52, italics mine)

"Do nothing from selfish ambition or conceit, but in humility count others more significant than yourselves. Let each of you look not only to his own interests, but also to the interests of others. Have this mind among yourselves, which is yours in Christ Jesus, who, though he was in the form of God, did not count equality with God a thing to be grasped, but emptied himself, by taking the form of a servant, being born in the likeness of men. And being found in human form, he humbled himself by becoming obedient to the point of death, even death on a cross." (Philippians 2:3-8)

∞ *Do you show unconditional love towards your athletes or performance-based acceptance? Do your theology and methodology honor God by showing that you value your athletes?*

"What do you want me to do for you?" That seems like an odd question that Jesus asks the blind man. But it shows that he loves and values the man, which is not the response the man seemed to be getting from all his friends and neighbors, who were trying to get him to shut up. In contrast, Jesus allows the blind man to speak, to express his desires. Do you allow your athletes to share what is on their hearts? Or do you presume to always know what is best for them? How you interact with your athletes on this level goes a long way in revealing a humble-servant attitude that expresses your desire to be a transformational coach rather than a transactional one. Try it and see what happens. "What do you want me to do for you? How can I encourage you? How can I help make your life better?"

> Transactional coaches [are] the kind of coaches who use players as tools to meet their personal needs for validation, status, and identity. They held their power over us to elicit the response they wanted... Transformational coaches are other-centered. They use their power and platform to nurture and transform players.[26]

Asking "What can I do for you?" shows your athletes that you value them as people. You are seeking to cultivate their time, talents, and treasures so that each of them can grow as people and athletes, not so you can use them to pad your own profile. It is critical that you love, value, and honor each athlete you coach, because they are made in the image of God. Love, value, and honor are not based upon an athlete's performance, but rather upon being the apex of God's creation, and the beneficiaries of Christ's performance on the cross. This, however, does not give your athletes carte blanche to behave in any way they please. On the contrary, it sets the tone for the entire team.

If you love, value, and honor your athletes in the way that you interact with them, than you expect the same in their behavior towards you and each other. Attitude reflects leadership.[27]

If you as a coach are seeking to live out the dictates of Colossians 3:23, "Whatever you do, work heartily, as for the Lord and not for men," than as a team, you will be setting high standards. These will be based upon your conversations with individuals and your experience as a coach. Then you will seek to help your athletes achieve these goals through your role as a humble servant-leader. The transactional alternative is ugly:

Kelly Greenberg recently finished her 10th season at Boston University. Unfortunately, her tenure has twice been sullied by accusations from players that she treated them in a bullying and demeaning manner. Eight players have publicly criticized Greenberg's coaching style and claimed that she was emotionally abusive. These accusations first surfaced in 2008 from Jacy Schulz and Brianne Ozimok. Both players transferred from the program. After the initial report in 2008, in an internal review, BU Athletic Director Mike Lynch said in a statement that the complaints "helped Coach Greenberg appreciate that her style has been difficult, and that she has also made substantive mistakes that she deeply regrets." Apparently it didn't stick.

Four players recently left the team due to what they described as "emotional bullying." Dana Theobald was struggling with an eating disorder, depression, and anxiety. When she asked for a leave of absence to deal with these issues, all Greenberg said, according to Theobald, was, "You look horrible out there, absolutely horrible." She also apparently told Theobald, "It's not my problem." Melissa Gallo was also dealing with depression. Not surprising if her claims against Greenberg are true. Gallo told the Daily Free Press. "… I told her I was speaking to someone in Student Health [Services] … She told me I was high maintenance for having depression. She attacked me on a personal level, saying things like, 'definitely change your hair, I hate that low bun,' or, 'you look sick and should put on some makeup'… She abused her powers."

Dionna Joynes said she felt suicidal after her coach told her she was uncaring and selfish as a teammate for being out of the lineup with a concussion. At one point, Joynes was taken by ambulance to a hospital because of emotional stress. Joynes told the Boston Globe, "Giving up a $60,000-a-year scholarship is the hardest thing I've ever done; I hate that I'm not in school, but it had to be done. My spirit was broken." A winning record of 186-127 and a contract extension through 2017 could not contend against the allegations. Greenberg has resigned her position. Boston University and head women's basketball coach Kelly Greenberg have parted ways.

Your athletes need to know that you genuinely love them and are concerned about their overall development as people and athletes. And don't think this is something that only needs to occur with older athletes. It needs to start from the very first time a child is part of a team. If this type of foundation is built, fewer children will drop out of the sporting scene by the time they are twelve. Those that do remain due to your coaching in this manner will know that they are loved.

Does that seem an odd thing to say about a coach, that she loves her athletes? If you are a disciple of Jesus, there is no greater calling upon your life than to love those you are mentoring. It doesn't matter whether they are just learning which goal is theirs on a soccer field or they are playing for the NCAA National Championship. Transformational coaches humbly serve their athletes by listening to them, challenging them and helping them to set high standards, and then shepherding them in their journeys.

Love will always be a stronger, longer-lasting, transformative power than any type of tactics involving intimidation, fear, or coercion. "Love is patient and kind; love does not envy or boast; it is not arrogant or rude. It does not insist on its own way; it is not irritable or resentful; it does not rejoice at wrongdoing, but rejoices with the truth. Love bears all things, believes all things, hopes all things, endures all things."[28] What might this look like? How about helping your athletes enjoy their time with you to such a degree that they enjoy the sport and their teammates more than when the season began – and they genuinely look forward to doing it all again.

The health of your athletes is also a critical component of your role as a humble servant. Are you taking unnecessary risks with your athletes who are made in the image of God? What value are you placing on reaching goals versus being a caretaker of your athletes? You must realize that just because someone is not injured under your watch doesn't mean that you aren't culpable to a degree. Many injuries of our youth can be cumulative in nature. You may not be the one that places the proverbial last straw upon the camel's back, but that doesn't mean you didn't unnecessarily increase the load previously. Continually be seeking to assess what effects your coaching may have on your athletes years down the road.

Sometimes, however, you may need to intervene in your athletes' lives because they are causing unnecessary harm to their bodies. They are the problem. You may have some athletes who are willing to risk their health in order to be 'successful.' They've heard the stories of professionals playing with broken bones, gulping down handfuls of anti-inflammatories, and doing a host of other absurd things that no one should imitate. It's at those moments when you as the servant-coach need to intervene and not allow them to continue until they are healthy again. You need to be the one who has the maturity and the eternal perspective to know when to call it a day.

∞ *Do you take the time to continually study your athletes in an effort to determine the best methods to train and equip them for their sport and life?*

When it comes to training and equipping, there is no such thing as one-size-fits-all. Are there basic tools necessary to learn for your sport and for life? Absolutely! But how you go about imparting those building blocks can be as varied as the individual personalities on your team. Coaching is an art and a science. Simply knowing the nuts and bolts of your sport is only part of the equation – the scientific part. A humble-servant artist/coach will continually be learning and adapting his coaching and mentoring style to meet the needs of individuals and the team as a whole. Just because something worked in the past is not a guarantee that it will work in the present.

Square pegs do not fit in round holes, no matter how hard you hammer away at them. You can talk to two athletes with the exact same tone and the exact same words, and find one encouraged and the other discouraged. Why is that? God created each of your athletes differently. It is imperative that you seek to understand what works best to motivate your athletes to learn new skills, practice those skills, and gain competency in those skills, whether they are for the playing field, for life, or for both. An artist will continually be on the lookout for the best ways, and continually be adjusting. Yes, that takes more time and effort than treating your athletes as plug-and-play modules that must solely adapt to a particular coaching methodology. But you are called to be a humble servant in order to point them to the Servant.

> One thing I have realized is that you can't change a personality so you have to understand it and be able to adapt to it. Or try to get that person to work with you and not against you... I work very hard at getting to know my players well enough that if something is bothering them, that is the most important thing for me at that moment. Because if I don't deal with that, practice and the game and everything else is irrelevant. (Mike Candrea, University of Arizona Head Softball Coach)[29]

Eyes that look and ears that merely hear sounds are common place. But eyes that truly see and ears that comprehend with the goal of transforming lives are all too rare. Consider two examples from Scripture. The first illustrates eyes that do not see and ears that do not hear because they are attached to self-centered hearts. The second example demonstrates what happens when eyes and ears are connected to a humble servant heart:

> And as they [Peter and John] were speaking to the people, the priests and the captain of the temple and the Sadducees came upon them, greatly annoyed because they were teaching the people and proclaiming in Jesus the resurrection from the dead. And they arrested them and put them in custody until the next day, for it was already evening. But many of those who had heard the word believed, and the number of the men came to about five thousand. Now when they saw the boldness of Peter and John, and perceived that they were uneducated, common men, they were astonished. And they recognized that they had been with Jesus. (Acts 4:1-4, 13)

> Some time after this, the cupbearer of the king of Egypt and his baker committed an offense against their lord the king of Egypt. And Pharaoh was angry with his two officers, the chief cupbearer and the chief baker, and he put them in custody in the house of the captain of the guard, in the prison where Joseph was confined. The captain of the guard appointed Joseph to be with them, and he attended them. They continued for some time in custody. And one night they both dreamed— the cupbearer and the baker of the king of Egypt, who were confined in the prison—each his own dream, and each dream with its own interpretation. When Joseph came to them in the morning, he saw that they were troubled. So he asked Pharaoh's officers who were with him in custody in his master's house, "Why are your faces downcast today?" They said to him, "We have had dreams, and there is no one to interpret them." And Joseph said to them, "Do not interpretations belong to God? Please tell them to me. (Genesis 40:1-8)

Would your athletes say your pattern more closely resembles that of the priests and Sadducees or Joseph? The religious leaders looked at Peter and John and merely saw common, uneducated men who were performing far above their station in life. They had no idea what to do with these men who were annoying them and ruining their leadership paradigm. Joseph, on the other hand, had eyes and ears connected to a humble-servant's heart. He saw that something was troubling the cupbearer and the baker, took the time to ask what was going on, and then sought to help remedy the problem, by the power of God.

How well do you know your athletes? I'm not talking about their on-the-field tendencies and abilities. How well do you know them as people? If you take the time to get to know what is going on off the field, you may be surprised. Rather than scratching your head or getting angry at an athlete practicing or playing at a sub-par level, find out what they are experiencing when they are not under your watchful eye. It may give you a direct clue about what is occurring on the field. But more importantly, it will also demonstrate that you care about them as living, breathing people, not just as parts of a machine. Their lives involve so much more than sports. Take the time to ask, listen, and learn.

TOOLS

Ω How well do you know your athletes as people?

Pray for the Holy Spirit to help your eyes and ears be connected to a humble servant's heart. Design a schedule to make sure that you have conversations during the season with each of your athletes in order to get to know who they are and what is going on in their lives. You should also be constantly aware of opportunities that arise anytime during practices, games, and life.

Ω How can you improve at serving as an artist?

Daily pray for the Holy Spirit to give you eyes to see, ears to hear, and a heart to respond. When you find yourself getting frustrated because practices, games, and/or the lives of your athletes are going askew, keep praying and seeking wisdom on the best way to serve them that will glorify God and bring joy to your athletes.

Ω What can I do to help each athlete today?

It is critical that you daily ask this question of yourself. Yes, you should ask your athletes what they want you to do for them. But it must not stop there or it can lead to the tail wagging the dog. You need to take their expressed desires and combine them with your education, experience, and Spirit-wrought wisdom to best train and equip your athletes.

Ω Write out 1 Corinthians 13:4-7 on an index card or put it on your phone or some other place where you will see it at regular intervals throughout the day. Put your name in every blank and ask the Holy Spirit to make it a reality today.

"_____ is patient and kind; _____ does not envy or boast; _____ is not arrogant or rude. _____ does not insist on its own way; _____ is not irritable or resentful; _____ does not rejoice at wrongdoing, but rejoices with the truth. _____ bears all things, believes all things, hopes all things, endures all things."

Ω PRAYER

"Lord Jesus, transform my heart to be like yours. Let me do nothing from selfish ambition or conceit, but in humility count my athletes more significant than me. Let me look not only to my own interests, but also to the interests of my athletes. For you did not count equality with your Father a thing to be grasped, but you emptied yourself, by taking the form of a servant, being born in the likeness of men. And being found in human form, you humbled yourself by becoming obedient to the point of death, even death on a cross. Therefore, anything that I might give up in working with my athletes is nothing in comparison to your ultimate sacrifice. So help me to not fear asking my athletes, 'What do you want me to do for you?' Connect my eyes and ears to a humble servant's heart so that I see when something is troubling my athletes, take the time to ask what is going on, and then seek to help remedy the problem, by your empowering, so my athletes may recognize that I have been with you, Lord Jesus." (Philippians 2:3-8; Mark 10:51; Acts 4:13)

THE OPPONENTS

"Atheism [the Christian faith] has been specially advanced through the loving service rendered to strangers, and through their care for the burial of the dead. It is a scandal there is not a single Jew who is a beggar, and that the godless Galileans care not only for their own poor but for ours as well; while those who belong to us look in vain for the help that we should render them" (Roman Emperor Julian, 332-363 A.D.).[30]

"So whatever you wish that others would do to you, do also to them, for this is the Law and the Prophets." (Matthew 7:12)

∞ *What can you learn from Jesus' life and his teaching about loving your 'opponents'?*

"And behold, a lawyer stood up to put him to the test, saying, 'Teacher, what shall I do to inherit eternal life?'"[31]

"He said to him, 'What is written in the Law? How do you read it?'"[32] There's a great lesson for you to learn in Jesus' short reply. Point your athletes to God's Word whenever it can be used to answer their questions. You don't have to give them chapter and verse for it to be impactful on their lives. In fact, if you are working in a secular environment, that is often a great way to proceed. Then, if your athlete asks you where you came up with your answer, you can answer directly without fear that you are proselytizing. Don't merely give your opinion. Let the living and active Word do its job.

"And he answered, 'You shall love the Lord your God with all your heart and with all your soul and with all your strength and with all your mind, and your neighbor as yourself.' And he said to him, 'You have answered correctly; do this, and you will live.'"[33]

Now this should have been the end of the story. The expert answered correctly by quoting from Deuteronomy 6:5 (the *Shema* that Jews prayed every day) and Leviticus 19:18. But God's Word was obviously not this man's final authority when it contradicted his desires.

"But he, desiring to justify himself, said to Jesus, 'And who is my neighbor?'"[34] He knew the correct answer but would not apply it to his own life. In his eyes, there were obviously those who could be defined as 'non-neighbors.'

"Jesus replied, 'A man was going down from Jerusalem to Jericho, and he fell among robbers, who stripped him and beat him and departed, leaving him half dead. Now by chance a priest was going down that road, and when he saw him he passed by on the other side. So likewise a Levite, when he came to the place and saw him, passed by on the other side.'"[35]

A priest comes upon this naked, beaten, half-dead man and what does he do? Does his heart go out to the man? Does he seek to serve him in any way? No. Many scholars believe the priest's supposed religious 'duty' kept him from being compassionate. "Priests were supposed to avoid especially impurity from a corpse; Pharisees thought one would contract it if even one's shadow touched the corpse... although the rule of mercy would take precedence if the man were clearly alive, the man looked as if he might be dead, and the priest did not wish to take the chance. The task was better left to a Levite or ordinary Israelite. [36]

The Law was used as an excuse to leave rather than an imperative to love. And what did the priest's helper, the Levite, do when he encountered the same man lying in need of help? He slowed down, did a bit of rubber-necking at the accident site, and then quickly headed down the road. He learned well from the one who went before him.

"But a Samaritan, as he journeyed, came to where he was, and when he saw him, he had compassion. He went to him and bound up his wounds, pouring on oil and wine. Then he set him on his own animal and brought him to an inn and took care of him. And the next day he took out two denarii and gave them to the innkeeper, saying, 'Take care of him, and whatever more you spend, I will repay you when I come back.' "[37]

"What? A Samaritan? That's impossible," the expert in the Law would say. "How can a Samaritan be the hero of the story?" For most Jews, a neighbor was another Jew, end of discussion. For instance, some of them said that it was illegal to help a gentile woman in her sorest time of need, the time of childbirth, for that would only have been to bring another gentile into the world.[38]

"'Which of these three, do you think, proved to be a neighbor to the man who fell among the robbers?' He said, 'The one who showed him mercy.' And Jesus said to him, 'You go, and do likewise.'"[39]

Perhaps we could all learn a valuable lesson from the Samaritan on loving our opponents. But let's allow C.S. Lewis to drive the point home:

"It is a serious thing to live in a society of possible gods and goddesses, to remember that the dullest and most uninteresting person that you talk to may one day be a creature which, if you saw it now, you would be strongly tempted to worship, or else a horror and a corruption such as you now meet, if at all, only in a nightmare. All day long we are, in some degree, helping each other to one or the other of these destinations…There are no *ordinary* people. You have never talked to a mere mortal."[40]

If Jesus and C.S. Lewis are correct, then the idea some coaches promote that their athletes should show contempt, disdain, and borderline hatred towards their opponents, all in the name of competition, is a sin. The goal is not the utter humiliation of your opponents. Just because they are on the opposite side of a 'game' in no ways justifies treating them as some kind of evil beings who need to be crushed. Quite the opposite. "Do nothing from selfish ambition or conceit, but in humility count others more significant than yourselves. Let each of you look not only to his own interests, but also to the interests of others."[41]

If you didn't have opponents, you would not have a sporting event. You must teach your athletes to rejoice when they are blessed with worthy competitors rather than allow them to demonize their opponents. Are you telling me that your opponents and their coaches don't work hard, don't want to win, don't have parents, family, and friends that are cheering for them? Good competitors help your individuals and teams reach higher levels. Your opponents should always be respected and never ridiculed. Respect honors God. Ridicule does not. You must always keep the cross at the center or you will develop an unhealthy perspective. "When I perceive what God has done for me through the death of his Son on the cross for my sins …I will esteem my teammates, and even my opponents, as more important than myself."[42] Follow Christ's example and show your athletes how to love their opponents.

For, "If you love those who love you, what benefit is that to you? For even sinners love those who love them. And if you do good to those who do good to you, what benefit is that to you? For even sinners do the same. And if you lend to those from whom you expect to receive, what credit is that to you? Even sinners lend to sinners, to get back the same amount. But love your enemies, and do good, and lend, expecting nothing in return, and your reward will be great, and you will be sons of the Most High, for he is kind to the ungrateful and the evil. Be merciful, even as your Father is merciful." (Luke 6:32–36)

∞ On a practical level, what might it look like for your team to love their opponents?

It's a story that perhaps only Hollywood could script. 5'2" Sara Tucholsky stepped up to the plate with her team, Western Oregon University, trailing in a game that would propel the winner into the NCAA DII softball playoffs. With two runners on base and a strike against her, the senior with the .153 batting average did something she had never done before. The ball cleared the centerfield fence and Sara had the first homerun of her career, high school or college. But the game changing hit would be short-lived. In her excitement, she sprinted to first base but missed tagging the bag as she rounded the corner heading towards second base. When she pivoted to turn back to first, her knee gave out and she crumpled to the ground in a heap. She literally crawled back to first base because she would be called out if anyone on her team assisted her. Then the real dilemma set in. Western Oregon coach Pam Knox ran onto the field and talked to the umpires. They said the coach could place a substitute runner at first, but then Tucholsky would only be credited with a single, not the homerun that put her team in the lead.

What two members of the Central Washington University team did next stunned the crowd and set social media ablaze. Mallory Holtman, the career home run leader in the Great Northwest Athletic Conference, asked the umpire if she and her teammates could help Sara 'run' the bases. The umpire said there was nothing in the rule book against it. So Holtman and her teammate, Liz Wallace, literally carried their opponent around the base path, stopping at every base so she could gently tap the bag with the foot of her good leg. A mixture of cheers and tears ensued when the trio reached home plate. Eventually that gesture led to Central Washington being eliminated from making the playoffs, as Western Oregon won the game 4-2. Central Washington coach Gary Frederick, 70, a fourteen-year coaching veteran, called the act of sportsmanship "unbelievable." Holtman's response? "In the end, it is not about winning and losing so much. It was about this girl. She hit it over the fence and was in pain, and she deserved a home run."

Winning at all costs disregards the dignity of your athletes and their opponents. This story would have never happened if somewhere along the way these young ladies hadn't learned valuable life lessons about loving, valuing, and honoring their opponents. Do you and your athletes know how to lose with style, class, dignity, and honor? There is a chasm between being disappointed and being distraught when you have lost. What do your words and actions, overtly or covertly, teach your team about God's loving sovereign rule and reign? About the ultimate reason why you coach? Consider the impression that Messiah College women's soccer program leaves with their opponents after winning and losing.

"I just wanted to commend your team. I was extremely impressed with the women I played against tonight. I am not only referring to their undeniable skill, but also their sportsmanship on and off the field. Playing against them was an experience that I never have had. Not only were they gracious after defeating us, but they were the nicest girls I have had the pleasure of playing. You should be proud of the impression that they leave on their opponents. I wanted you to know how much

I appreciate them... (They) are not only talented soccer players, but wonderful people... Good luck with the rest of your season!"

Messiah doesn't experience defeat much, but they were the classiest program in defeat that we ever faced. Even with their streak ending and losing the [National] Championship... everything after the game was complete class. All my girls were saying "we've never played a team like that." A lot of teams would be bitter, saying we just bunkered in and play defense to protect the lead. But the Messiah girls were saying "you deserve it, you're a class act, your team is great, enjoy it" - things that are very difficult to say when you're dealing with your own emotions.[43]

Respect all your opponents. Fear none. In order to honor God, you must focus on doing your utmost to prepare yourself and your team to perform to their highest potential on any given day, regardless of who will be on the other sideline. And when the dust settles, may you bless your team by showing them how to win and lose with class.

TOOLS

Ω Teach your athletes, "Do unto others as you would have them do unto you."

Have them continually measure their actions against The Golden Rule. How would they feel if they were treated likewise? Would they be okay with an opponent treating their teammate in a similar fashion? Would you ever behave similarly towards the person you claim to love the most?"

Ω Have you ever spent time teaching your athletes the true meaning behind the postgame handshake ritual? Do you have something similar you can use in your sport to show respect for your team's opponents after a game?

It is a way to thank your opponents for pushing you to excel in a manner that would not ever have happened if they weren't on the other sideline. It says, "We're in this thing called life together." This ritual is not a meaningless throwaway if done with the proper motive. It is an opportunity to bless your opponents, not to flaunt superiority in an attempt to shame the losing team.

Ω PRAYER

"Father God, grant me wisdom how to teach our athletes how to love, value, and honor their opponents, no matter how they may behave towards us in any given game. Grant me the wisdom to know how to lead them well by my interactions with the opposing team's coaching staff. Empower me to pray for whatever team we will be facing each week, and to treat them as I would want to be treated. Let me be a blessing to all opponents we face throughout this season so that you will be glorified and joy will be brought to many athletes and coaches throughout our sport. For you said that we are to love our enemies and pray for those who persecute us. We are to feed our enemies if they are hungry, and give them something to drink if they are thirsty. If we are to do that to people that are truly our enemies, how much more should we love, value, and honor those people who are merely our opponents in a game? Do not allow me to be overcome by evil, but help me overcome evil with good." (Matthew 5:43-44; Romans 12:20-21)

THE TRAINING

"Let the wise hear and increase in learning, and the one who understands obtain guidance." (Proverbs 1:5)

"Humble people are teachable people who realize that there is always more for them to learn."[44]

∞ *Why should your athletes listen to you? What do you bring to the table that should cause them to want to follow your lead? How are you learning to become more competent in coaching your sport?*

If you want your athletes to have confidence in you as their coach, you need to have a solid foundation of knowledge about your sport. That might seem like a no-brainer, but there are scores of coaches in this country who have little or no training. They are handed a whistle, a roster, and a game schedule and are sent on their way. As discussed in previous chapters, this is not a problem inherent just in youth leagues. There are too many uneducated coaches in high school and some smaller colleges. Why? Because expediency, budgets, or both, often dictate who is hired. Just as important as having the knowledge about your sport, you must be able to teach it in a way that is easily understood by your athletes so they can then practice the implementation of those skill sets.

This coaching education, however, is not a one-time process. Yes, credentialing or certification may happen at one set place in time. But the learning process of a humble-servant coach must be for a lifetime. Even once you have learned the fundamentals and strategies of your sport, you are just beginning. As long as you are a coach you need to always seek to be acquiring knowledge and wisdom. Coaching is a science and an art. Yes, the best coaches understand the nuts and bolts of the game, but they don't stop there. They regularly experiment with different ways to implement that basic knowledge in a manner that will help transform their athletes. Artists know their athletes' strengths and weaknesses, and are regularly seeking how to best teach within those present boundaries. Just as you can have two siblings raised in the same home that don't learn the same way, so it is with the myriad of athletes on your team. Scientific knowledge is readily available. Artistic wisdom is harder to achieve.

Regardless which you are trying to acquire, you must realize that you cannot pursue such excellence by yourself. You need others who have gone before you, and those who are presently your peers. Never stop learning. An honest assessment of your strengths and weaknesses will keep you firmly tethered to the cross and humbly walking side-by-side with others. If you want to grow in your coaching competence, you need to learn to ask, listen, study, and teach.

Ask

"If any of you lacks wisdom, let him ask God, who gives generously to all without reproach, and it will be given him."[45]

Asking for help is a true sign of humility. There is no sense in pretending you know it all, because you don't. There are always ways to fine-tune your coaching. When you know your weaknesses, ask for help to bolster them. Don't just seek the advice of coaches. If you are in a school setting, or you know EMTs or physicians, seek out their wisdom on issues like injury prevention and treatment, CPR, and first aid. This is all part of learning how to coach your sport in a manner that will benefit all involved. If you don't know, ask.

> University of Nebraska softball coach Rhonda Revelle invested the time to build her confidence early in her coaching career. After being a standout pitcher for the Huskers, Revelle eventually became the head coach of the team. While she knew pitching like the back of her hand, hitting was another story. Instead of trying to hide her lack of hitting knowledge, she willingly admitted her desire to learn and sought out University of Arizona softball coach Mike Candrea, who is considered one of the gurus of hitting.[46]

Listen

"Listen to advice and accept instruction, that you may gain wisdom in the future."[47]

Don't bother asking if you're not going to listen. Too many times we ask questions in order to validate what we think we already know, or to show how much we do know. A humble-servant coach listens intently to the person they are seeking to follow as their mentor. Don't be thinking about a witty response to what is being said. Rather, prayerfully and respectfully take in the teaching and meditate upon it. Don't be hasty to add anything to your coaching repertoire or to cast off the new information as being worthless. Listen, learn, meditate, and pray about what you have been told. No matter how long you coach, don't stop listening. For, "Without counsel plans fail, but with many advisers they succeed."[48]

But what do you do about your critics? Yes, you will have critics, because not everyone is going to be happy with your coaching all the time. So do you listen to them or just blow them off because they seem like they're just trying to tear you down, or at least not be on your game plan? In this case, I don't think there is any better advice than that of Samuel Brengle, who was a teacher and preacher in the Salvation Army movement:

> Samuel Brengle, noted for his sense of holiness, felt the heat of caustic criticism. Instead of rushing to defend himself, he replied: "From my heart. I thank you for your review. I think I deserved it. Will you, my friend, remember me in prayer?" When another critic attacked his spiritual life, Brengle replied: "I thank you for your criticism of my life. It set me to self-examination and heart-searching and prayer, which always leads me into a deeper sense of my utter dependence on Jesus for holiness of heart, and into sweeter fellowship with him."[49]

A humble-servant coach is teachable, whether advice comes from friends or foes. Having critics is not necessarily a bad thing. They may be the tool God is using to help you improve as a person and as a coach, or God may be allowing them in your life to help you stay tethered tightly to him through prayer and study of the Word. "Woe to you, when all people speak well of you, for so their fathers did to the false prophets."[50]

Study

"For Ezra had set his heart to study the Law of the LORD, and to do it and to teach his statutes and rules in Israel."[51]

What does this verse have to do with coaching? It gives leadership principles. If someone or something is important to you, your heart will be engaged. You will desire to have a fuller knowledge of that person or thing. And not just a fuller knowledge of facts, but a depth of understanding that calls for you to engage your mind and heart together, so that your passion will be inflamed. When the heart and mind are engaged in the study of that person or thing, the overflow will be a delight that causes you to teach others. That is the call of a coach.

Treasuring Jesus is what coaching is ultimately about, but that doesn't mean that coaching should be a lifeless venture. Coaching, in and of itself, is not the chief reason you exist. On the contrary, you need to ask yourself what you are going to do to engage your heart and mind in the study of your sport so that you are a passion-filled, credible teacher. Your athletes should sense your delight in the sport you coach so that they willingly join you in pursuing excellence through it, because it is a tool you will use to point them to Jesus.

Find out what instructional materials are available to help you study your sport. Ask about books, DVDs, conferences, and clinics. If you want your athletes to have a desire to learn and grow, you must show them the way. Don't be content with what you know at the present time. Take your coaching to the next level. Meeting the minimum requirement is not doing everything for the glory of God. Ask, Listen, Study, Teach.

Teach

" May my teaching drop as the rain, my speech distill as the dew, like gentle rain upon the tender grass, and like showers upon the herb. For I will proclaim the name of the LORD; ascribe greatness to our God!" (Deuteronomy 32:2-3)

Does this describe your teaching? Do your athletes feel rejuvenated when you teach them skill sets that you have studied? Or is your teaching more likely to come down like hail with peals of thunder, causing everyone to flee for safety? It's not enough to be knowledgeable about the sport you coach. Are you able to teach it in a manner that is readily understood, implemented, and enjoyed? I'm not saying hard work isn't necessary. But do your athletes enjoy the process of learning under you because you know what you're talking about and how to transfer that knowledge?

Doing so will increase the odds of attaining excellence and transforming lives. Your athletes will even have more fun if you are a lifelong learner of your sport and seek to teach it in a relevant and respectful manner. "I can tell you from experience that this is where the real 'fun' is in sports participation, especially for young adult athletes. There is nothing like being able to perform something, whether in an individual sport or a team sport, to the point where it is so effortless and smooth, it is almost as if you could perform that skill in your sleep. It is at this point that you realize all the hard work and efforts you have put in have been more than worth it. It transcends sports participation itself, creating an understanding of what true success is really all about."[52]

Like a shepherd leading the flock to green pastures and still waters, a coach must take the lead in exposing her athletes to what she is studying so they, too, will be well fed.

TOOLS

Ω **Make a list of coaches that you respect in your immediate area. Contact them and ask for help in overcoming your weaknesses. From there, expand your search area and contact coaches in an even wider circle via the internet and email.**

Any true coach is excited to share what he knows with other coaches who desire to excel in their craft. They are not afraid of letting some secret out of the bag that will ruin their chances to pursue excellence.

Ω Keep a tool with you at all times to record what you are learning about your sport, your team, your individual athletes, and yourself.

It can be as old school as a small pad of paper or as modern as a digital voice recorder or the notepad on your phone. The key is to make sure that you always have some way to record what you learn. Do not rely on your memory!

Ω Find one tool, like a book or DVD about your specific sport.

Make a reading/viewing schedule to help you stay on task. Pray for wisdom before you read or watch! Take notes as you progress through the material, and then try implementing ideas you think might help your team.

Ω Change how you deal with critics in the future.

Prayerfully find out if there is even a hint of truth in what they are saying. Ask the Holy Spirit to reveal the true condition of your heart in regards to the criticism you have received. If truth has been revealed, seek wisdom and empowering to change it. Regardless of the veracity of the criticism, consider taking Samuel Brengle's approach rather than vilifying the critic.

Ω PRAYER

"Heavenly Father, your Word tells us that 'without counsel plans fail, but with many advisers they succeed.' Bless me with wise counselors in my midst that I can learn from so that I grow intimately with you, and competently in my coaching. Fill me to overflowing with your Spirit so that I am wise and listen well, so that I will increase in my learning and obtain guidance for the path that lies ahead of me as a disciple and as a discipler. When criticism is levied at me, help me to run straight to you so that I can find out if there is any truth in what has been said. Help me to remember that even if the critic is an opponent, I must treat him with love and respect. Remind me in these moments that you, Lord Jesus, warned that all men speaking well of me is not a blessing. So inspire me to teach rightly. Let me be humble in the training and equipping of my athletes so that they know they are loved, valued, and honored, because they are made in your image." (Proverbs 15:22; Proverbs 1:5; Luke 6:26; Exodus 35:34; Psalm 25:9)

Notes

1. Mark Driscoll, Sermon: *Vintage Jesus - Why Did Jesus Come to Earth* (Seattle: Mars Hill Church, Dec. 12, 2006).
2. John 15:5.
3. Jeremiah 9:23-24.

[4]   John Piper, *The Dangerous Duty of Delight: The Glorified God and the Satisfied Soul* (Sisters: Multnomah, 2001), 34.

[5]   Galatians 5:13-14.

[6]   Wikipedia, Etymonline, Steve Ogne & Tim Roehl in Scott Thomas and Tom Wood, *Gospel Coach: Shepherding Leaders to Glorify God* (Grand Rapids: Zondervan, 2012), 24.

[7]   Reggie McNeal, *Practicing Greatness: 7 Disciplines of Extraordinary Leaders* (San Francisco: Jossey-Bass, 2006), 1-2.

[8]   Larry Ellis, Adapted from "3200," *Running Times Magazine*, Oct. 2009, pgs. 50-53.

[9]   Proverbs 16:18.

[10]   Debbie Colberg in Jim Thompson, *The Double-Goal Coach: Positive Coaching Tools for Honoring the Game and Developing Winners in Sports and Life* (New York: Harper Collins, 2003), 217.

[11]   C.J. Mahaney, *Don't Waste Your Sports*, (Gaithersburg: Sovereign Grace Ministries, 2008), www.sovereigngraceministries.com.

[12]   Hans Finzel, *The Top Ten Mistakes Leaders Make* (Colorado Springs: David C. Cook, 2007), 32-33.

[13]   Timothy Keller, *Counterfeit Gods: The Empty Promises of Money, Sex, and Power, and the Only Hope that Matters* (New York: Dutton, 2009), 75.

[14]   Mahaney, op. cit.

[15]   *USA Today* poll in Dave Kraft, *Leaders Who Last* (Wheaton: Crossway, 2010), 47.

[16]   Mark 1:1-8.

[17]   Luke 3:15.

[18]   John 1:19-20.

[19]   John 1:23.

[20]   John 3:30.

[21]   These categories are based on the work of Matthew Henry in Henry, M. (1996, c1991). *Matthew Henry's commentary on the whole Bible: Complete and unabridged in one volume* (1 Ki 19:19). Peabody: Hendrickson.

[22]   Henry, M. (1996, c1991). *Matthew Henry's commentary on the whole Bible: Complete and unabridged in one volume* (1 Ki 19:19). Peabody: Hendrickson.

[23]   Matthew 16:24-26.

[24]   Bill Price, "Clemson Football Coach Dabo Swinney Under Fire from Freedom From Religion Foundation," *The Daily News*, 4/17/2014, Accessed 7/18/2014. www.nydailynews.com/sports/college/clemson-coach-accused-violating-separation-church-state-article-1.1760450.

[25]   Ann Spangler and Lois Tverberg, *Sitting at the Feet of Rabbi Jesus* (Grand Rapids: Zondervan, 2009), 55.

[26]   Joe Ehrmann with Paula Ehrmann and Gregory Jordan, *Inside Out Coaching: How Sports Can Transform Lives* (New York: Simon & Schuster, 2011), 5-6, 94.

[27]   From the movie, *Remember the Titans*.

[28]   1 Corinthians 13:4-7.

[29]   Mike Candrea in Jeff Janssen and Greg Dale, *The Seven Secrets of Successful Coaches: How to Unlock and Unleash Your Team's Full Potential* (Carey: Quality, 2006), 53.

[30]   Roman Emperor Julian in John Piper, *Don't Waste Your Life* (Wheaton: Crossway, 2003), 87.

[31]   Luke 10:25.

[32]   Luke 10:26.

[33]   Luke 10:27-28.

[34]   Luke 10:29.

[35]   Luke 10:30-32.

[36]   C.S. Keener, *The IVP Bible background commentary: New Testament* (Downers Grove: InterVarsity Press, 2003), Luke 10:31.

[37]   Luke 10:33-35.

[38]   William Barclay, *The Gospel of Luke* (Philadelphia: Westminster, 2000, Rev. ed.), 140.

[39]   Luke 10:36-37.

[40] C.S. Lewis, "The Weight of Glory," in *The Weight of Glory: And Other Addresses* (New York: HarperCollins, 1949/2001), 45-46.

[41] Philippians 2:3-4.

[42] Mahaney, op. cit.

[43] Dickenson College Women's Soccer Player & HSU Coach Marcus Wood in Michael Zigarelli, *The Messiah Method: The Seven Disciplines of the Winningest College Soccer Program in America* (USA: Xulon, 2011), 90, 49.

[44] Kent Millard & Judith Cebula, *Lead Like Butler: Six Principles for Values-Based Leadership* (Nashville, Abingdon, 2013), 3-4.

[45] James 1:5.

[46] Jeff Janssen and Greg Dale, *The Seven Secrets of Successful Coaches: How to Unlock and Unleash Your Team's Full Potential* (Carey: Quality, 2006), 99-100.

[47] Proverbs 19:20.

[48] Proverbs 15:22.

[49] Samuel Brengle in J. Oswald Sanders, *Spiritual Leadership: Principle of Excellence for Every Believer* (Chicago: Moody, 2007), 120.

[50] Luke 6:26.

[51] Ezra 7:10.

[52] Kirk Mango, "Where Burnout Ends and "Fun" Begins in Sports Participation," *Chicago Now*, 8/12/2013, Accessed 10/26/2013. www.chicagonow.com/the-athletes-sports-experience-making-a-difference/2013/08/where-burnout-ends-and-fun-begins-in-sports-participation/.

7

ACCOUNTABLE SHEPHERD

"You ought to coach each player like they are going to be your son-in-law" (Coach Eddie Robinson, Grambling University).

"Either make the tree good and its fruit good, or make the tree bad and its fruit bad, for the tree is known by its fruit. You brood of vipers! How can you speak good, when you are evil? For out of the abundance of the heart the mouth speaks. The good person out of his good treasure brings forth good, and the evil person out of his evil treasure brings forth evil. I tell you, on the day of judgment people will give account for every careless word they speak, for by your words you will be justified, and by your words you will be condemned." (Matthew 12:33-37)

"So then each of us will give an account of himself to God" (Romans 14:12).

∞ *What does 'accountable' mean for a coach?*

In simplest terms, to be accountable means that you are held responsible for your words and actions. You do not have free reign to do as you like with no consequences if you act inappropriately. But, in order to be held accountable, there must be a standard by which your words and actions are being measured. You must have people in your life who are willing and able to hold you accountable to biblical standards. Your ministry through coaching will be viewed against the silhouette of Scripture. That is the tool benchmark by which you will ultimately give an account of yourself to God. But it is imperative that you understand that biblical accountability does not entail people lurking around, ready to pounce on you the instant you deviate from the straight and narrow path.

That type of accountability does not mesh with the God of Scripture, who is "merciful and gracious, slow to anger, and abounding in steadfast love and faithfulness."[1] I am talking about accountability partners who love you and desire the best for you, the type of people who will speak the truth in love, in the hope that "your love may abound more and more, with knowledge and all discernment, so that you may approve what is excellent, and so be pure and blameless for the day of Christ, filled with the fruit of righteousness that comes through Jesus Christ, to the glory and praise of God."[2] Did you catch the source of your righteousness, your right living as a coach? It comes "through Jesus Christ." Keep this in the forefront of your heart and mind. The power to perform comes from Jesus Christ himself.

But what types of overarching questions need to be asked in your quest to be held accountable to biblical standards through the empowering of Jesus?

- "Do you accept responsibility when appropriate, or do you always look to place the blame on others?
- Do you live with integrity?
- Are you loyal?
- Are you comfortable with not being the most knowledgeable person in the room?
- Are you secure enough to teach and share with others the things you know that will help them to be better at what they do?
- Are you the same person in public as you are in private?
- Are you shepherding those around you? Are you willing to change?"[3]
- Are your decisions made from your convictions or what is convenient?

You are responsible to set the tone for the entire team. When the world sees your team, they will see those athletes as a reflection of you, their leader. And when the world sees and hears your behavior, it is a direct reflection on Jesus, your Leader. So what are your athletes learning from observing your life?

∞ *Who is walking beside you to encourage, reprove, and correct you?*

If you are a man reading this, I feel sorry for you. Don't take it personally – it's just a fact for those of us carrying the XY chromosome package. We are often adrift at sea by ourselves. It seems more probable to spot Bigfoot than find a man who has a genuine friend, someone he can and will be vulnerable around, share what is going on in his life, and from whom he can seek wisdom, counsel, and prayer. Until you reach that point with other men, you will never truly know what it means to be loved as a brother in Christ.

For those women who understand this need and have those nurturing, open, and honest relationships, keep showing the way, and maybe we men will get it. For those of you who have become more influenced by the male way of thinking, pay attention. You need God-fearing, Christ-exalting, Bible-saturated women in your life; women who will encourage you and build you up, and confront you and help you correct your course. Do you have those types of peers in your life that will help enable you to be a transformational coach for the glory of God?

TOOLS

Ω **What are the potential benefits of being an accountable-shepherd coach? Post the following questions somewhere that you cannot avoid seeing them, praying for them to be a reality in your life, and to be held accountable for them in your coaching.**

"In his booklet, *Leadership: How to Guide Others with Integrity,* Stephen Viars asks these instructive, recalibrating questions:

1. Do people understand more of *God's mercy* because of the way I respond to their mistakes?
2. Do people understand more of *God's holiness* because of my high ethical standards?
3. Do people understand more of *God's patience* because of the time I give to grow and develop?
4. Do people understand more of *God's truthfulness* because of the way I communicate honestly?
5. Do people understand more of *God's faithfulness* because they see me keep my promises?
6. Do people understand more of *God's kindness* because of the tone of my voice?
7. Do people understand more of *God's love* because I go out of my way to help and serve them as I lead?
8. Do people understand more of *God's grace* because I avoid being harsh and unreasonably demanding?"[4]

Ω **Do you have a *Coach's Code of Ethics* to which you will be held accountable? Consider the questions above and topics below as a framework to develop your own code, along with the appropriate scriptural references. These can be drafted for use in 'sacred' or 'secular' programs and with all age levels.**

Consider the following topics for your code:

- Lead by example.
- Teach the rules of the sport.
- Provide a safe environment.
- Know basic first aid.
- Have fun.
- Challenge athletes to master sport-specific skills.
- Coach them with their individual strengths and weaknesses in mind.

Ω **Do you live out the values you espouse in your coaching? Ask the Holy Spirit to reveal someone you can trust to help pray for you, encourage you, and hold you accountable to your *Coach's Code of Ethics.***

If your trusted counselor shows you a discrepancy between your stated code and your actions, prayerfully seek ways to change so that your words and actions are aligned. By doing this, you will honor Jesus and set the tone for your athletes if their behavior strays outside the agreed upon boundaries.

Ω Take the Bible Test first, then the CNN and Family Tests as supplements.

Before you take any action, find out how it meshes with Scripture. If it is outside the silhouette of God's Word, ask for wisdom and desire to take a new course of action. Do not be deceived by what 'looks' or 'feels' right or good. Remember, "The heart is deceitful above all things, and desperately sick; who can understand it?"[5] Follow God's prescriptions. Next, would you want the world to learn about your actions via CNN? Would you be embarrassed that the CNN vans were camped outside your home waiting to get a story? How would your family react if you had to be the one to explain the news story they just watched break across the screen?

Ω PRAYER

"Heavenly Father, I need help! I cannot possibly hope to be a shepherd after your own heart by myself, for my heart is deceitful above all things, and desperately sick. Bless me with God-fearing, Christ-exalting, Bible-saturated peers who will hold me accountable to the standard of your Word. I need a core group who will encourage me when I'm on the correct path and be willing to show me when I have strayed. But first and foremost, let me store up your Word in my heart so that I will not sin against you! Grant me wisdom to carefully measure my words before I speak, knowing that on the Day of Judgment I will give account for every careless word I speak. Forgive me for the many times I have carelessly blurted out the first thing that came to mind, with absolutely no thought of how it reflected on Jesus or how it might impact my athletes. May people 'understand more of your mercy because of the way I respond to their mistakes; understand more of your holiness because of my high ethical standards; understand more of your patience because of the time I give to grow and develop; understand more of your truthfulness because of the way I communicate honestly; understand more of your faithfulness because they see me keep my promises; understand more of your kindness because of my tone of voice; understand more of your love because I go out of my way to help and serve them as I lead; and understand more of your grace because I avoid being harsh and unreasonably demanding'[6]...so that Jesus may be seen as the ultimate Treasure, the ultimate example, the ultimate Power Source for changed lives." (Jeremiah 17:9; Psalm 119:11; Matthew 12:37)

∞ *What does it mean to be a shepherd?*

Written by the *Commission on Children at Risk*, a panel of leading children's doctors, research scientists and health service professionals, *Hardwired to Connect,* describes for the nation new strategies to reduce the currently high numbers of U.S. children who are suffering from emotional and behavioral problems such as depression, anxiety, attention deficit, conduct disorders, and thoughts of suicide. The Commission is basing its recommendations on recent scientific findings suggesting that children are biologically "hardwired" for enduring attachments to other people for moral and spiritual meaning. Meeting children's needs for enduring attachments and moral and spiritual meaning is the best way to ensure their healthy development.[7]

> This report makes the case that young people have three basic needs. One, they need someone to believe in them and to affirm and validate their inherent value and potential [KNOW]. Two, they need a belief system [FEED]. According to the study, our youth are seeking some kind of spirituality to help them find meaning and purpose in life [LEAD]. Third, they need a place to belong [PROTECT] - a community built on well-defined principles with expectations and boundaries that provide structure and safeguards in the treacherous journey to adulthood. They need to belong to a team! They need a teacher-coach, a mentor.[8]

KNOW THE SHEEP

"You can impress people at a distance, but you can impact them only up close" (Howard Hendricks).[9]

"The LORD is my shepherd; I shall not want. He makes me lie down in green pastures. He leads me beside still waters. He restores my soul. He leads me in paths of righteousness for his name's sake. Even though I walk through the valley of the shadow of death, I will fear no evil, for you are with me; your rod and your staff, they comfort me. You prepare a table before me in the presence of my enemies; you anoint my head with oil; my cup overflows. Surely goodness and mercy shall follow me all the days of my life, and I shall dwell in the house of the LORD forever." (Psalm 23)

∞ *What does it mean to 'know' your athletes?*

An accountable shepherd coach provides his athletes with a sense of belonging.

"The LORD is *my* shepherd…" (Psalm 23:1, italics mine)

"Know that the LORD, he is God! It is he who made us, and we are his; we are his people, and the sheep of his pasture" (Psalm 100:3).

An accountable shepherd coach knows his athletes.

"I am the good shepherd. I know my own and my own know me, just as the Father knows me and I know the Father..." (John 10:14-15)

"My sheep hear my voice, and I know them." (John 10:27)

An accountable shepherd coach knows his athletes by name, implies that he cherishes each one as unique and valuable to him as a coach, and to the team as a whole.

"The sheep hear his voice, and he calls his own sheep by name..." (John 10:3)

"And I have other sheep that are not of this fold. I must bring them also, and they will listen to my voice. So there will be one flock, one shepherd... but you do not believe because you are not among my sheep." (John 10:16, 26)

This, however, is not a mere surface knowledge of the athlete. The word 'to know' points to a loving, deep relationship. It is the same root word used in describing the marriage relationship between Adam and Eve, "Now Adam knew Eve his wife, and she conceived and bore Cain, saying, 'I have gotten a man with the help of the LORD.'"[10] An accountable shepherd coach does not merely blow a whistle and shout instructions in the hopes that his athletes will go where he points and do what he says. Rather, he seeks to know his athletes like a shepherd knows his sheep. Have you ever seen a flock of sheep? If you're like me, they all pretty much look the same. But shepherd of that flock knows the name, character, family line, and strengths and weaknesses of each sheep. Can you say you are seeking this type of 'knowing' with your athletes? This can only occur in a hands-on, face-to-face relational setting. Look to God's example. He didn't post on Facebook:

"In the past God spoke to our ancestors through the prophets at many times and in various ways, but in these last days he has spoken to us by his Son, whom he appointed heir of all things, and through whom also he made the universe."[11]

God did not choose social networking to get our attention, to show us his majesty, to reveal his love, to offer us a way to make it back home. Our heavenly Father desires a true intimacy with us, an offer to be part of his family...not just an invitation to merely be 'friends' - so he sent his Son. "The Word became flesh and made his dwelling among us. We have seen his glory, the glory of the One and Only, who came from the Father, full of grace and truth. John testifies concerning him. He cries out saying, 'This was he of whom I said, 'He who comes after me has surpassed me because he was before me'"[12].

The Word became flesh and literally 'tented' among us. "I think what pitching a tent implies is that God wants to be on familiar terms with us. He wants us to be close. He wants a lot of interaction. If you come into a community and build a huge palace with a wall around it, it says one thing about your desires to be with people. But if you pitch a tent in my back yard you will probably use my bathroom and eat often at my table. This is why God became human. He came to pitch a tent in our backyard so we would have a lot of dealings with him."[13]

No sitting on high directing events from a distance for Jesus. He did not count on posting pics from heaven with the caption, "Wishing you were here]" to help us see the inestimable worth of spending eternity in heaven with him. He came down from heaven into the filth of a barn to be born, to have most people misunderstand him throughout his life, to end up on a cross, in order to demonstrate God's love for us, his desire for intimacy with us – while we were still sinners. Because "Greater love has no one than this: to lay down one's life for one's friends."[14]

It is apparent from the beginning of man's history that God never intended to simply give us a list of rules to live by and then disappear from the picture. For Genesis 3:8 tells us, "Then the man and his wife heard the sound of the Lord God as he was walking in the garden in the cool of the day..." What a beautiful picture of how it was meant to be - and how someday again it will be for those who are his children.

God has always desired that his people know He is with them. He has never been the God that created the world and stepped back to let it run its course. He has always sought to be intimately involved with his people. The Supreme Example, Jesus, came out of our heavenly Father's desire to lead us home in order that we might know him and feel his embrace. So he sent Jesus to be our Shepherd. And in like manner, Jesus has sent us to shepherd others: "Peace be with you. As the Father has sent me, even so I am sending you."[15]

As wearying a task as this may seem, you must in some way name, appreciate, and count your athletes every day if you are going to truly know them. What does that mean if you volunteer and only see your athletes twice a week? You can daily cover them in prayer, seeking to know how to best intercede before the Shepherd's throne on their behalf. What does that mean if you have a large team? You need to recruit your assistant coaches and/or parents, or others in your circle of relationships into this process. They don't have to be Christians in order for you to train them in the majority of relational coaching methods, and it might just be the tool the Spirit uses to open up their eyes and ears to the gospel!

What might this look like from a heart-perspective? "Shepherd the flock of God that is among you, exercising oversight, not under compulsion, but willingly, as God would have you; not for shameful gain, but eagerly; not domineering over those in your charge, but being examples to the flock."[16] This principle can be applied to athletic coaches just as assuredly as it does to pastors and teachers. The flock that God has assigned to you is your team and the individual athletes that comprise it.

You should be coaching because you desire to, not because you have been forced into the position. Trust me, everyone knows the coaches who don't want to be there striving towards knowing, caring and tending for their team. Furthermore, if your primary motivation is a desire for financial gain or a boost in your reputation, this often leads to a domineering spirit. If you want your athletes to follow you, then you must be willing to interact with them as people, not just as athletes. The most profound influence you can have with your athletes will be face-to-face. Don't be a stranger.[17] Get involved and change lives!

TOOLS

Ω Do you know your athletes up close and personal?

Begin praying today for opportunities to get to know each of your athletes as people. Develop an age-appropriate, simple questionnaire to help spur on this process. If you were in their shoes, what would you want the coach to know about you? But don't rely solely on the questionnaire. Always be looking for moments when you can learn more about your athletes as you interact with them.

Ω What does your heart-attitude need to be if you want to develop as an accountable shepherd who knows your athletes?

"Let every day be a day of humility; condescend to all the weaknesses and infirmities of your fellow-creature, cover their frailties, love their excellencies, encourage their virtues, relieve their wants, rejoice in their prosperities, compassionate over their distress, receive their friendship, overlook the unkindness, forgive their malice, be servant of servants, and condescend to do the lowliest offices of the lowliest of mankind" (William Law).[18] If you live out this type of loving-kindness, you cannot help but know your athletes at a depth of level necessary to shepherd them in a biblically consistent manner.

Ω How can you shepherd your athletes in a way that shows you truly desire the best for them as people as well as competitors, even if you are in a secular setting?

If you want to truly love your athletes, you must seek ways to know them, and from that knowing, seek further wisdom on the best way to present the gospel to them in word and deed. They must hear and see the love of Jesus manifested in their lives. "We make much of Christ in our secular work [or volunteering] by treating the web of relationships it creates as a gift of God to be loved by sharing the Gospel and by practical deeds of help…*speaking* the good news of Christ is part of why God put you in your job [or volunteer position]… 'But you are a chosen race, a royal priesthood, a holy nation, a people for his own possession, that you may proclaim the excellencies of him who called you out of darkness into his marvelous light.'" (1 Peter 2:9)[19]

Ω PRAYER

"I praise you, Father, that you have been my shepherd all my life until this very day. And you will lead me in paths of righteousness until the very end. So let me give thanks to you forever, from generation to generation let me praise your name, and teach others to do likewise. May my legacy show that I sought to sow seeds of salvation and sanctification through word and deed to my athletes and those impacted by our program. For you are my God, my Shepherd, and I am one of many sheep of your pasture. So let me never be like the foolish shepherds who failed to inquire of you. For their work failed and their flock scattered. Rather, grant me the eyes to see you every day, the ears to hear you, and the heart to follow you as I seek to lay down my life so others might live. To you alone belong all glory, and honor, and praise." (Genesis 48:15, Psalm 79:13, Psalm 95:7)

FEED THE SHEEP

An accountable shepherd coach provides for the basic needs of her athletes.

"The LORD is my shepherd; I shall not want." (Psalm 23:1)

"When they had finished breakfast, Jesus said to Simon Peter, 'Simon, son of John, do you love me more than these?' He said to him, 'Yes, Lord; you know that I love you.' He said to him, 'Feed my lambs.' He said to him a second time, 'Simon, son of John, do you love me?' He said to him, 'Yes, Lord; you know that I love you.' He said to him, 'Tend my sheep.' He said to him the third time, 'Simon, son of John, do you love me?' Peter was grieved because he said to him the third time, 'Do you love me?' and he said to him, 'Lord, you know everything; you know that I love you.' Jesus said to him, 'Feed my sheep.' " (John 21:15-17)

The team under your care should have a peace and assurance that their basic needs as athletes will be taken care of, so there is no need for them to fear or be anxious. This would be a reminder of God's shepherding care for the nation of Israel in the wilderness: "For the LORD your God has blessed you in all the work of your hands. He knows you are going through this great wilderness. These forty years the LORD your God has been with you. You have lacked nothing."[20] They never lacked physical or spiritual food in their forty year journey, nor did they lack an understanding of the Source of that nourishment.

An accountable shepherd coach provides rest and sustenance for her athletes.

"He makes me lie down in green pastures…" (Psalm 23:2)

"I will feed them with good pasture, and on the mountain heights of Israel shall be their grazing land. There they shall lie down in good grazing land, and on rich pasture they shall feed on the mountains of Israel. I myself will be the shepherd of my sheep, and I myself will make them lie down, declares the Lord GOD." (Ezekiel 34:14-15)

You need to provide regular rhythms of rest and refueling in the lives of your athletes during workouts and during the week. They need times when they not only know that it is okay to rest, but that you want them to take a break. But that is only part of the equation. In order to help them excel as athletes, you must feed them the necessary knowledge and understanding to develop as athletes and people. They need solid nourishment that comes from your continually learning about the Lord, the sport, and your athletes.

An accountable shepherd coach must guide her athletes towards good training and equipping to prepare them to compete.

"You prepare a table before me in the presence of my enemies [competitors]…" (Psalm 23:5)

As a coach, you need to provide an atmosphere where your athletes do not have to be afraid of their competitors because you have prepared them heart, mind, soul, and strength to the best of your and their abilities. Hence, there is no need to fear competition.

An accountable shepherd coach is generous towards his athletes.

"…my cup overflows." (Psalm 23:5)

"And my God will supply every need of yours according to his riches in glory in Christ Jesus." (Philippians 4:19)

"The thief comes only to steal and kill and destroy. I came that they may have life and have it abundantly." (John 10:10)

Consider these words carefully - overflows, riches, abundantly. How does your treatment of your athletes compare? Are you providing a trickle of lukewarm water or a drink at a cold mountain stream when it comes to sharing your time, talents, and treasures?

∞ *What balanced diet should you be feeding your athletes?*

Purpose for Playing – Loving God and Others

Depending on where you coach, you may be somewhat restricted by what others consider acceptable references to God. That, however, should not deter you from letting your athletes know the reasons why you coach. For, "[I]f sport is only focused on mere material performance, it will fall short of realizing its necessary social dimension. In the end, sporting activity must help one [your athletes] to recognize their own talents and capacities, their very efforts in their own very life as gifts that come from God. For this reason, sport should always have God our Creator has its ultimate point of reference."[21] That is a key facet in fulfilling the call to feed your athletes with "knowledge and understanding."[22]

The second element that segues into this part of the athletes' diet is diligence in seeking to help them understand what it means to love and respect others because they are made in the image of

God. Are you regularly providing life lessons to help build these virtues into your athletes through the power of sports? Teach them to understand that success in sports is measured by much more than the scoreboard. One of those assessment tools is respecting and honoring those they have competed against, win or lose.

Feeding your athletes a steady diet that keeps "loving God and loving others" as the foundation takes discipline. "Do you not know that in a race all the runners run, but only one receives the prize? So run that you may obtain it. Every athlete exercises self-control in all things. They do it to receive a perishable wreath, but we an imperishable. So I do not run aimlessly; I do not box as one beating the air. But I discipline my body and keep it under control...."[23]

Pursuit of Success – The 4:13 Kool-Aid

> Part of your coaches' education program should involve a direct discussion of the importance of winning to a successful program... At one extreme is the belief that winning is unimportant in youth sports; at the other extreme is the belief that winning is the only thing... Clearly, there can be too much emphasis on winning; however, those who advocate the position that winning is not important often miss the point that without an attempt to win the contest, the activity is no longer sport... A key point is to acknowledge that while winning is an important part of sport, it must be kept in perspective with the other valuable aspects of youth sports such as social development, fun, fitness, etc.[24]

For the Christian coach, it's not about winning *or* sowing seeds of salvation and sanctification. It's about seeking to win a competition *while* sowing those seeds! If you're prone to use coffee cup verses like Philippians 4:13 to pump up your team on game day, stop it! Quoting "I can do all things through Christ who strengthens me" does not magically give you higher powers to take on all opponents. The verse has been hijacked by way too many coaches as a secret talisman, a rabbit's foot in the hope that something miraculous will happen. You can be competitive and wildly successful, even if the scoreboard doesn't say so.

Does that sound like a nice, "we're all winners, kum-ba-yah" mantra? It's not meant to be. The aim is to give you a realigned perspective. Yes, you strive to win every game. But losing will occur. Sometimes that is the best tool God has to help refocus our priorities. And few had their priorities more on target than the oft-quoted John Wooden, "There is a standard higher than merely winning the race: Effort is the ultimate measure of success." And that philosophy was the benchmark by which Steve Prefontaine measured ever race he competed in:

> All of my life, man and boy, I have operated under the assumption that the main idea in running was to win the damn race. Actually, when I became a coach I tried to teach people how to do that. I tried to teach Pre how to do that. I tried like hell to teach Pre. And Pre taught me. Taught me, I was wrong. Pre, you see,

was troubled by knowing that a mediocre effort can win a race and a magnificent effort can lose one. Winning a race wouldn't necessarily demand that he give it everything he had from start to finish. He never ran any other way. I tried to get him to. God knows I tried. But Pre was stubborn. He insisted on holding himself to a higher standard than victory. A race is a work of art. That's what he said. That's what he believed. And he was out to make it one every step of the way. Of course, he wanted to win. Those who saw him compete, those who competed against him, were never in any doubt about how much he wanted to win. But how he won mattered to him more. Pre thought I was a hard case. But he finally got it through my head that the real purpose of running isn't to win a race. It's to test the limits of the human heart. And that he did. Nobody did it more often. Nobody did it better (Head Oregon Track Coach, Bill Bowerman speaking at Steve Prefontaine's eulogy).[25]

Principles for Participation – How You Play the Game

Related to the steady diet of pursuing success is the complementary nutritional component of sportsmanship. Your athletes must learn from your words and actions that winning outside of the bounds of the spirit and letter of the rules is unacceptable. To win on a scoreboard while skirting the rules means you are biblically unsuccessful. Your team's example must be of the highest standard, pouring out your best effort to win while honoring your opponents simultaneously. Too often, however, this is not how many Christians are perceived. You must be one of the coaches that helps counter this travesty.

How can you train your athletes to make sure they honor the game by honoring the rules and their opponents? Constantly remind them of the guiding principles of your program. If you have a locker room, post the team standards, the code of ethics. If not, post them in a well-lit, well-traveled pathway where your team works out. Help your athletes to memorize these principles so they become ingrained in their minds and actions. Most importantly, give them an example to follow!

Practice towards Perfection – Learning Skill Sets to Compete

The final component in a balanced diet is making sure that you have the knowledge necessary to help your athletes work towards mastery of their sport. But, being well-educated in your sport is not enough. You must have the ability to present the information in a manner that makes it transferrable. In other words, can your athletes regularly take your instructions and implement them because you present them in a clear, cogent, and enjoyable style? If you do this, then your athletes will be prepared to the best of your ability, by the empowering of the Holy Spirit, to compete to the best of their abilities. The score will take care of itself.

The more you feed your team training and equipping that aids them in growing as athletes and people, the more confident they will become when they take the field, the court, stand on the starting line, or participate in the race called life. That confidence in their preparation will overflow into their performance. But it's critical to remember what Coach Jim Bevan of Rice University has often told me: "Inch-by-inch, it's a cinch. Yard-by-yard makes it hard." Positive reinforcement through incremental steps is a key to helping your athletes enjoy the process by celebrating forward progress!

TOOLS

Ω Find one topic per week throughout the season to keep your athletes well-fed regarding the purpose for playing or the principles for participation.

Use 5-10 minutes before practices and games to discuss the topic. If you see it implemented during practice, stop, point it out, and take advantage of the teachable moment so all members of the team can learn. If you see it exhibited in a game, take note of it and use it as part of your post-game discussion.

Ω Provide access to articles or books that show athletes living out what you are seeking to teach.

"The reading of good biography forms an important part of a Christian's [athlete's] education. It provides him with numberless illustrations for use in his own service. He learns to assess the true worth of character, to glimpse a work goal for his own life, to decide how best to attain it, what self-denial is needed to curb unworthy aspirations; and all the time he learns how God breaks into the dedicated life to bring about his own purposes" (Ransome W. Cooper).[26]

Ω Teach your athletes how to deal with officials.

"As a former basketball coach, one of the areas I identified where our athletes needed to behave correctly involved responding to referees' decisions. In order to practice this behavior, we chose a time prior to the first game where we had referees at a scrimmage. After several quarters of action, we had a break in which I quietly asked the referees to make a lot of 'wrong' calls during the next few minutes of the scrimmage....The results were very insightful. After about five minutes of 'wrong' calls, we stopped the action and called the team together with the two referees and explained what we had asked the officials to do. Then, we asked the players how they thought they had done, since we had intentionally not corrected any of their actions during this part of practice. Next, we went to videotape of that section of practice and replayed it for all the players to see... It also gave us a non-threatening way to discuss the repercussions would be if that happened in a game, or even in a practice. Later, we were able to speak privately with those athletes who were most out of line."[27]

Ω Inch-by-Inch

Don't overwhelm your athletes with too much information at one time. Give them bite-sized portions so that they don't choke on trying to digest it. The same thing holds true for the physical nature of workouts. Help them to progress step-by-step so that they have periodic victories over the course of a season rather than crushing blow after crushing blow from not ever being able to adequately adapt to the physical demands placed upon them.

"Look for situations in which players try hard but fail to make the play. Then praise them for the effort… Help players set Effort Goals as well as Outcome Goals. Effort Goals are more within the control of players; Outcome Goals tend to depend on the quality of the opponent."[28]

Ω PRAYER

"Heavenly Father, help grant me the desire and wisdom to shepherd my team well. Place on my heart a passion to know each of them as uniquely designed in your image. And bless me with daily doses of wisdom to discern how to feed them in a manner that will help them to mature as athletes and people. Show me how to train them up in the way they should go so they will be well-nourished. Then when they are old they will not depart from it. Sports mastery apart from pointing them towards the Master is an epic failure. Bless me with a shepherd's heart so that I will feed my athletes with knowledge and understanding of the gospel, and the game which they play. For man does not live by bread alone, but by every word that comes forth from your mouth! Never let the ultimate purpose for my coaching be far from my heart and mind. For faith without works is dead. Let my faith and works paint the same picture through every aspect of my coaching: loving you with all of my heart, all of my soul, all of my mind, and all of my strength…and my neighbor as myself." (Proverbs 22:6; Jeremiah 3:25; James 2:14-18; Deuteronomy 8:3; Mark 12:30-31)

LEAD THE SHEEP

An accountable shepherd coach will seek to find the safest ways to lead his athletes towards maturation as people and mastery as athletes.

"…He leads me beside still waters." (Psalm 23:2)

"Save me, O God! For the waters have come up to my neck. I sink in deep mire, where there is no foothold; I have come into deep waters, and the flood sweeps over me." (Psalm 69:1-2)

A shepherd lived a lonely and strenuous life, accented by hardships and dangers. His workday was twenty-four hours long, watching his flock day and night. He was outside most of the year in all extremes of weather, from the blazing summer sun to the cold, harsh winter rainstorms. His main task was providing water and grass for his flock (Psalm 23:1-2). This required moving the flock from place to place. In summer the shepherd led the sheep to the cooler mountain pastures. The valleys and plains were home for the flock in winter.[29]

As you might imagine, there are not a lot of sources of water in the wilderness areas of the Middle East. One of the sources of dangers comes when a sudden storm deluges the landscape. Because it cannot soak into the rock-hard soil, the water barrels down the wadis (the canyons), and they become death traps. Even if the water source was something less dangerous, like a river, sheep still don't stand a chance. They cannot drink from fast moving water, because they will drown. Once the rain storms stop and the waters subside, however, pools of water are left in the wadis. These are the types of places where the sheep can drink. Yet, even these pools hold imminent danger for sheep. If the shepherd does not lead them on to dry places beside the still water, the sheep will walk into the mud where they cannot extricate themselves. The shepherd must pull them out of the muck and the mire if they are to survive and thrive. It's not enough to lead them to food and water. The shepherd must be ever-vigilant to protect them.

You, too, must be willing to get into the trenches with your athletes in an effort to lead them towards still waters, places where they can learn and grow without physical, mental, spiritual, or emotional damage happening to them. When the water comes rushing down and threatens to overwhelm one of your athletes or she gets stuck in the muck and mire of life, you have to be willing to enter the wadi and get her back to still waters. Chaos and drama will happen on every team. The question is, are you willing to enter the fray in order to lead them back to calm waters?

An accountable shepherd coach is known and trusted by his athletes, and they will enthusiastically follow him. He goes in front of them and leads by example.

"My sheep hear my voice, and I know them, and they follow me" (John 10:27).

"So I exhort the elders among you, as a fellow elder and a witness of the sufferings of Christ, as well as a partaker in the glory that is going to be revealed: shepherd the flock of God that is among you, exercising oversight, not under compulsion, but willingly, as God would have you; not for shameful gain, but eagerly; not domineering over those in your charge, but being examples to the flock. And when the chief Shepherd appears, you will receive the unfading crown of glory." (1 Peter 5:1-4)

An accountable shepherd coach joyfully desires to lead his athletes. He is not forced into the position, but willingly seeks to coach his team, because he sees it as an opportunity to serve and honor God. He doesn't do it primarily for personal gain, but out of delight. He leads his athletes by example, not pushing them in a domineering, militaristic fashion. If you sow love into the lives of your athletes, you will reap a harvest of young men and women that will joyfully follow your lead.

Follow Me as I Follow Jesus

Coaches need to demonstrate what they want their athletes to learn and be willing to say, "Follow me." In Eastern cultures, the shepherd goes in front of the sheep and leads them on the safest paths. If there is danger in the pathway, the shepherd will encounter it first. But in the midst of this leading, another danger lurks. Are you promoting hero worship or holy emulation to your athletes? Do they see you as a celebrity or as a servant? Too many Christians in this arena have been sadly influenced by the cultural air they breathe. "John Erickson [former Fellowship of Christian Athletes president] says, 'We think we've harnessed hero worship,' and he states that resolutely. It is unlikely that the Fellowship, at least under Erickson, will completely renounce its star cast."[30] The only way to make sure that this does not become an issue for you is if you hold tightly to Jesus as your Greatest Treasure so that your athletes can witness you following the Great Shepherd.

Follow My Passionate Lead

Are you passionate about your athletes, your sport? Why do I ask that question? Because passion is contagious. It is the wind that stokes the fire. If your athletes see that you are genuinely enthusiastic about them and the sport, it will fuel a desire in them to pursue excellence. Don't celebrate mediocrity. Don't be the coach who tries to figure out the minimum he has to do to get a passing grade. Love what you do and watch the fire spread.

Follow My Physical Fitness

Bringing this up gets a little sticky. I'm afraid it goes along with the lack of discussion regarding physical fitness in the Church as a whole. Why is it that the ransacking of the temple of the Holy Spirit with lack of exercise and poor diet choices is considered off-limits in most Christian settings? It's kind of like discussing religion or politics in the rest of the world. But, if you want to be an accountable shepherd coach, your physical fitness is important. Otherwise you're back to the "do as I say, not as I do" coaching paradigm. I'm not saying you need to be juicing with testosterone therapy to get back some glory-days body. But it's critical that your athletes see you making strides to improve your physical condition. Be honest, did you have ever an out-of-shape coach? Did it bother you?

It did me. Imagine my dismay when I saw one of my coaches smoking a cigarette. Or the portly coach I saw passed out on one of the training tables when I went to use the ice bath. These were the same men that were constantly yelling at us for not performing to their satisfaction in workouts or track meets. It was hard to take them seriously. I kept wanting to invite them to try even part of a workout with us so we could watch them gasp in misery at the mere attempt. Conversely, when

I see someone like Rick Barnes, the University of Texas men's basketball coach, running around the track trying to care for the body he has been blessed with, I cheer inside. I love seeing these types of coaches get in the middle of practices and show their athletes how to play, rather than tell them. No one in their right mind believes they can actually compete against their athletes. But watching them sweat goes a long way in creating credibility among their players. Sweat equity works both directions!

Follow My Example

A good demonstration will always trump a good description. A good description married to a good demonstration is gold. The more that you can show your athletes how to perform a certain skill set, the greater the likelihood that they will be able to eventually repeat the movement…and continue towards mastery of their sport. Consider the following true story:

> In 2005, Ange Sabin Peter, an accomplished potter, served a six-month apprenticeship under Masaaki Shibata, a famous Japanese potter… She envisioned herself shaping beautiful pottery on his wheel, his decades of skill sharpening her own expertise… At the start of her apprenticeship, Ange knew little or nothing of an ancient Japanese tradition… of becoming an *uchi deshi*, an apprentice to a skilled craftsman [literally, *an inside learner* – a closeness that allows the apprentice to observe all of the craftsman's life]…
>
> "You cannot separate life from work," Shibata told Ange, his new apprentice, one day. "The way you do the most insignificant activity in your daily life will reflect in your work." Then he sent her to the rice fields to dig for clay instead of inviting her to sit down at his wheel. Her pride chafed at not being asked to demonstrate her own skill. In fact, Shibata did not allow her to throw even one piece of pottery during her six-month stay in Japan… Still, as she toiled at her humble chores she snatched every chance to watch the master potter at work.
>
> Returning home, she felt deflated and defeated, afraid that her six months in Japan had been a complete waste. But when she sat down at her wheel, she began to sense a subtle difference. Something had changed. Then, as the kiln door opened on her new work, she marveled at the result. Without knowing it, she had been absorbing a new way of doing things… Thanks to her time with Masaaki Shibata, Ange Peter's approach to her craft had been transformed. Delightedly she caressed each new vessel, admiring how the influence of her Japanese master had blended beautifully with her own personality to transform each of her new creations."[31]

So why do I tell you a story about a Japanese potter? What does that have to do with understanding what it means to be an accountable shepherd coach? We need to examine teaching and coaching through a different lens. In places like America, we often think of athletes merely as students – people who want to know what the coach knows. In the Eastern culture, however, learning is a passionate commitment to not only know 'what' your teacher knows, but to live like he lives. The usual method of learning was much like the story I just told you – through hands-on learning, through imitating someone who possessed the skills they wanted to acquire.

An accountable shepherd coach seeks to lead her athletes to the gospel by example. She desires that her athletes keep their eyes upon her and imitate her example because she desires that her athletes have their citizenship in heaven.

"…He leads me in paths of righteousness for his name's sake." (Psalm 23:3)

"Brothers, join in imitating me, and keep your eyes on those who walk according to the example you have in us. For many, of whom I have often told you and now tell you even with tears, walk as enemies of the cross of Christ. Their end is destruction, their god is their belly, and they glory in their shame, with minds set on earthly things. But our citizenship is in heaven, and from it we await a Savior, the Lord Jesus Christ, who will transform our lowly body to be like his glorious body, by the power that enables him even to subject all things to himself." (Philippians 3:17-21)

Are you encouraging your athletes to follow you as you seek to follow Christ? Who is watching your life right now? Do you have the confidence that Paul had when he proclaimed, "Be imitators of me, as I am of Christ"?[32] If you feel inadequate to say such a thing, remember that Paul is the same man who also said, "Here is a trustworthy saying that deserves full acceptance: Christ Jesus came into the world to save sinners – of whom I am the worst." [33] Paul knew that the only reason he was worthy to be followed was because his life was focused on staying in step with Jesus. Let that be an encouragement to you!

As an accountable shepherd coach, you must be able to explain to your athletes why you are leading them down certain paths, and why one route is better than another for their well-being. Stay in the Word and prayer so you are able to clearly see the path that leads to Jesus. The ultimate reason for your coaching is to glorify God so that Jesus, the Chief Shepherd, will be seen as the Greatest Treasure. Your athletes will experience this as you lead them from the front, giving them an example to follow. It is not enough to be able to demonstrate skill sets that will help mastery of your sport. You must be able to exhibit a lifestyle that will help point them to the Master of your sport. Is there a fire in your life whose embers will ignite your athletes' lives when they get close? Do your words and actions work in synch, on and off the court? You have a great calling, responsibility, and empowering to lead your athletes down the straight and narrow path that leads to life. Are you fulfilling that call?

TOOLS

Ω Still Waters: Are you making sure that your athletes get adequate sleep, rest, and recuperation?

Encourage your athletes to have daily 'Sabbath rests' away from technology tethers and 'to-do' lists, and to simply celebrate the gift of life and all that it entails.

Ω Follow Me: "Jesus Christ is the same yesterday and today and forever."[34]

What kind of a coach are you? Are you consistent in how your leadership or are your athletes always left guessing what you want from day to day? Do your athletes truly enjoy playing for you on a consistent basis? Do you treat all your athletes equitably, whether they are starters or non-starters? In other words, would you want to be treated in a similar passion if your athletes imitated you and roles were reversed? Or more importantly, would you coach Jesus in the same manner that you coach your athletes?

Ω Paths of Righteousness: Finding the right route for you and your athletes.

1. "*Is it helpful?* 'Everything is permissible for me' – but not everything is beneficial. 'Everything is permissible for me' – but I will not be mastered by anything.'(1 Cor. 6:12)… Is whatever I'm about to do helpful to [my athletes] *physically*, or will it harm [them]? Does it help [them], *mentally*, or does it tend to get [their] mind on things that draw [them] into sin? Does it help [them] *spiritually*? Does it help [them] grow, or does it hurt [their] spiritual development?
2. *Does it get [them] in its power?* Does it enslave [them]?
3. *Will it cause others to stumble?* …I may be the only example of a Christian that somebody has. So I must think of others when I decide on my activities.
4. *Is it glorifying to God?*"[35]

Ω Follow Me: Contemplating whether you need to take new paths for practices.

"1. Did you fill players' emotional tanks to the degree that you wanted?
2. Did you cover all the most important things?
3. Did the instruction take hold, or do you need to repeat the same material next time?
4. I find it helpful to jot down points that I don't want to risk forgetting as soon after practice as possible, starting with my objectives and priorities for the next practice."[36]

Ω PRAYER

"Give ear to my prayer, O Shepherd of Israel, you who led out your people like sheep and guided them in the wilderness like a flock. In every aspect of my coaching, help me to trust in you with all my heart, and not lean on my own understanding. But in all my ways may I acknowledge you, and you will make straight my paths. Then with an upright heart may I, likewise, shepherd my athletes and guide them with skillful hands. For you give wisdom; from your mouth comes knowledge and understanding; you store up sound wisdom for the upright; you are a shield to those who walk in integrity, guarding the paths of justice and watching over the way of your saints. Then I will understand righteousness and justice and equity, and every good path on which to lead my athletes. So empower me to joyfully shepherd the athletes you have placed under my care, exercising oversight, not under compulsion, but willingly, as you would have me; not for shameful gain, but eagerly; not domineering over those in my charge, but being an example to my team so I may encourage them to imitate me as I seek to imitate Jesus!" (Psalm 78:52; Proverbs 3:5-7; Psalm 78:72; Proverbs 2:6-9; 1 Peter 5:2-3; 1 Corinthians 11:1)

PROTECT THE SHEEP

An accountable shepherd coach seeks to know what threatens the spiritual and physical health and well-being of her athletes in order to protect them from unnecessary exhaustion and weariness of the soul. When they cross this line, she goes into action to revive and restore them.

"The ultimate measure of a man is not where he stands in moments of comfort and convenience but where he stands at times of challenge and controversy" (Martin Luther King Jr.).[37]

"He restores my soul…" (Psalm 23:3).

"Pay careful attention to yourselves and to all the flock, in which the Holy Spirit has made you overseers, to care for the church of God, which he obtained with his own blood. I know that after my departure fierce wolves will come in among you, not sparing the flock; and from among your own selves will arise men speaking twisted things, to draw away the disciples after them." (Acts 20:28-30)

She protects her team. She does not look to her needs first, but the needs of her athletes. She strengthens those who are weak through encouragement and patience. She works on healing those athletes who are injured in order to get them back into team participation. If she finds out that any of her athletes are straying, she seeks them out in order to gather them back into the culture and fold of the team. "What do you think? If a man has a hundred sheep, and one of them has gone astray, does he not leave the ninety-nine on the mountains and go in search of the one that went astray? And if he finds it, truly, I say to you, he rejoices over it more than over the ninety-nine that never went astray."[38] She leads them with compassion, which sometimes is tough and sometimes tender. By keeping the Word of God central in all her activities, she protects them from outsiders, wolves, who seek to devour them with deceitfulness and lies. "The law of the LORD is perfect, reviving the soul."[39]

> The good shepherd in Mt. 18 was in a position to notice when only *one* of the one hundred in his flock was missing…How can you know what the sheep need to balance their spiritual diets unless you are interacting with them on a personal level? How can you know the direction in which to lead the flock as a whole unless you are in touch with the gifts of the individual members? How can you effectively protect the church [your athletes] if you do not know the challenges, struggles, and temptations that your sheep face?[40]

For this to happen, you must keep a close eye on your athletes in order to detect when trouble begins to arise, not waiting until it festers into a full-blown path-altering problem. Conversely, the following from the prophet Ezekiel is a negative portrait of how shepherds behave who do not seek to protect their flock, those whose focus is on themselves:

> "Son of man, prophesy against the shepherds of Israel; prophesy, and say to them, even to the shepherds, 'Thus says the Lord GOD: Ah, shepherds of Israel who have been feeding yourselves! Should not shepherds feed the sheep? You eat the fat, you clothe yourselves with the wool, you slaughter the fat ones, but you do not feed the sheep. The weak you have not strengthened, the sick you have not healed, the injured you have not bound up, the strayed you have not brought back, the lost you have not sought, and with force and harshness you have ruled them. So they were scattered, because there was no shepherd, and they became food for all the wild beasts. My sheep were scattered; they wandered over all the mountains and on every high hill. My sheep were scattered over all the face of the earth, with none to search or seek for them. Therefore, you shepherds, hear the word of the LORD: As I live, declares the Lord GOD, surely because my sheep have become a prey, and my sheep have become food for all the wild beasts, since there was no shepherd, and because my shepherds have not searched for my sheep, but the shepherds have fed themselves, and have not fed my sheep, therefore, you shepherds, hear the word of the LORD: Thus says the Lord GOD, Behold, I am against the shepherds, and I will require my sheep at their hand and put a stop to their feeding the sheep. No longer shall the shepherds feed themselves. I will rescue my sheep from their mouths, that they may not be food for them'" (Ezekiel 34:2-10).

An accountable shepherd coach will provide visible protection for her athletes that will enable them to train and compete without fear. She must be willing to fight for her athletes to protect them from others. But, she also disciplines and corrects them to protect them from themselves.

"Even though I walk through the valley of the shadow of death, I will fear no evil, for you are with me; your rod and your staff, they comfort me." (Psalm 23:4)

"So Jesus again said to them, 'Truly, truly, I say to you, I am the door of the sheep. All who came before me are thieves and robbers, but the sheep did not listen to them. I am the door. If anyone enters by me, he will be saved and will go in and out and find pasture. The thief comes only to steal and kill and destroy. I came that they may have life and have it abundantly. I am the good shepherd. The good shepherd lays down his life for the sheep. He who is a hired hand and not a shepherd, who does not own the sheep, sees the wolf coming and leaves the sheep and flees, and the wolf snatches them and scatters them. He flees because he is a hired hand and cares nothing for the sheep.' " (John 10:7-13)

The rod, staff, and door were all tools for protecting the sheep from predators and would-be rustlers. The rod was used like a club, or baseball bat, to beat off wild animals and thieves. "But David said to Saul, 'Your servant used to keep sheep for his father. And when there came a lion, or a bear, and took a lamb from the flock, I went after him and struck him and delivered it out of his mouth. And if he arose against me, I caught him by his beard and struck him and killed him.'"[41] The staff is used to gently guide the sheep. No matter how dark a situation seems, the sheep are comforted by the presence of their shepherd with his protective tools in hand. And, they never feared that the rod would be used against them. Do your athletes feel similarly about your protection of them? Are you more like the good shepherd or the hired hand?

The door takes your responsibility as a shepherd coach to another level. Unlike the rod and staff, it did not give the shepherd an additional tool to wield – it made him into one. The shepherd literally became the door for a sheepfold.

> When sheep were penned in at night outside the city, the shepherd himself would often construct a makeshift fold. He would take brush and bushes and construct them in a "u" shape or some other formation depending on what was already at hand. He would then place thorny branches on top of the brush to both inhibit the sheep from jumping out and from wild animals and thieves jumping into the enclosure to hurt or kill the sheep. (Robbers would accomplish their goal by climbing over the enclosure, slitting the throat of the sheep and heaving the body/ bodies over the wall...) The only way in and out of the fold was through a space he would leave open. The shepherd himself would actually lie across the opening, becoming the door in and out of the sheepfold. The shepherd's own comfort and sleep were secondary to the comfort and safety of the sheep.[42]

This is a picture of "dying to yourself," which every Christian is called to do. "I have been crucified with Christ. It is no longer I who live, but Christ who lives in me. And the life I now live in the flesh I live by faith in the Son of God, who loved me and gave himself for me."[43] "We who are strong have an obligation to bear with the failings of the weak, and not to please ourselves. Let each of us please his neighbor [athlete] for his good, to build him up."[44] In all of this, we are seeking to follow God's example by God's empowering. "I myself will be the shepherd of my sheep, and I myself will make them lie down, declares the Lord GOD. I will seek the lost, and I will bring back the strayed, and I will bind up the injured, and I will strengthen the weak."[45] This is what it means to follow the example of the Protector.

> If the world is to hear the church's voice today, leaders [coaches] are needed who are authoritative, spiritual, and sacrificial. Authoritative, because people [athletes] desire reliable leaders who know where they are going and are confident of getting there. Spiritual, because without a strong relationship to God, even the most attractive and competent person cannot lead people to God. Sacrificial, because this trait follows the model of Jesus, who gave Himself for the whole world and calls us to follow in His steps.[46]

An accountable shepherd coach provides protection and a hospitable environment to her athletes, and in doing so, shows them that they are valued.

"…you anoint my head with oil…" (Psalm 23:5)

For the sheep, the anointing with oil was used as a protective measure to keep harmful insects and parasites from causing extreme discomfort and infections. For humans in that culture, a guest was received into a home by the host's anointing him with oil mixed with perfume. It was a symbol of gladness and hospitality, showing that nothing was too good for the guest. The opposite occurred when Simon the Pharisee entertained Jesus in his home:

> "A certain moneylender had two debtors. One owed five hundred denarii, and the other fifty. When they could not pay, he cancelled the debt of both. Now which of them will love him more?" Simon answered, "The one, I suppose, for whom he cancelled the larger debt." And he said to him, "You have judged rightly." Then turning toward the woman he said to Simon, "Do you see this woman? I entered your house; you gave me no water for my feet, but she has wet my feet with her tears and wiped them with her hair. You gave me no kiss, but from the time I came in she has not ceased to kiss my feet. You did not anoint my head with oil, but she has anointed my feet with ointment." (Luke 7:41-46)

"Is anyone among you sick? Let him call for the elders of the church, and let them pray over him, anointing him with oil in the name of the Lord." (James 5:14)

What type of environment surrounds your coaching? Is it a place of faith, hope, and love or distrust, despair, and dissension? You are the primary individual that will set the tone for your entire program. If you truly seek to help your team develop their potential as people and athletes, they must never be treated as intrusions, unwelcome guests, or strangers. Do you honestly seek to treat each of your athletes as if he or she were Christ Jesus himself? May the significance of the following passage for your coaching drive you to your knees as you seek the Spirit's empowering to love your athletes well:

> When the Son of Man comes in his glory, and all the angels with him, then he will sit on his glorious throne. Before him will be gathered all the nations, and he will separate people one from another as a shepherd separates the sheep from the goats. And he will place the sheep on his right, but the goats on the left. Then the King will say to those on his right, "Come, you who are blessed by my Father, inherit the kingdom prepared for you from the foundation of the world. For I was hungry and you gave me food, I was thirsty and you gave me drink, I was a stranger and you welcomed me, I was naked and you clothed me, I was sick and you visited me, I was in prison and you came to me." Then the righteous will answer him, saying, "Lord, when did we see you hungry and feed you, or thirsty and give you drink? And when did we see you a stranger and welcome you, or naked and clothe you? And when did we see you sick or in prison and visit you?" And the King will answer them, "Truly, I say to you, as you did it to one of the least of these my brothers, you did it to me." (Matthew 25:31-40)

An accountable shepherd coach will seek to do good and show mercy to her athletes. She will be patient with her athletes, especially with mistakes made in the context of the sport.

"Success is a false indicator of God's love for us; neither does it tell us anything about God's lack of love for us."[47]

"Surely goodness and mercy shall follow me all the days of my life..." (Psalm 23:6)

"He will tend his flock like a shepherd; he will gather the lambs in his arms; he will carry them in his bosom, and gently lead those that are with young." (Isaiah 40:11)

Do not tie your athletes' value as people to their performance as athletes! I've never met a coach yet that didn't say that they value effort. But many of them seem to forget their convictions regarding effort as soon as the game begins and the score is kept. As I've stated before, attempting to win is not the problem. It's placing so much emphasis on the scoreboard that your athletes fail to focus on performing what they practice because their valuation is going up and down along with the scoreboard. Can you honestly say that you never made any mistakes when you were learning the intricacies of a sport? Why do you think it will be any different for those you shepherd - no matter how proficient you are as a coach? If you desire for your athletes to master anything you teach them, prepare for inevitable mistakes.

If you want to shower goodness and mercy upon your athletes, then help them on a regular basis to see the progress they are making. Too much of the world is about comparison with other people. That will never give an accurate portrait of what progress is being made because there are a multitude of factors regarding another athlete that cannot be controlled by the one factor you are focusing on. "For if anyone thinks he is something, when he is nothing, he deceives himself. But let each one test his own work, and then his reason to boast will be in himself alone and not in his neighbor."[48] Again, your team can be wildly successful even if they lose a game. Sometimes you are just outgunned, and there's nothing you can do. You can make a conscious decision to keep a tally of areas where each of your athletes are improving and enthusiastically share that good news with them.

Too many adults act on their tendencies to want to point out and to correct every mistake a child makes during practices and games. This intimidates developing players. They are afraid to be creative and to take risks. They often play a game that is less about themselves and more about what their coaches say.[49]

[Furthermore, if you coach pre-teen athletes:] Scholars who have studied child development have found that most children only *begin* around age 8 to develop the cognitive and social abilities necessary to understand the complex relationships and competitive, action-oriented team sports. Sports sociologist Jay Coakley notes that parents and volunteer coaches often plead loudly with children to "stay in position!" Or "get back where you belong!" without realizing kids' brains just aren't formed that way yet. Understanding the concept of positional play asks that a participant do three things simultaneously: mentally visualize where his teammates and opponents are on the field at a given moment, assess their relationships to one another and the ball, and decide where he or she needs to be. Most children do not fully develop the skills until 12. Adults "mistakenly think that children are not concentrating or trying hard," Coakley says. "This frustrates children who *are* doing the best they can at their level of psychosocial development." Many of the frustrated kids quit the game.[50]

An accountable shepherd coach provides a 'home' atmosphere where each athlete is welcomed, nourished, cherished, and protected.

"…and I shall dwell in the house of the LORD forever." (Psalm 23:6)

"One thing have I asked of the LORD, that will I seek after: that I may dwell in the house of the LORD all the days of my life, to gaze upon the beauty of the LORD and to inquire in his temple." (Psalm 27:4)

Your ultimate desire should be that your athletes will dwell in the house of the Lord forever, to continually be in the presence of the Lord experiencing constant communion with him. One of your responsibilities as a coach is to give them a foretaste of that reality – a time when the children of God will be gathered around his banquet table in peace and security, and all their enemies have been defeated.

∞ *What are some of the ways you can exhibit a cherishing attitude and loving protection towards each one of your athletes?*

Never stop growing as a disciple of Jesus and as a coach. You show your athletes that you cherish them and desire to protect them from unnecessary pain and suffering by staying committed to your own growth. Are you trained and equipped to coach? Can you become certified as a coach in your sport? This singular passion on your part will set you apart from many coaches in America who have little or no sports-specific training, and definitely nothing regarding character development. And this appalling lack of training in many sports, especially for youth, is a top-down issue.

> Want some guidance from USA Basketball at how to coach kids? Don't bother. A couple years ago, Brian McCormick, the private trainer from Sacramento, wrote USA Basketball to ask if he could get certified as a coach... "The Federation responded by telling me they don't do certification," McCormack said...In 2003, *The Seattle Times* and the AAU checked the rosters of 4,236 coaches and volunteers in Washington and Idaho and found 38 felons... AAU president Bobby Dodd told the *Times* that he considered a one percent rate to be low - but promised to examine the ways to perform background checks nationwide. By the time I met up with Dodd three years later, he had talked himself out of mandatory checks. He said an insurance advisor suggested that random checks would be sufficient to protect the organization legally. Besides, Dodd said, he wasn't sure which screening company to trust. [51]

Do your research! Do not be content with a paper mill-type of certification process that takes little effort on your part. You are an ambassador of Jesus Christ. Constantly pursue excellence in your preparation as a coach. Athletes do not need another "what's the minimum I need to do?" coach. "Need an AAU coach? My dog is now available. Out of curiosity, I went to aausports.org, launched in the name, kennel, and birth date of my Nova Scotia Duck Tolling Retriever, clicked 'No' when asked 'have you ever been convicted of a sex offense or felony?,' And supplied my credit card information ($33.95 for a two-year membership, with free T-shirt). Just like that, her printable AAU Membership Card showed up in my e-mail box."[52] And, if you have been blessed with excellent education and experience, make yourself available to those who desire the same. There are not a lot of your peers out there who have been taught how to pursue excellence as disciples and coaches so that they can help transform lives for the glory of God and the joy of their athletes.

It is a high and holy calling you are participating in as a coach to Know, Feed, Lead, and Protect those athletes under your care.

> Lastly... the Holy Father [Pope] then gave us a blueprint for sport, describing how he sees, within a Christian perspective, the sporting ideal that the church should promote and uphold: "a sport that protects the weak and excludes no one, that frees young people from the snares of apathy and indifference, and arouses a healthy sense of competition in them; sport that is a factor of emancipation for poorer countries and helps eradicate intolerance and build a more fraternal and united world; sport which contributes to the love of life, teaches sacrifice, respect and responsibility, leading to the full development of every human person."[53]

TOOLS

Ω Five Ways to Protect Your Athletes. Pray for the Spirit to develop each of these practices in your life.

"1. *Protect with compassion (love)…* Love for Jesus and love for [your athletes] are essential to effectively shepherding [coaching] another person.
2. *Protect with courage (faith)…* The coach pursues the disciple [athlete] in their rebellion, apathy, or sin, and holds them accountable [in love].
3. *Protect by contact (community)…* A shepherd [coach] is…watching for deviancy and a disciple's [athlete's] tendency to escape or wander away in isolation.
4. *Protect with calling (passion)*. Coaches must examine their hearts, their motivation, and the cost to their lives as they follow this calling.
5. *Protect with commitment (generosity)*. Shepherding others requires a generous commitment of time, relational energy, and focus."[54]

Ω Game Day Protection: Post-game Tools

1. "Players talk first: They can better hear what you have to say if they get the chance to talk first... It also provides information that you may not get if you talk first.
2. Have your athletes focus on sharing based on questions like: "What worked well?" "What didn't turn out so well?" "What was the most fun for you today?" "Any thoughts on what you'd like to work on before the next game?"
3. Coach speaks last: You may want to reinforce something one of the players said... This will encourage players to continue to analyze or play in future. You can also gently disagree with players when you think they are making a misdiagnosis.
4. End with a positive: Find something hopeful and motivating to help players come to the next practice excited about their sport and their team."[55]

Ω In our 'selfie'- enthralled world, how can you protect your athletes from the social media barrage that can either put them on a pedestal or bury them under a pile?

1. Have your athletes memorize Galatians 6:2-3, "For if anyone thinks he is something, when he is nothing, he deceives himself. But let each one test his own work, and then his reason to boast will be in himself alone and not in his neighbor." Notice that there is no mention of God or Jesus in this passage, so it can be used in 'sacred' or 'secular' settings to get your point across. With your Christian athletes, you can explain it in context.
2. Post the poem, *If*, by Rudyard Kipling as another reminder to take all social media, press, and clippings with a grain of salt.

If

If you can keep your head when all about you
Are losing theirs and blaming it on you,
If you can trust yourself when all men doubt you,
But make allowance for their doubting too;
If you can wait and not be tired by waiting,
Or being lied about, don't deal in lies,
Or being hated, don't give way to hating,
And yet don't look too good, nor talk too wise:

If you can dream—and not make dreams your master;
If you can think—and not make thoughts your aim;
If you can meet with Triumph and Disaster
And treat those two impostors just the same;
If you can bear to hear the truth you've spoken
Twisted by knaves to make a trap for fools,
Or watch the things you gave your life to, broken,

And stoop and build 'em up with worn-out tools:

If you can make one heap of all your winnings
And risk it on one turn of pitch-and-toss,
And lose, and start again at your beginnings
And never breathe a word about your loss;
If you can force your heart and nerve and sinew
To serve your turn long after they are gone,
And so hold on when there is nothing in you
Except the Will which says to them: 'Hold on!'

If you can talk with crowds and keep your virtue,
Or walk with Kings—nor lose the common touch,
If neither foes nor loving friends can hurt you,
If all men count with you, but none too much;
If you can fill the unforgiving minute
With sixty seconds' worth of distance run,
Yours is the Earth and everything that's in it,
And—which is more—you'll be a Man, my son![56]

3. "[Messiah College Coach] Brandt even went so far as to forbid his players from reading Internet posts about D3 soccer, what he calls 'the *National Enquirer* of men's soccer.' Reading that stuff, he insists, perniciously shifts the team mindset from 'substance' to 'image,' from playing for what really matters to playing for reputation and rankings."[57]

PRAYER

"Heavenly Father, plant in my heart a desire, compassion, and wisdom to provide protection for my athletes. Let them not be afraid, dismayed, or wandering about outside the fold of the team. But if some of them do wander, let me be like a shepherd who seeks out his flock when he is among his sheep that have been scattered. So will I seek out my sheep, and I will rescue them from all places where they have been scattered. Bless them with a peace in knowing that I want the very best for them in heart, mind, soul, and strength. Show me when I need to fight to protect them from others, themselves, or even from myself. Holy Spirit, grant me discernment the moment I turn from thinking about any athlete (on my team or other teams) as a mere commodity to meet my desires. For I have been called to love my neighbor (athletes) as I love myself, and I hated being treated as merely a tool to pad a coach's portfolio. Grant me eyes to see the beauty in each athlete because they are made in your image for your purposes. So I bring them to you. May each of them learn to take your yoke upon their lives, and learn from you, Lord Jesus. For you are gentle and lowly in heart, and they will find rest for their souls. For your yoke is easy, and your burden is light." (Jeremiah 23:4; Matthew 11:28-30; Ezekiel 34:12; Galatians 5:15)

Notes

[1] Exodus 34:6.

[2] Philippians 1:9-11.

[3] Tony Dungy, *The Mentor Leader: Secrets to Building People and Teams that Win Consistently* (Carol Stream: Tyndale, 2010) 95-97.

[4] Stephen Viars in Thabiti Anyabwile, "Does Your Leadership Reveal the Character of God?" *The Gospel Coalition*, 9/25/2013, Accessed 8/2/2014. www.thegospelcoalition.org/blogs/thabitianyabwile/2013/09/25/does-your-leadership-reveal-the-character-of-god/

[5] Jeremiah 17:9.

[6] Anyabwile, op. cit.

[7] Commission on Children at Risk, "Hardwired to Connect: The New Scientific Case for Authoritative Communities," *Institute for American Values*, 2003, Accessed 6/15/14. www.americanvalues.org/search/item.php?id-17#survey.

[8] *Hardwired to Connect* study in Ehrmann, Ehrmann, and Jordan, op. cit., 73.

[9] Howard Hendricks in Dave Kraft, *Leaders Who Last* (Wheaton: Crossway, 2010), 129.

[10] Genesis 4:1.

[11] Hebrews 1:1-2.

[12] John 1:14-15.

[13] John Piper, *Sermon on John 1:14-18*: Bethlehem Baptist Church, Minneapolis, MN.

[14] John 15:13.

15 John 20:21.

16 1 Peter 5:2-3.

17 John 10:5 – sheep will flee from strangers.

18 William Law in J. Oswald Sanders, *Spiritual Leadership: Principles of Excellence for Every Believer* (Chicago: Moody, 2007), 63.

19 John Piper, *Don't Waste Your Life* (Wheaton: Crossway, 2010), 151-152.

20 Deuteronomy 2:7.

21 Edited by Kevin Lixey, L.C., Christoph Hubenthal, Dietmar Mieth, and Norbert Muller, *Sport & Christianity: A Sign of the Times in the Light of Faith* (Washington, D.C.: The Catholic University of America Press, 2012), 151-152.

22 Jeremiah 3:15.

23 1 Corinthians 9:24-27)

24 David A. Feigley, Ph.D., "The Role of Winning in Youth Sports," *Rutgers*, Accessed 1/3/2014. www.youthsports.rutgers.edu/general-interest/24-articles/44-the-role-of-winning-in-youth-sports

25 *Without Limits* movie, 1998. Coach Bill Bowerman at Steve Prefontaine's Eulogy.

26 Ransome W. Cooper in Sanders, op. cit., 63.

27 Brown, op. cit., 80.

28 Jim Thompson, *The Double-Goal Coach: Positive Coaching Tools for Honoring the Game and Developing Winners in Sports and Life* (New York: Harper Collins, 2003), 60.

29 Ray Vanderlaan, cd-rom.

30 Frank DeFord, The Word according to Tom," *Sports Illustrated*, 4/26/1976, Accessed 12/18/2013. www.sportsillustrated.cnn.com/valut/article/magazine/MAG1091031/index.htm

31 Ann Spangler and Lois Tverberg, *Sitting at The Feet of Rabbi Jesus*, (Grand Rapids: Zondervan, 2009), 52-53.

32 1 Corinthians 11:1.

33 1 Timothy 1:15.

34 Hebrews 13:8.

35 Eims, op. cit., 32-33.

36 Thompson, op. cit., 205.

37 Martin Luther King Jr., *Strength to Love*, quoted at "10 Famous Quotes from Dr. Martin Luther King, Jr., *Constitution Daily*, 1/19/2014, Accessed 6/3/2014. www.blog.constitutioncenter.org/2014/01/10-famous-quotes-from-dr-martin-luther-king-jr-2/.

38 Matthew 18:12-13.

39 Psalm 19:7.

40 Timothy Z. Witmer, *The Shepherd Leader: Achieving Effective Shepherding in Your Church* (Phillipsburg: P&R, 2010), 186-187.

41 1 Samuel 17:34-35.

42 I had this quote from a study I did in the past. Unfortunately I have not been able to trace the original. It is not mine.

43 Galatians 2:20.

44 Romans 15:1-2.

45 Ezekiel 34:15-16.

46 Sanders, op. cit., 18.

47 Scott Thomas and Tom Wood, *Gospel Coach: Shepherding Leaders to Glorify God* (Grand Rapids: Zondervan, 2012), 67.

48 Galatians 6:3-4.

49 Big Bigelow, Tom Moroney, and Linda Hill, *Just Let The Kids Play: How to Stop Other Adults from Ruining Your Child's Fun and Success in Youth Sports*, (Deerfield Beach, FL: Health Communications, 2001), 163.

50 Jay Coakley in Tom Farrey, *Game On: The All-American Race to Make Champions of our Children* (New York: ESPN, 2008), 98-99.

[51] Tom Farrey, *Game On: The All-American Race to Make Champions of our Children* (New York: ESPN, 2008), 201.

[52] Tom Farrey, *Game On: The All-American Race to Make Champions of our Children* (New York: ESPN, 2008), 203.

[53] Lixey, Hubenthal, Mieth, and, op. cit., 4.

[54] Thomas and Wood, op. cit., 140-141.

[55] Ibid., 233-237.

[56] *A Choice of Kipling's Verse* (1943)

[57] Dave Brandt in Michael Zigarelli, *The Messiah Method: The Seven Disciplines of the Winningest College Soccer Program in America* (USA: Xulon, 2011), 41.

8

GRACE DISPENSER

"Rather, speaking the truth in love, we are to grow up in every way into him who is the head, into Christ, from whom the whole body, joined and held together by every joint with which it is equipped, when each part is working properly, makes the body grow so that it builds itself up in love." (Ephesians 4:15-16)

Would your athletes say that this verse exemplifies your coaching style and the culture of your team? What does it mean to speak the truth "in love"? Unfortunately in the world in which we live today, "love" for all too many people means only affirmation and encouragement. Every word must be positive. If you correct someone, you may hurt their 'self-esteem.' That, however, is not the biblical portrait of being loving, because not every situation you encounter as a coach calls for affirmation or encouragement. Sometimes the most loving thing you can do is to correct someone. Failure to do so would be truly unloving.

Consider the gospel message as the ultimate example of speaking the truth in love. What were the first recorded words of John the Baptizer and Jesus as they began their ministries?

> John appeared, baptizing in the wilderness and proclaiming a baptism of *repentance for the forgiveness of sins.* (Mark 1:4, italics mine)

> From that time Jesus began to preach, saying, "*Repent*, for the kingdom of heaven is at hand." "...I have not come to call the righteous but *sinners to repentance*" (Matthew 4:17; Luke 5:32 italics mine)

Sinners? Not a very loving thing to call people, is it? Try using that terminology and see what kind of response you get. One of the first articles I had published was seen as unloving even by some in the church because I used that very word. To not use it, however, would be to deny the reality of the gospel message: we are great sinners in need of a great Savior. Without Christ's death on the cross to cover our sins, God's wrath would be poured out upon us through eternal suffering in hell. Only through a corrective stance in regard to sin can anyone hope to know the encouragement of eternal life in heaven.

> But when the goodness and loving kindness of God our Savior appeared, he saved us, not because of works done by us in righteousness, but according to his own mercy, by the washing of regeneration and renewal of the Holy Spirit, whom he poured out on us richly through Jesus Christ our Savior, so that being justified by his grace we might become heirs according to the hope of eternal life. (Titus 3:4-7)

I know that's heavy for a book on coaching, but we need to keep an eternal perspective. Through affirmation, encouragement, and correction lovingly and clearly communicated, your team will operate more smoothly and more biblically.

∞ *How do you make "speaking the truth in love" a reality for your team?*

LISTEN

"The first service that one owes to others in the Fellowship consists in listening to them. Just as love to God begins with listening to his word, so the beginning of love for the brethren is learning to listen to them. It is God's love for us that he not only gives us his word, but also lends us his ear. So it is his work that we do for our brother when we learn to listen to him." (Dietrich Bonhoeffer)[1]

"Know this, my beloved brothers: let every person be quick to hear [listen], slow to speak, slow to anger; for the anger of man does not produce the righteousness of God." (James 1:19-20)

How well would your athletes say you listen to them, really hear what they are saying? If someone talks a lot about a specific topic, the odds are that subject is important to them. Keeping that in mind, realize that "listen" occurs more than 200 times in the Bible. If you truly want to let your athletes know that they are important to you, listen with your heart and your mind. This is an activity in which virtually every human being needs to continually strive to improve. Listening to your athletes is a gift. Failure to listen to those under a person's authority has had grave consequences throughout history:

Sunday evening April 14, 1912 was a calm, clear night. Standing on the bridge of the mighty *Titanic*, the ship's crew witnessed an awe-inspiring spectacle. Stars sparkled like diamonds against the velvet backdrop of the heavens. Below deck, saloons and smoking rooms contained merrily entertained travelers Staterooms held deep-sleeping passengers such as John Jacob Astor, one of the world's wealthiest men. All was well aboard the *Titanic* for "not even God could sink that mighty vessel" with its fifteen watertight steel compartments. No need to fear. 2,340 passengers, twenty lifeboats with a capacity of about 1,100 – far more than would ever be needed.

Earlier that day, the German steamship *Amerika* radioed a warning reporting large icebergs directly in the *Titanic's* proposed path. Despite this warning she forged ahead at her normal operating speed of about twenty-six miles per hour. The alarm rang. The snooze button was hit. Sometime after 11:15 p.m., lookouts in the *Titanic's* crow's nest thought they spotted an iceberg off the bow. They telephoned the bridge to relay the information to the captain but no immediate answer was forthcoming. Two or three minutes passed before an officer on the bridge even answered the lookouts' call. What could have been so important that kept the phone from being answered? Alarm #2 went unheeded.

Too late. One does not alter the course of an 882-foot long ocean liner as if it were a Porsche handling hairpin turns. The movement of the *Titanic* was so imperceptible that the passengers didn't even know evasive action was taking place. At 11:40 p.m. the iceberg began shredding the underside of the *Titanic* as if she were a tin can. Water poured into the 'air-tight' compartments and the unthinkable scenario began. Alarm #3 was sounded: "Within a few minutes stewards and other members of the crew were sent round to arouse the people. Some utterly refused to get up. The stewards had almost to force the doors of the staterooms to make the somnolent appreciate their peril, and many of them, it is believed, were drowned like rats in a trap."[2]

What kind of coaches did you have throughout your playing days? Did they listen to you, or were they too busy to hear what you had to say, even if you could see an iceberg ahead? I'm not sure whether it's mainly coaches' sinful natures, personality flaws or insecurity that leaves so many athletes frustrated. Countless coaches may say they want to hear from their athletes, but when the time comes for those 'conversations,' these coaches aren't really engaged. The problem? "Too many strong personalities are compulsive talkers. 'He won't listen to me'... 'He gives the answer before I have had a chance to state the problem.'...Leaders who want to show sensitivity should listen often and long, and talk short and seldom. Many so-called leaders are too busy to listen. True leaders know that time spent listening is well invested."[3]

It is impossible for you to know everything that is going on with your athletes individually and your team as a whole unless you listen to them. You need that information if you are going to make wise decisions as a coach. Speaking the truth in love entails a desire to keep your finger on the pulse of your team. This will only happen if you are an avid listener. Are you taking the time to try to understand the complex lives of your athletes? Yes, it's time-consuming and can mire you in drama. But remember, "Time spent listening is well invested."

Even if some athletes disagree with you, it is well worth your time to listen. In fact, you may find out that they have valid points that need to be addressed. If you try something new and it works, it's a win-win. If it doesn't pan out, it can still be a win-win because you are affirming the value of those under your authority by taking them seriously, and still do things 'your way.' At those times, however, you may need to restate your position and ideas so that they can clearly grasp why you are sticking with your methodology. Don't look at asking questions and listening to your athletes as a sign of weakness. On the contrary, it is a sign of wisdom and strength to seek feedback from them, and from your assistants, if you are so fortunate to have any. Furthermore, you are helping to train and equip everyone involved to further comprehend what it means to be a team on which:

The body does not consist of one member but of many. If the foot should say, "Because I am not a hand, I do not belong to the body," that would not make it any less a part of the body. And if the ear should say, "Because I am not an eye, I do not belong to the body," that would not make it any less a part of the body. If the whole body were an eye, where would be the sense of hearing? If the whole body were an ear, where would be the sense of smell? But as it is, God arranged the members in the body, each one of them, as he chose. If all were a single member, where would the body be? As it is, there are many parts, yet one body. (1 Corinthians 12:14-20)

Affirming all the parts of the body through active listening is only part of the equation. You also need to make sure that you surround yourself with assistants, or others who are trustworthy if you do not have the luxury of assistants, who will speak the truth in love to you. Do you have people who are willing to speak truth into your life in order to help you improve as a coach and as a disciple of Jesus? Moses had Jethro:

The next day Moses sat to judge the people, and the people stood around Moses from morning till evening. When Moses' father-in-law saw all that he was doing for the people, he said, "What is this that you are doing for the people? Why do you sit alone, and all the people stand around you from morning till evening?" And Moses said to his father-in-law, "Because the people come to me to inquire of God; when they have a dispute, they come to me and I decide between one person and another, and I make them know the statutes of God and his laws." Moses' father-in-law said to him, "What you are doing is not good. You and the people with you will certainly wear yourselves out, for the thing is too heavy for you. You are not able to do it alone. Now obey my voice; I will give you advice, and God be with you! You shall represent the people before God and bring their cases to God, and you shall warn them about the statutes and the laws, and make them know the way in which they must walk and what they must do. Moreover, look for able men from all the people, men who fear God, who are trustworthy and hate a bribe, and place such men over the people as chiefs of thousands, of hundreds, of fifties, and of tens. And let them judge the people at all times. Every great matter they shall bring to you, but any small matter they shall decide themselves. So it will be easier for you, and they will bear the burden with you. If you do this, God will direct you, you will be able to endure, and all these people also will go to their place in peace." So Moses listened to the voice of his father-in-law and did all that he had said. (Exodus 18:13-24)

Moses listened to the voice of his father-in-law and implemented his ideas. Why? Because Jethro was trustworthy, Moses listened attentively and realized the wisdom in the suggestions being offered. Jethro had nothing to gain from speaking the truth into Moses' life. He was merely seeking to help his son-in-law. May God so anoint your ears, heart, and mind to hear what is burdening your athletes so that you can point them towards hope and healing. If you don't know what is causing stress and pain in your athletes' lives, you may inadvertently add to it, rather than helping them to properly deal with it. Coaching is much greater than merely helping them become faster, higher, and stronger. "Bear one another's burdens, and so fulfill the law of Christ."[4] In this way, you will be actively pointing them towards Jesus' promise:

> Come to me, all who labor and are heavy laden, and I will give you rest. Take my yoke upon you, and learn from me, for I am gentle and lowly in heart, and you will find rest for your souls. For my yoke is easy, and my burden is light. (Matthew 11:28-30)

TOOLS

Ω Gospel Listening – The Foundations

1. "The gospel reminds us that listening is an *act of grace* extended to the other person.
2. Listening is an *act of love...* when we listen to others with the motivation to care for them.
3. Listening is an *act of compassion*. When we listen to another person, we are displaying empathy and sympathy for the issues, challenges, and celebrations they are experiencing.
4. Listening is an *act of participation with the Holy Spirit*. We must listen responsively to the Spirit, who may want to reveal Scriptures and their applications that we may never come up with through our own wisdom."[5]

Ω Listening 101 – The Practice

1. "*Pay attention.* Give the speaker your undivided attention and acknowledge the message...
2. *Show that you are listening.* Use your own body language, tone, and gestures to convey that you are paying attention...
3. *Provide feedback.* Ask questions to clarify certain points. 'What do you mean when you say...?' Or 'Is this what you mean?'
4. *Defer judgment.* ...Allow the disciple [athlete] an opportunity to finish. Don't interrupt with counter arguments.
5. *Respond appropriately.* ... Be candid, open, and honest in your response. Assert your opinions respectfully."[6]

Ω Making the Time to Listen

1. Schedule regular times to meet with each one of your athletes during the season. Depending on your setting, this can happen during school hours or before and after practices.
2. Have athletes over to your home for a meal.

3. Visit the training room to spend informal time with athletes receiving treatment. It is especially critical to listen to athletes who are rehabbing in order to encourage them. And listen to what the trainers learn through their interactions with these same athletes.

4. Always be on the lookout for slices of unplanned time when you can listen to your athletes and gain insights into their lives.

Ω Ask for Input

1. Ask your support staff, whether it's just one volunteer assistant, or a cadre of helpers, to evaluate how you are doing. Prayerfully discuss their feedback and seek ways to implement changes that will positively impact the program.

2. Ask your athletes similar questions. If you are truly a team, it is important to find out how they perceive you are doing as a coach. It is also imperative that this process allow their identities to remain anonymous or they may not be completely honest. That can be done simply by having another trusted person administer the survey and gather them when the athletes are finished. When you receive their comments, prayerfully sift through them with your support staff seeking wisdom how to implement changes based upon the feedback of your athletes and staff.

Ω PRAYER

"Heavenly Father, bless my tongue so that it is a fountain of life for my athletes. Empower me to speak the truth in love so that our entire team is transformed more into Christlikeness through sowing seeds of salvation and sanctification. Grant me discernment, Holy Spirit, when I need to be tough and when I need to be tender. Help me to be quick to listen, slow to speak, and slow to become angry so that I hear correctly and respond properly. Just as you stoop down to listen to the prayers of your people, help me to serve my athletes well by listening to them and affirming their value as people. When I receive input from others, help me to place their ideas against the silhouette of Scripture first, and then prayerfully respond in the best manner that will glorify you and bring joy to our team. In all of this, may my compassion grow so that I desire to help bear the burdens that I hear and see in my athletes, all the while bringing them to you, Lord Jesus, where they must ultimately come to find rest for their souls." (Proverbs 10:11; Ephesians 4:15-16; James 1:19-20; Galatians 6:2; Matthew 11:28)

CORRECT – "SLOW TO SPEAK, SLOW TO BECOME ANGRY"

"The most powerful thing we can do is to speak out and end the silence toward poor, unsportsmanlike behavior while simultaneously lifting up and highlighting those shining moments where civility and class come first."[7]

"Therefore, having put away falsehood, let each one of you speak the truth with his neighbor, for we are members one of another. Be angry and do not sin; do not let the sun go down on your anger, and give no opportunity to the devil… Let no corrupting talk come out of your mouths, but only such as is good for building up, as fits the occasion, that it may give grace to those who hear. And do not grieve the Holy Spirit of God, by whom you were sealed for the day of redemption. Let all bitterness and wrath and anger and clamor and slander be put away from you, along with all malice. Be kind to one another, tenderhearted, forgiving one another, as God in Christ forgave you." (Ephesians 4:25-32)

Matt Labrum is a high school football coach who is obviously not afraid to make waves. In 2013 he suspended nearly every player on his team. Reports about some of his players being involved in cyber-bullying, plus skipping class and the poor grades that ensued, caused the coach to put drastic measures in place. Why? Because he believes that the most important thing they do is build character. To the shock of his players, he sat all of them down in the locker room after a game and told them to turn in their uniforms and all their equipment. If they wanted to play for the Union Football team, they would have to earn the right. The day after the suspensions, Coach Labrum handed out a letter titled "Union Football Character," that outlined what the boys had to do to get back on the team. They had to attend all practices, be on time, have no discipline problems, complete a community service project, and memorize a quote about good character. In other words, they had to prove themselves as human beings, not football players.

The following Monday and Tuesday they were putting this new code of conduct into practice. Monday they did service projects. Tuesday they were at a senior citizens center playing games with the residents and listening to their stories. This all occurred with the support of Labrum's coaching staff, the school administration, and the players' parents. One parent even stated, "It's not a punishment. I see it as an opportunity to do some good in the community." Wednesday's practice entailed a study hall and team meeting – followed by the news that thirty-two out of the original forty-one players had earned their jerseys back. "We want to help our parents raise their sons. We want to be a positive influence. We want to be an asset," said Coach Labrum. Bravo! They are definitely headed in the right direction.

Correction sometimes focuses on character issues and other times on mastery of skills. Regardless of what sport or age group you coach, there will be times when you will have to correct your athletes for errors in judgment and simply for making mistakes. In other words, there are times when you should be upset with their behavior and other times when you need to relax, because mistakes happen at every level of the sporting world. Whether it's character issues or skill mastery issues you are dealing with, however, your attitude towards your athletes will have consequences. "There's a time when love gets in the loved one's face with correction. While such correction can be done gently and tactfully, it must be done and not abandoned altogether as though love never confronts. Love offers correction… [But] Our listeners will be more inclined to hear us if they believe *we're* not angry at them, but grateful for them."[8] If you seek to intimidate your athletes into exhibiting the correct behavior, realize that the 'positive' results will be short-lived compared to what will occur if you 'speak the truth in love' and affirm their value as people.

So before correction ensues, check your attitude at the door. Are you looking at your athletes as God's image-bearers? Are you truly grateful they are part of the team, or do you wish they would vanish? You won't be able to hide your true feelings very long. As an ambassador of Jesus Christ, you must clearly address issues as they arise. But also remember that if your correction takes the form of discipline, you will always have those on the sidelines who disagree with you. Stand firm on God's Word and heed the words of Jesus: "Woe to you, when all people speak well of you."[9] You will not always be popular. But that is not the calling God has placed on your life. You are called to speak the truth in love, through the empowering of the Holy Spirit, so that, in the end, your athletes are built up.

In this process, you must never humiliate or demean your athletes in any way. You are commanded to put away all "bitterness and wrath and anger and clamor and slander." So pray for the Golden Rule to flow forth in and through your correction. Would you want to be treated in a similar fashion in which you treat your athletes? If not, rethink your approach before proceeding! If your athletes see you speaking to one of their teammates in an unbiblical manner, what message will that send to them? If that happens, do not be surprised if your athletes imitate your behavior when they speak with each other. Unity will be sacrificed upon the altar of your anger.

When your athletes make mistakes, how should you properly correct them so that their confidence is not shredded? Do not demean them by criticizing them as people or their abilities. Rather, help them to understand what they 'did' wrong and then instruct them on how to correct it. Regardless of whether the error occurs due to carelessness, or simply because of a lack of skill, the first goal is seeking to help the athlete understand what they need to physically do to correct the mistake. Secondarily, address an attitude if it also needs to be corrected.

Your goal should be to help your athletes succeed in growing in the mastery of the skills necessary to compete in your sport. Correction is not a form of punishment. On the contrary, by seeking to correct your athletes, you are letting them know that you believe they have the ability to improve. If you move from correction to punishment when your athletes make mistakes, however, you will build a culture of fear and caution which will hinder the growth of your team as people and athletes. Does punishment have its place as a corrective measure in sports? Absolutely! But not for making mistakes in playing a game. Save that, if necessary, to help bring correction to character issues like those that were plaguing the Union High School football team. And when punishment of an individual needs to take place, do it in private, and do it in love. Because when you must punish an athlete, it is critical that they know that you believe in them and their ability to change.

There are two foundational questions you must ask yourself regarding the correction of your team: "Are your corrections driven by your own preferences, your own disappointments and frustrations? Or are your corrections driven by what God desires for each person?[10] Remember the foundational calling God has placed upon your life. The pursuit of excellence in your sport is a tool to point your athletes to Jesus, who is the ultimate definition of Excellence. Those mistakes that arise for every member of your team are reminders to them, and you, that we are called to pursue perfection, but we will never attain it on this earth. "You therefore must be perfect, as your heavenly Father is perfect."[11] Those character issues that need correction are further proof why you need to continually seek wisdom and empowering to sow seeds of salvation and sanctification into the lives of your athletes. "For there is no distinction: for all have sinned and fall short of the glory of God,"[12] and "Surely there is not a righteous man on earth who does good and never sins."[13]

TOOLS

Ω Correction when disciplinary action is necessary.

"1. First conduct a thorough and impartial inquiry [Quick to Listen].
2. Then consider the overall benefit of the disciplinary action to the work and to the individual [Build Up].
3. Do all in the spirit of love - be considerate, always [Speak the Truth in Love].
4. Always keep the spiritual restoration of the offender in view [Forgiving One Another].
5. Pray it through [Pray without Ceasing]."[14]

Ω Correction when your athlete fails to perform a skill/makes a mistake.

1. "Be understanding…Most are athletes already upset when they make a mistake and become overly tough on themselves.
2. Give them the chance to correct themselves within the game rather than always pulling them out or offering your feedback right away.
3. Avoid making it personal. [Focus on the issue that needs correction, not the athlete].
4. Avoid using sarcasm to embarrass athletes into performing better.
5. Focus on the solution.
6. Make it a 'we' project. For example, if one of your athletes needs to develop more strength. You can tell him, 'We need to get you stronger.'"[15]
7. "Avoid non-teachable moments… [For instance,] The moment after your player missed a layup that would have tied the game is not the time to give technical instruction in which foot he should be leading with."[16]

Ω PRAYER

"Heavenly Father, empower me with your Spirit so that I am quick to listen, slow to speak, and slow to become angry. Too often in the heat of competition I forget that my call to coach is not primarily about winning a game or ever about gaining personal glory. Forgive me for losing my focus and making it about me. Apart from you, Lord Jesus, I can't do anything. With you, I can conquer sinful anger that arises in my heart. Enable my words to be grace-filled, a fountain of life for my athletes when I need to correct them. Let no corrupting talk come out of my mouth but only words that will build up my athletes. I desperately need your wisdom for every situation I encounter, whether it's correcting a mistake or willful disobedience that may require some type of punishment. Let all bitterness and wrath and anger and clamor and slander be put away from my life, along with all malice. I desire to be kind towards my athletes, tenderhearted, forgiving each when necessary, just as you forgave me. Grant me eyes to see that each athlete I am blessed to coach is made in your image. Let me be truly grateful that they are part of the team. And let any correction be done with a heart of love and a deep desire for that athlete to be drawn nearer to you, Father, who is slow to anger and abounding in steadfast love." (James 1:19; Ephesians 4:25-32; Numbers 14:18)

AFFIRM

"If God is sovereign, and every good gift is from above, then not praising the good in others is a kind of sacrilege and soul-sickness. When our mouths are empty of praise for others, it is probably because our hearts are full of love for self."[17] (John Piper)

"Let each of us please his neighbor for his good, *to build him up.*" (Romans 15:2, italics mine)

Who doesn't want to be praised, to be built up? Everyone needs that type of blessing from those they esteem, admire, or love. Think back to your own playing days, for example. Can you remember how you felt when your parents or coach were paying attention to you and celebrated your abilities? Few things in life match the power of praise from someone you value. It can be as simple as a pat on the back letting you know that your efforts and actions were seen and appreciated. Have today's athletes changed in that regard? But is that all that 'affirmation' means – praising another person for their strengths and abilities, for something they've done? "Affirmation is truthfully declaring by complimentary word or action the goodness of something. Good affirmation attests, certifies, or confirms that which honors God, that which is morally upright."[18]

> Christian organizations are sometimes the worst, because there is the attitude that "they are working for God, and he will reward them for their labors." Some even argue that it builds egos to give men praise, therefore, it is unspiritual and is to be avoided at all costs. I find that a pretty sad argument against lavishing your coworkers [athletes] with affirmation and recognition for a job well done. Yes, I am working for that final pat on the back in the sky, "Well done, good and faithful servant." But I think God expects me to pat others on the back along the way.[19]

May you be wary of falling into this way of thinking. [For] "If an overly corrective under-affirming pattern continues, three things can happen: First *others stop hearing our corrections…*

Second, *they stop hearing us altogether, not just our corrections, but us as persons... Third, the relationship itself becomes oppositional.*"[20] It is not unspiritual to give men praise, not if it is done correctly, for the glory of God. Remember, "Good affirmation attests, certifies, or confirms that which honors God." Does God want us to give others a pat on the back? How can you be sure of this? Because Jesus can be seen doing this very thing. For example, he praises the faith of the centurion who had a sick servant, and the faith of the widow who gave liberally from the little that she had.

> Now a centurion had a servant who was sick and at the point of death, who was highly valued by him. When the centurion heard about Jesus, he sent to him elders of the Jews, asking him to come and heal his servant. And when they came to Jesus, they pleaded with him earnestly, saying, "He is worthy to have you do this for him, for he loves our nation, and he is the one who built us our synagogue." And Jesus went with them. When he was not far from the house, the centurion sent friends, saying to him, "Lord, do not trouble yourself, for I am not worthy to have you come under my roof. Therefore I did not presume to come to you. But say the word, and let my servant be healed. For I too am a man set under authority, with soldiers under me: and I say to one, 'Go,' and he goes; and to another, 'Come,' and he comes; and to my servant, 'Do this,' and he does it." When Jesus heard these things, he marveled at him, and turning to the crowd that followed him, said, "I tell you, not even in Israel have I found such faith." And when those who had been sent returned to the house, they found the servant well. (Luke 7:2-10)

> Jesus looked up and saw the rich putting their gifts into the offering box, and he saw a poor widow put in two small copper coins. And he said, "Truly, I tell you, this poor widow has put in more than all of them. For they all contributed out of their abundance, but she out of her poverty put in all she had to live on." (Luke 21:1-4)

Affirmation, in and of itself, is not the problem. The quandary arises when we desire the accolades for the wrong reason – to point to our own awesomeness. Praise is a tool. When wielded correctly, it will point to Jesus, the Source of any proper motivation and concordant action that ensues. Praise without Jesus as the focal point will more often than not lead to pride. "What do you have that you did not receive? If then you received it, why do you boast as if you did not receive it?"[21]

Other problems arise when coaches offer continual positive words to their athletes in the hope that it will somehow magically transform them into better athletes. I call that "The Little Engine that Could Theology." That flattery has nothing to do with affirmation. "While affirmation commends virtues, flattery exaggerates them, glosses over flaws, offers excessive input, and is insincere, not chiefly building up the recipient in Christlikeness, but interested chiefly in obtaining some kind of direct favor."[22] This attempt at building up often leads athletes to drink the

Philippians 4:13 Kool-Aid: "I can do all things through Christ who strengthens me." As discussed in a previous chapter, this is utter Scripture twisting, a vain attempt to 'force' God to fulfill his Word by holding it up like a genie's lamp. On the flip side, however, "Affirmation is [also] not about lowering standards. It is about commending incremental progress toward those standards as those standards reflect the character of Christ [inch-by-inch]."[23]

So how should you affirm your athletes so that they do not become prideful in themselves, deluded into literally thinking they can do 'anything,' or on the flip-side, become satisfied with mediocrity and failing to pursue excellence? Like everything else in your coaching arsenal, affirmation should ultimately point your athletes to Jesus: "For from him and through him and to him are all things. To him be glory forever."[24] "[A] good, proper healthy, important, and necessary way to praise *people* is to the glory of God."[25] Does it need to look like these affirmations from the Apostle Paul?

> But thanks be to God, that you who were once slaves of sin have become obedient from the heart to the standard of teaching to which you were committed. (Romans 6:17)

> But thanks be to God, who put into the heart of Titus the same earnest care I have for you. (2 Corinthians 8:16)

> We always thank God, the Father of our Lord Jesus Christ, when we pray for you, since we heard of your faith in Christ Jesus and of the love that you have for all the saints. (Colossians 1:3-4)

> We ought always to give thanks to God for you, brothers, as is right, because your faith is growing abundantly. (2 Thessalonians 1:3)

You would be hard-pressed to imitate Paul's words if you are employed or volunteer in a secular organization. Does that mean that you can't affirm people biblically? Not at all. If you have athletes who are Christians, you can, at the appropriate times, use the full array of biblical texts and nuances. If you are dealing with non-Christian athletes, or you find yourself in a public setting where you are more limited in your open, unswerving public proclamation of the gospel, does that keep you from praising God for your athletes? No! For instance, just because someone "took prayer out of public schools" doesn't mean that prayer in school has been stopped. Secondly, God's common grace is exhibited in the lives of believers and nonbelievers. "For he makes his sun rise on the evil and on the good, and sends rain on the just and on the unjust."[26]

So when you see godly qualities in the lives of your non-believing athletes, affirm them. Praise them when they pursue excellence, when they put forth daily effort, when they fall and get back up, when they have a positive attitude, and you will be sowing seeds of salvation and sanctification. If your athletes know you are a Christian and that you model a godly life, then your affirmation of godly qualities in their lives may be the seeds God uses to open their eyes, ears, and hearts to the gospel.

> By commending Christlike qualities, and celebrating them when we spot them, affirmation showcases the character of God, giving him honor for being the kind of God he is. Andy Stanley adds, "Celebration reinforces value…." By affirming, we teach. We make explicit what is important.[27]

So constantly be on the lookout for attitudes and effort, behaviors, and characteristics in which God is pleased. For instance, years ago during an early stint coaching cross country in high school, I was impressed with one young man, Peter. To this day, he is still the slowest male runner I have ever coached. In my ignorance and pride, I could not for the life of me understand why he showed up to practice each day, and with a smile on his face. I cannot ever remember him seemingly having a bad day. He genuinely seemed enthusiastic for every practice. And yet, he would arrive back at the school a full thirty minutes after everyone else. One day I asked him why he decided to run cross country. His answer was simple, "I like to run and I like being part of a team."

At our awards banquet that year, it was a simple choice for me who would receive the coach's award for attitude, effort, and perseverance. Peter was genuinely shocked when I announced his name and explained why I had chosen him. His teammates gave him a rousing ovation and his parents were beaming from ear-to-ear. Peter never got much faster, but his heart was always in the right place. For all I know, he may have honored God more with his talents than those who were part of the Jr. Olympic National Championship team later that year, but I was too immature to fully grasp that concept. But I did see glimpses. Be watchful. Be amazed. Affirm!

When you affirm your athletes by pointing out the positives that you see in their lives, you will help build their confidence. And that confidence will produce more success. But remember, success in God's eyes will not necessarily square up with the final tally on the scoreboard. "Coaches who communicate well develop a level of trust with their athletes. This trust allows them to dignify honest mistakes by sending the message, 'mistakes are part of learning and as long as you are giving your complete attention and full effort, you will improve'… Small successes lead to bigger successes [inch-by-inch]. It doesn't take much to let an individual athlete know you have seen him improve."[28] Affirm successes and efforts! By doing so, you will motivate them to continue on that same pathway. Affirming those godly characteristics in your Christian athletes has an added dimension: "To affirm Christlikeness in transformed believers [athletes] is to affirm what Christ purchased with his blood."[29]

TOOLS

Ω "Four Characteristics of Good Affirmations

1. *Detached from Correction*: Correction packaged with the affirmation will contaminate and weaken the affirmation, perhaps making it altogether fruitless... Corrections tend to cancel affirmations, and the closer the proximity to correction, the more crippled the affirmation. [The 'sandwich method' (affirmation/correction/affirmation) can make others reticent to hear your affirmations, because they're always waiting for the corrections to come.]
2. *Steady*: [T]here must be a steady stream of affirmations. Indifference and passive silence do not honor... Yesterday's refreshment doesn't refresh permanently. You can't stockpile freshness.
3. *Honest*: Commend only the commendable. It simply won't do to make up phony commendations... 'Truthful lips endure forever, but a lying tongue is *for a moment*' (Proverbs 10:19).
4. *God-Centered*: The aim is to glorify God by refreshing people as we help them see God at work in their lives, moving them toward Christlikeness... Even when someone fails in his performance, there are ways to commend good character."[30]

Ω Moments of Greatness

Teach you athletes how to look for positive actions in their teammates lives – in practices, games, and outside the sport. At the end of practices or games, take the time to affirm your players by pointing out those individual moments to the entire team. Encourage them to join you in looking for examples of how their teammates are living in ways that positively impact those around them. Give them opportunities to affirm those actions at the same time you affirm the moments of greatness. Doing this also helps you to train the next generation of Grace Dispensers by allowing them to practice the art of affirming what they see in their teammates on and off the field. Consider also sending individual/group texts as reminders and encouragements for your players to continue traveling down that road.

Ω Affirm Your Athletes to Other People

"1. Not only commend people to their faces (or in letters), but commend them behind their backs, *whether or not* the report ever gets back to them.
2. Let God be your reward for doing your good deeds 'secretly.'
3. Commending the qualities of persons who are absent nevertheless affirms the characteristic in focus and serves as a teachable moment for others and a reminder to yourself, holding up a commendable standard.
4. It makes positive use of the grapevine rather than the negative gossipy use."[31]

Ω PRAYER

"I praise you, Father, the One to whom all glory, and honor, and praise is due. Open my eyes to see where you are working in the lives of my athletes. Grant me a passion to diligently seek to affirm the godly qualities that they exhibit, so that all are drawn towards you. May the athletes I coach desire to hear, "Well done, good and faithful servant," when they have been faithful with the talents you have bestowed upon them. For you are sovereign, and every good and perfect gift comes down from heaven, from your very hand, to saints and sinners alike. So empower me to praise my athletes, to affirm those things that honor you, Father, so they are built up and you are praised. Let it be that the affirmations that I give are bathed in the truth, saturated with love, and help improve the hearing of my athletes. Holy Spirit, daily grant me wisdom how to be a grace dispenser through affirmation in a way that glorifies Jesus and brings joy, now and forevermore, to each member of the team." (Matthew 25:21-22; James 1:17)

ENCOURAGE

"Though related, affirmation and encouragement are not the same…encouragement looks forward and affirmation looks backward… Encouragement, like cheerleading, often aims for something that has not *yet* been done (win that game, pass that test, get that job, fight that cancer, etc.) while affirmation rewards what has *already* been demonstrated (determination in winning that game, diligence in studying for that test, perseverance in searching for that job, endurance in fighting that cancer, etc.)" (Sam Crabtree).[32]

"And let us consider how to stir up one another to love and good works." (Hebrews 10:24)

"And we urge you, brothers, admonish the idle, encourage the fainthearted, help the weak, be patient with them all." (1 Thessalonians 5:14)

Christian coaches should pursue excellence, and teach their athletes to do likewise, because it glorifies God. Yet in this pursuit of excellence, each one of your athletes will fall short at varying times during any given season. You must have wisdom in balancing out challenging your athletes to reach further ahead than where they are presently, and blessing them with encouraging words and practical action steps when they fall short. Mistakes and the ensuing frustration are inevitable if your athletes are truly seeking to become the best they can be during a season. Watch any professional sporting event, and it becomes glaringly obvious how unattainable the goal of 'perfection' is. For instance, why is a .400 batting average seen as being rarified air, yet if you scored 40/100 on a test in school, it would be deemed a miserable performance? The pursuit of perfection does not mean that it will be attained. Everyone loses eventually.

The fact of the matter is, no one likes to fail, and most everyone fears failure to some degree. However, it is important to understand that because you are a Christian, you really have nothing to be afraid of. Christ will always be with you! He will be with you when you win and he will be with you when you lose. No matter what the outcome of your performance is, he will love you, just the same.[33]

For I am sure that neither death nor life, nor angels nor rulers, nor things present nor things to come, nor powers, nor height nor depth, nor anything else in all creation, will be able to separate us from the love of God in Christ Jesus our Lord. (Romans 8:38-39)

But what do you do with non-Christian athletes? How do you encourage them when they fail? Regardless of an athlete's beliefs in relationship to Jesus, your actions should be similar. You need to show that your love for them, your concern for their well-being, and your respect for them as people does not waver when mistakes are made, when losses come. They need to see and feel that you will not cast them aside like yesterday's trash. That, however, does not mean that athletes are sometimes benched in place of a teammate who is playing better.

In those critical moments when those decisions must be made, they need to be based upon a pattern of mistakes. Too many coaches show their athletes that they are only valued if they continuously perform up to the coach's expectations, which can be nebulous at best. When an athlete gets yanked for making a singular mistake, not only is it discouraging - it promotes a culture of fear. Athletes become tentative. They will do everything within their power to keep from having to take on any tasks that might put them in harm's way of their coach.

Athletes become resentful of these types of coaches and feel that they are perfectionists, which is a far cry from a pursuit of excellence. At those critical junctures when you must replace/substitute one athlete for another, take at least a moment and acknowledge the value of the athlete coming out of the game as a person, as an athlete, and as a teammate. Get them back in the game as soon as possible, and help them work on whatever weakness you believe is at the root of their cycle of errors. That is encouragement.

"Encouragement is the fuel that powers our efforts to engage, educate, and equip. Nothing does more to lubricate the rough spots than a good dose of encouragement. Mentor leaders care. Mentor leaders lift others up. Mentor leaders encourage."[34] One of the key components of encouragement is helping your athletes to see their potential. Again, I'm not talking about the pie-in-the-sky, I-think-I-can-because-Jesus-rose-from-the-dead-theology. I mean their potential as best as you can assess it through prayer and the empowering of the Holy Spirit, together with your training, equipping, and experience. When you plant seeds of success, help your athletes have stepping stone goals that they can celebrate reaching, and diligently coach them in acquiring the necessary skill sets, encouragement will daily rain down and fear will disperse because your athletes will know they are loved. "There is no fear in love, but perfect love casts out fear. For fear has to do with punishment, and whoever fears has not been perfected in love... And this commandment we have from him: whoever loves God must also love his brother."[35]

It was the goal of a long journey. The training, recuperating, and multiple competitions were behind them. Descending down the ramp, they boarded the plane with the boundless energy that only comes with youth. The belief was still intact, "We can compete with the best." Soon they headed due east out of Los Angeles. The destination was Fort Sam Houston in San Antonio, Texas. December 15, 1984. One coach and eight young men had come seeking to fulfill a dream - capturing the *Junior Olympic Cross Country National Championship*. Eight young men hoping to be crowned the best under-18 age-group team in the nation, knowing their dreams would only be a reality if they ran the 5,000 meters as one unit, trusting in each other and their preparation.

The morning of the race the starting line stretched from one end of the field to the other. If you stood at one end, you couldn't even tell what colors the runners on the other end were brandishing. Some of the best high school runners in the United States paced about nervously as the frigid rain continued to descend. Their furrowed brows spoke volumes. One long strand of anxious athletes awaiting the sound of the starter's pistol. An eerie fog hung over the course making it impossible to tell which way the course veered a mere quarter of a mile from the start.

Seeing the heavy breathing and nervous twitches in his runners' bodies, the coach went over to say one last word of encouragement. "We've done the preparation, there's nothing more to do but run. We have what it takes to win it all. I'll be all over the course to encourage you, but I can't run for you. I believe in you! Believe in each other!" Turning to walk away, he overheard one of the runners say, "He really believes we can win!"

A lot of coaches use the word *we*, but this was different. Never were any of these eight young men merely handed a workout as their coach idly sat by yelling out their times as he eyed a stopwatch. It wasn't a matter of Xeroxing off the "how-to's" of the sport, the do's and the don'ts of distance running. He was involved. In the truest sense of the word, they were a *team*.

These young men had seen their coach succeed, fatigue, sweat, tire, even fail. But, they never saw him quit. Every race they ran, he traversed a myriad of routes in order to see his runners at every imaginable, and unimaginable, point in order to encourage them to stay strong. Those times when the runners couldn't see him, they somehow still sensed his presence. They remembered what he had taught them through word and deed. He could not run in the flesh with his runners, but in spirit he was right beside them each step of the way.

And, he would be there for them at the finish line, when hearts are pounding, lungs are searing, and legs have turned to jell-o. When they jettisoned down that final straightaway, the roar of the crowd was but an echo compared to the jubilation that enveloped his very soul - all in an effort to guide them to becoming accomplished runners and true teammates. By the way, they did win it all that day thirty years ago.[36]

Do you want to encourage your athletes? Then be all in. Don't play the "I did my time" card and blah, blah, blah about the glory days. Seriously, who wants to be taught, mentored, trained, or coached by the person who exemplifies, "Do as I say, not as I do"? I seem to remember Jesus having some harsh words for leaders who lived like that. That is the antithesis of encouragement. Are you placing expectations on your athletes' shoulders but doing nothing to help them to carry that load, so that it eventually becomes a crushing burden? There is no better way to encourage your athletes than being a selfless servant rather than a selfish master.

Then Jesus said to the crowds and to his disciples, "The scribes and the Pharisees sit on Moses' seat, so do and observe whatever they tell you, but not the works they do. For they preach, but do not practice. They tie up heavy burdens, hard to bear, and lay them on people's shoulders, but they themselves are not willing to move them with their finger. They do all their deeds to be seen by others. For they make their phylacteries broad and their fringes long, and they love the place of honor at feasts and the best seats in the synagogues and greetings in the marketplaces and being called rabbi by others. But you are not to be called rabbi, for you have one teacher, and you are all brothers. And call no man your father on earth, for you have one Father, who is in heaven. Neither be called instructors, for you have one instructor, the Christ. The greatest among you shall be your servant. Whoever exalts himself will be humbled, and whoever humbles himself will be exalted. (Matthew 23:1-12)

Encourage them by helping them to have fun, to rejoice in the fact that they are blessed to be able to participate. Who do you think performs better on a more consistent basis, joy-filled individuals or direct descendants of Eyeore? It's a game. Inherent in that reality is the fact that it is supposed to be fun. So help your athletes to celebrate well, even when they're tired and hurting or they've made a mistake and lost on the scoreboard. Rejoicing is not based upon circumstances, but on the Savior! "Rejoice in the Lord *always*; again I will say, rejoice… The Lord is at hand; do not be anxious about anything, but in everything by prayer and supplication with thanksgiving let your requests be made known to God. And the peace of God, which surpasses all understanding, will guard your hearts and your minds in Christ Jesus."[37] Teach them by your words and actions to pursue excellence, to focus on what they have practiced, and love them – win, lose, or draw.

> While others will judge you strictly in relation to somebody or something else - the final score, the bottom line, or championship - that is neither the most demanding nor the most productive standard... The highest, purest, and most difficult standard of all, the one that ultimately produces one's finest performance - and the great treasure called "peace of mind" - is that which measures the quality of your personal effort to reach Competitive Greatness.[38] (John Wooden)

I think Coach Wooden must have been meditating on the words of the Apostle Paul when he wrote that. "If anyone thinks he is something, when he is nothing, he deceives himself. But let each one test his own work, and then his reason to boast will be in himself alone and not in his neighbor."[39]

TOOLS

Ω Encouraging Notes

Take time throughout the season to hand write actual notes encouraging each one of your athletes. Yes, I encourage you to text, email, or use the team's Facebook page also. But there's something unique about receiving a handwritten note, especially in the twenty-first century. It's one more way to let them know that you care about them and want the best for them as people and athletes.

Ω Mistake Rituals

"What's Important Now"

Every athlete and coach has those moments crop up when they let their minds wonder and start focusing on past mistakes. At those moments, the most encouraging thing to do is focus on what needs to happen now. This will help everyone to more quickly forget what has occurred in order to reboot and be prepared for what's coming next. "The acronym that can be used to remind athletes to recover quickly from a mistake of theirs or a mistake of a teammate is 'WIN.' It stands for 'what's important now.'[40] It has been said, "One of the best skills an athlete can possess is a short memory." Develop a mistake ritual that is culture-appropriate for your team.

"Flush It"

When one of Mike's players [Mike Legarza, basketball coach at Canada College] made a mistake on the court, his teammates moved their hands up and down as if they were flushing a toilet. This quickly and effectively says that it's okay to make a mistake, let's get past it and focus on the next play. Sometimes they'd yell out 'Flush it!' to each other.[41]

Ω Find the Silver Lining

Let's say you've been teaching your young baseball team how to turn a double play. Game time comes and a ball gets hit sharply to your shortstop. He scoops it up, tosses it the second baseman who steps on the bag, then bobbles the ball getting it out of his glove so he can throw it to first base. In his anxiousness to get it to first base, he throws it harder than usual, and it sails over the first baseman's head. Time to find the silver lining: "Pete, great job scooping up that ball and getting it over to Bill. Bill, you did an excellent job getting that out at second and then firing the ball over to first base. We'll get two next time! Great effort guys, keep it up! Play on!"

Ω PRAYER

"Heavenly Father, the God of endurance and encouragement, your Word tells us that 'We who are strong have an obligation to bear with the failings of the weak, and not to please ourselves.' So empower me to build up and bless my athletes for their own good. For your Son did not come to this earth to please himself, but to honor you by being a Servant. And your Word has been given to instruct your children and give us hope and encouragement. So let my words and actions be inextricably intertwined with your Word so that I live in harmony with my athletes, that together we may glorify you! Holy Spirit, grant me daily discernment how to stir up my athletes to love and good works, to encourage the fainthearted, help the weak, and to be patient with all, so that the souls of your disciples will be encouraged to continue in the faith, and those who do not know you will be drawn towards you by your love. Let my words rain down encouragement and strengthening so that my athletes will not fear making mistakes or failing, but rather that they will wholeheartedly pursue excellence. Enable me to show them the love that you have poured down upon me. For you are my light and my salvation; whom shall I fear? You are the stronghold of my life; of whom shall I be afraid?" (Romans 15:1-6; Hebrews 10:24; 1 Thessalonians 5:14; Acts 15:32; Psalm 27:1)

COMMUNICATE

"Word selection matters. 'The right word is like a drug,' says Amanda Knoke. She means that it diminishes pain and fosters health."[42]

"Let your speech always be gracious, seasoned with salt, so that you may know how you ought to answer each person." (Colossians 4:6)

"There's glory for you!"

"I don't know what you mean by 'glory,'" Alice said.

Humpty Dumpty smiled contemptuously. "Of course you don't – till I tell you. I meant 'there is a nice knock-down argument for you!'"

"But 'glory' doesn't mean 'a nice knock-down argument,'" Alice objected.

"When I use a word," Humpty Dumpty said, in a rather scornful tone, "it means just what I choose it to mean, neither more nor less."[43]

Behavior

This is not how Grace Dispensers communicate. If your athletes need a decoder ring to decipher your messages, you are not extending grace to them. You are not blessing them with the ability to understand what is expected of them. Clarity in communication is critical. Do your athletes have a code of conduct that spells out how they are expected to behave as members of your team? If not, then how are they being held accountable? Guessing games like this will promote a culture of fear. Athletes will always be waiting for the coach's hammer to come crashing down because of behavior or attitude that was deemed 'wrong' for that day, and they will not know whether the same standards will be applicable tomorrow.

Discipline

I'll bet when you read 'discipline' you immediately connected it to the 'behavior' paragraph above. But that's not what I'm talking about here. The type of discipline I'm referring to is what you need to develop in your own life in order to be a Grace Dispenser in all areas of communication with your athletes.

> For me, the two virtues of mindful communication are clarity and discipline. Clarity in verbal communication means conveying intentions, plans, and requirements as precisely as possible… Communication discipline entails coaches constantly weighing the effect of their words and body language and the importance of placing players' needs above their own… To be able to communicate across the generational, gender, and cultural divides requires a connection that helps players understand what we are saying and why we are saying it.[44]

Unfortunately for all of us, we have at one time or another lacked restraint in our communication; which is why I would recommend waiting 24 hours to speak to your athletes if you truly don't have anything positive to tell them. When I look back at my early years coaching, I can't believe some of the ways I communicated through my words and actions. But again, that is one of the main reasons I felt compelled to write this book: "Those who fail to study history are doomed to repeat it." May the words of the Apostle Paul help your future be altered.

'Let no corrupting talk come out of your mouths, but only such as is good for building up, as fits the occasion, that it may give grace to those who hear." (Ephesians 4:29)

Roles

Do your athletes know what role they play on the team? For instance, everyone needs to grasp what it takes to become a 'starter' and to remain one. Do you communicate clearly what individual athletes need to do if they want a different role on the team? New team members need to have these issues spelled out clearly in order to minimize drama and maximize efficiency by showing that each athlete is valued. Veterans need reminders lest they get lax in their attitudes and efforts and start believing that longevity somehow grants them inherent privileges. Failure to help your athletes discern their roles will also create a culture of fear/anxiety.

Gail Goestenkors, the [former] women's basketball coach at Duke University, says it's very important to her to be brutally honest with her players about the roles they have on her team. She has an individual meeting with each player early in the season and lets the athletes know which "piece of the puzzle" the player represents and the success of the team. In addition to telling each athlete where she fits into the scheme of the team, and Gale provides her with feedback on ways to change that role if she is not happy with it. This is a key aspect of this process because she gives the athlete concrete aspects of her game to work on to improve her role if she isn't happy with it.[45]

Listening

Here we come back to where we started this entire chapter: "Be quick to listen." Communication needs to be a two-way street. Are you secure enough in your identity in Christ to allow questions from your athletes? There are many times they seek clarification on a myriad of subjects. Just because you thought you communicated clearly, effectively, and repeatedly does not insure that everyone comprehended your message. If you are married, ask your spouse if you've ever stood there, hands on hips, shaking your head, absolutely befuddled when communication lines failed between the two of you, because you were 'crystal clear' in what you said. The truth is that different personalities learn in different ways. Different athletes have all kinds of thoughts rushing through their minds at any given time. As hard as this might be to swallow, sometimes you just don't communicate as effectively as you think. So you must welcome questions and learn to listen with love in order that everyone may grow in grace together.

Everyone's hearing improves on a team when all voices are perceived as valuable. Respectfully listening to your athletes is probably the best hearing aid you can provide for them! This helps tie together all that we have been discussing in this chapter: "People are more willing to listen to us when they have experienced the refreshment of affirmation from us… People are influenced by those who praise them. Giving praise does wonders for the other person's sense of hearing."[46]

TOOLS

Ω Communicating Clearly During Competition

1. "Communications should be simple and to the point.
2. Beware of your body language. Remember that your athletes will not hear what you say if your body is saying something different.
3. When you give instructions during a timeout… you should ask athletes to repeat what you said or ask them to tell you what they are supposed to do on the next play or in the next few moments… At least when they have to repeat it, you will know they heard what you wanted them to hear.
4. Avoid using the word 'don't' when giving instructions.
5. Following a mistake, try to ask your athletes questions like 'What did you see out there?' or 'What do you think you could have done differently in that situation?'"[47]

Ω Communicating Clearly During Practice

1. "Coaches need to ask themselves: what messages do I need to send to my athletes today at practice?
2. What do I expect from them this week and how will I design our lesson plans to deliver the message?
3. What sort of behavior do I expect from them off the field when they interact with their friends and families and in the community?
4. What do I need to communicate to empower them and prepare them to flourish as fathers [mothers], friends, and citizens of a community, country, and world?
5. We must communicate to them what we expect of ourselves as coaches: to love them and to help them become involved, responsible, and devoted men and women for others."[48]

Ω PRAYER

"Father, your Word tells me that if anyone thinks he is religious and does not bridle his tongue but deceives his heart, this person's religion is worthless. Let that not be true of my life. Fill me with your Holy Spirit so that the words that proceed from my mouth are joy-infusing, life-affirming, and unity-building. Grant me discernment to know when to praise and when to correct, and let it all be done with clarity and love. Help me to be quick to listen, slow to speak, and slow to become angry so that you are honored through all my communications. Let my 'yes' be 'yes,' and my 'no' be 'no' so that my athletes are not left guessing what my true intentions are regarding their behavior and the roles on the team. And when my athletes ask me questions, let my answers always be gracious, seasoned with salt, so that I may know how I ought to answer each person. Let no corrupting talk come out of my mouth, but only such as is good for building up, as fits the occasion, that it may give grace to those athletes who hear." (James 1:26, 1:19, 5:12; Colossians 4:6; Ephesians 4:29)

Notes

1   Dietrich Bonhoeffer, *Life Together: A Discussion of Christian Fellowship* (New York: Harper & Row, 1954), 97.
2   Caplan, Bruce M. (Editor), *The Sinking of the Titanic – 1912 Survivor Accounts* (Bellevue, WA: Seattle Miracle Press, 1997), 50.
3   J. Oswald Sanders, *Spiritual Leadership: Principles of Excellence for Every Believer* (Chicago: Moody, 2007), 73-74.
4   Galatians 6:2.
5   Scott Thomas and Tom Wood, *Gospel Coach: Shepherding Leaders to Glorify God* (Grand Rapids: Zondervan, 2012), 143.
6   Ibid., 152.
7   Bruce Lesley, "Youth Sports, Adult Conduct Disorders and One Shining Moment," *Huffington Post*, 2/19/2013, Accessed 10/26/2013. www.huffingtonpost.com/bruce-lesley/youth-sports_b_2679189.html.
8   Sam Crabtree, *Practicing Affirmation* (Wheaton: Crossway, 2011), 86, 21.
9   Luke 6:26.
10 Crabtree, op. cit., 146-147.
11 Matthew 5:48.
12 Romans 3:22-23.
13 Ecclesiastes 7:20.
14 Sanders, op. cit., 127.
15 Jeff Janssen and Greg Dale, *The Seven Secrets of Successful Coaches: How to Unlock and Unleash Your Team's Full Potential* (Carey: Quality, 2006), 154-160.
16 Jim Thompson, *The Double-Goal Coach: Positive Coaching Tools for Honoring the Game and Developing Winners in Sports and Life* (New York: Harper Collins, 2003), 93.
17 John Piper in Crabtree, op. cit., 7.
18 Ibid., 132.
19 Hans Finzel, *The Top Ten Mistakes Leaders Make* (Colorado Springs: David C. Cook, 2007), 62.
20 Crabtree, op. cit., 50-51.
21 1 Corinthians 4:7.
22 Crabtree, op. cit., 107.
23 Ibid., 71.
24 Romans 11:36.
25 Crabtree, op. cit., 107.

[26] Matthew 5:45.

[27] Crabtree, op. cit., 75.

[28] Brown, op. cit., 56

[29] Crabtree, op. cit., 32.

[30] Ibid., 64-70.

[31] Crabtree, op. cit., 109.

[32] Ibid., 99-101.

[33] Derek de la Pena, *Scripture and Sport Psychology: Mental-Game Techniques for the Christian Athlete* (Lincoln: iUniverse, 2004), 27.

[34] Tony Dungy, *The Mentor Leader: Secrets to Building People and Teams that Win Consistently* (Carol Stream: Tyndale, 2010) 177.

[35] 1 John 4:18, 21.

[36] Chris Schrader, *Catch of the Day* (Spring: Touch of Grace, 2000), 27-29.

[37] Philippians 4:4-7, italics mine.

[38] John Wooden and Steve Jamison, *Wooden on Leadership* (New York: McGraw-Hill, 2005), 57.

[39] Galatians 6:3-4.

[40] Brown, op. cit., 56.

[41] Thompson, op. cit., 52.

[42] Crabtree, op. cit., 146.

[43] Carroll, Lewis, *Through the Looking Glass* (Philadelphia, PA: David McKay, 1912), 110.

[44] Joe Ehrmann with Paula Ehrmann and Gregory Jordan, *Inside Out Coaching: How Sports Can Transform Lives* (New York: Simon & Schuster, 2011), 184-185.

[45] Gail Goestenkors in Jeff Janssen and Greg Dale, *The Seven Secrets of Successful Coaches: How to Unlock Your Team's Full Potential* (Cary: Quality, 2006), 81.

[46] Crabtree, op. cit., 72, 54.

[47] Janssen and Dale, op. cit., 173-174.

[48] Ehrmann, Ehrmann, and Jordan, op. cit., 187.

9

COMMUNITY BUILDER

∞ *How do you build team chemistry?*

"Your relationships with others must be based on your relationship to God through the cross."[1]

"'And you shall love the Lord your God with all your heart and with all your soul and with all your mind and with all your strength.' The second is this: 'You shall love your neighbor as yourself.' There is no other commandment greater than these." (Mark 12:30-31)

Love is the central element of team chemistry. Anything else used as your team's foundation will never allow you to reach the depths that will truly transform lives. Who doesn't want to be loved? Who doesn't need to be loved? We need each other because we are created in the image of God. He is eternally co-existent as Father, Son, and Holy Spirit. We are designed to be in relationships; the search for belonging is part of being human. Athletic teams are in a better position than most entities to provide that sense of belonging, that family. As a coach, you are in a prime position to help educate your athletes on what love truly entails. Let's look at four ways to "pursue love"[2] that will aid in building that chemistry you're looking for.

WE ARE FAMILY

In the movie, *Miracle on Ice*, there is a scene where a handful of Coach Herb Brooks' USA Hockey players confront him after a game. Twenty-one young men have been rigorously training for six months to get ready for the 1980 Winter Olympics. Only twenty will make the final cut. Yet, at this critical juncture, Coach Brooks decides to bring in another player who he thinks can help the team. When the players tell Herb they disagree with his strategy, he asks them why. They said, "Because we're a family!" Herb responds, "And this is the family you want to take with you to Lake Placid?" "Absolutely!" they say in unison.

When you can help the members of your team see one another in this light, they will be a consummate force to be reckoned with. It is one of the key reasons a group of twenty-one year old college hockey players were able to take down the Soviet hockey machine that had dominated international competition for the previous twenty years, including shellacking these same Americans 10-0 less than two weeks before the Olympic Games began. So why is this such a difficult task with most teams?

We live in an isolated world. Facebook friends are seen as normative, and the person sitting across from you gets less attention than the little screen you're holding in your hand. Despite all the technology available to us, our communication skills are at an all-time-low. This can't help but spill over onto our teams. We are "living together alone," and this is killing team chemistry. But Scripture tells us, "And though a man might prevail against one who is alone, two will withstand him—a threefold cord is not quickly broken."[3] The individual "I" falls apart at record paces compared to the three-fold "team."

It's time for you to help your team break free the model that trained individuals to stand alone, to be self-sufficient, and look to the Jewish model, which sought to build a community where followers supported, encouraged, and corrected each other. When you have this, you will have a tight-knit cord that will not easily be broken. Family then becomes a motivation and inspiration to pursue excellence. It's about the team, not any one individual, no matter how good they may be in comparison to their teammates.

These types of programs are not only competitive; they are fun. But how do you teach your athletes that they are playing for the person next to them? How do you get them off the path of self-centered egotism that pervades America today, where even some 'pastors' give sermons intimating that God's entire existence is about making us happy: "When we obey God, we're not doing it for God… We're doing it for ourselves, because God takes pleasure when we're happy. That's the thing that gives him the greatest joy."[4] This self-absorbed navel-gazing has to stop. Consider some of the methods Coach Brad Stevens used when he was at Butler University:

> Coach Stevens told each player to run four 'suicide drills.' They would be timed on each one. The players assumed that they would be evaluated on how fast they could complete it. When the exercise was over, the players' performance statistics were given the Coach Stevens. He stood before the exhausted players and threw the sheets on the floor. Coach Stevens said, "I don't really care how fast you can run 'suicide drills.' I did this exercise to see if any of you would encourage another player to improve their time on the 'suicide drill.' Only two of you did it. Only two of the fourteen players here encouraged another player while they were running this exercise."[5]

> …During an in-season basketball game, if a Butler player falls to the floor during the game, every Butler player on the court will be at his side in seconds… [W]henever a player is replaced on the court and returns to the bench, all the other players on the bench stand up and acknowledge that player for his contribution

to the team, regardless of how well he has done at any particular moment. Every player is spoken to and welcomed when he comes off the court by the coaches and all the players on the bench.[6]

To build this type of team chemistry, you must teach your athletes through word and deed that anything threatening the sanctity of the 'family' must be shunned. Your athletes are making a commitment to love, honor, respect, care, and fight for each other. It is one of the reasons gangs are so successful. You are a member for a lifetime and you know that your brothers or sisters always have your back. I'm obviously not advocating gangs - but they do have part of the concept correct. "A friend loves at all times, and a brother is born for adversity."[7] And Jesus told his disciples, "A new commandment I give to you, that you love one another: just as I have loved you, you also are to love one another. By this all people will know that you are my disciples, if you have love for one another."[8] Did you catch especially how critical it is for those on your team who are Christians to love one another? "By this all people will know that you are my disciples!" Loving each other equates to belonging to God.

The 'best place to play' means you love the guys you're playing with. It means you develop deep relationships that go well beyond [your sport]. It means you have awesome team chemistry where what the team needs is more important than what you need - and you fully buy-in to that. It means you fight for game time, but you don't hold that against your teammate - that you're not mad when you're subbed out, but instead, you're excited for the guy who came in for you. And it means that we have each other's back.[9]

To be a family means that your team members are continually looking for ways to "serve one another in love,"[10] to "outdo one another in showing honor."[11] As the coach, you need to help your athletes to be aware of times when selfish motives and ambitions are rising to the surface. When this happens, service and honor wane quickly. At those times you must remind them what a team is all about – when your teammates succeed, you succeed! "By this we know love, that he laid down his life for us, and we ought to lay down our lives for the brothers."[12] You want to develop athletes who understand that the goal is to become the best teammate. That is what family is all about - "us", not "I." Are you teaching your athletes to lay down their lives for their teammates?

TOOLS

Ω **How do you deal with the inevitable conflict that arises on your team, as it does in any family?**

"1.   **Have I Prayed?**
2.   **What is my motive?**
3.   **Am I striving to edify others?**

4. **Have I sought counsel?**
5. **Would I not rather be wronged?** When someone has criticized us, fairly or not, publicly or privately, it is not always necessary to respond...
6. **How will I treat the person with whom I disagree?** [With love or animosity?]
7. **Am I involving a bigger audience than necessary?** Is this a public or private matter?
8. **Am I the right person to engage?**
9. **What is my ultimate goal?** ...Will our engagement further advance the gospel and love for God and neighbor? ...
10. **Am I focused on God's glory?**"[13]

Ω A Checklist of Friendship Qualities.

Pray for these to be normative for your team, starting with you as the head of the family.

1. "*Integrity* – it means promises are backed up, confidences are kept, and people are treated with respect.
2. *Vulnerability* – Friendships do not develop without some degree of risk.
3. *Humility* – Some leaders cannot have friends because they are in competition with everyone else. Humility, on the other hand, allows leaders to accept that they are less talented than someone else in some areas [For instance, why have 'position' coaches in some sports?].
4. *Willingness to Listen* – Leaders are used to being heard. Great leaders know how to listen. The act of listening is a gift to a friend. It takes time to hear what someone is revealing about her heart, not just what she is saying with her lips.
5. *Sensitivity and Responsiveness* – Friends respond to friends with sensitivity in ways that are appropriate to the situation, that take into account the personalities involved, and that acknowledge the level of accountability and caring that the relationship can sustain. Friends know when to help and how to help.
6. *Realistic Expectations* – Many friendships fail to mature because of unrealistic expectations on the part of one or both parties. Friends will at some point fail us. Can we forgive them? Can others' shortcomings be overlooked for the sake of friendship? Are we willing to extend grace to others? Leaders with a landscape littered with broken relationships probably suffer from unrealistic expectations of others."[14]

Ω A Checklist of Family Qualities

1. [*Parental-type Love*] "Stan Morrison, when he was head basketball coach at San Jose State University, described how he told his recruits that he was available to them 24 hours a day for the rest of their lives... In essence, Morrison was telling his players that they could treat him like a father.

2. *Named and Known* – [M]ake it a point to greet each player by name at the beginning of *every* practice.
3. *Physical Greetings* - People thrive from supportive touching. Pats on the back, shaking hands… [or] The physical greeting I've used often is a simple fist tap.
4. *Communication Cues* - Teams with strong cultures have their own ways of communicating - the equivalent of a secret password that contributes to a feeling of family."[15]

Ω PRAYER

"Heavenly Father, build my team into a true family where we are kind to one another, tenderhearted, forgiving one another, as you have forgiven us through your Son. Help each of us to constantly be seeking ways we can serve one another in love. If we live this way, we will bear one another's burdens and fulfill the law of Christ, so you will be glorified and joy will be brought to the team. So empower us through your Holy Spirit to genuinely love one another, abhor evil and cling to what is good. Help us to love one another with brotherly affection and seek to outdo each other in showing honor. Let our team be so tightly knit together that we rejoice with those who rejoice and weep with those who weep. Let others see that we truly live in harmony and seek the best for each other. Let none of us be arrogant, but rather may we reach out our hands to lift up those who may not be as talented as we are. In all things let us honor one another and seek to live peaceably with all. For as we love each other as you have loved us, Lord Jesus, all people will know we are your disciples. May this type of love draw many to the cross where they will find forgiveness and eternal life, whether they are members of our team or are outside of our family." (Ephesians 4:32; Galatians 5:13; Romans 12:9-10, 15-18; John 13:34-35)

UNITY, NOT UNIFORMITY

"I'm not looking for the best players. I'm looking for the right players." (Herb Brooks, 1980 US Olympic hockey coach, *Miracle on Ice*)

"Now the full number of those who believed were of one heart and soul, and no one said that any of the things that belonged to him was his own, but they had everything in common." (Acts 4:32)

"Now there are varieties of gifts, but the same Spirit; and there are varieties of service, but the same Lord; and there are varieties of activities, but it is the same God who empowers them all in everyone. (1 Corinthians 12:4-6)

If you want to have a team that pursues excellence, a team where lives are transformed, they must have a united purpose – "of one heart and soul [mind]." A group of superstars playing together does not necessarily result in a successful team. Why not? Because more often than not, egos get in the way. Too many all-star teams rely upon individual talent.

> "The way a team plays as a whole determines its success. You may have the greatest bunch of individual stars in the world, but if they don't play together, the club won't be worth a dime." (Babe Ruth)

> "In order to have a winner, the team must have a feeling of unity; every player must put the team first – ahead of personal glory." (Paul 'Bear' Bryant)[16]

> Don't let jealousy and selfish ambition be a part of you. For where jealousy and selfish ambition exist, there will be disorder and every vile practice. (James 3:16)

A loving community where everyone is honored and respected is built upon the truth that all members are valuable. God has designed each athlete on your team to fulfill a specific purpose. In the spiritual realm, "Everyone has some gifts, therefore all should be encouraged. Nobody has all the gifts, therefore all should be humble. All gifts are from the Lord, therefore all should be contented."[17] The same holds true in the world of sports. An individual cannot win a team sport by himself or herself. Not even Lebron James or Michael Jordan could win without at least four other teammates playing alongside them. Your athletes are different, so don't try to fit them all into one mold. Celebrate unity, not uniformity.

∞ *What is the difference between unity and uniformity?*

Let's use evangelism as an example. I will venture to say that all justified, blood-bought Christians are unified in the belief that we are called to share the gospel with the world, to participate in The Great Commission. But who thinks that we should all be doing it exactly the same way? This is an example of uniformity.

> There are basically two kinds of evangelism – confrontational and relational. It's the confrontational one that is embedded in most people's minds. Confrontational evangelism is an all-or-nothing encounter that encourages a person to receive Christ right then and there and attempts to "close the deal," as it were, on the spot – from door-to-door calling, open air meetings, campus blitzes with *Four Spiritual Law* booklets, to the sweat-drenched revival preacher and the zealot on the street corner.

> The apostle Peter was the master of this genre. On the day of Pentecost in Acts 2, Peter proclaimed, "Would you like to know why the Messiah isn't here? Because you killed him!" Not very politically correct, but it worked. It was perfect for that setting. His hearers were "cut to the heart" and 3,000 came to Christ that very day.

In Luke Chapter 3, we see an example of the relational method of evangelism. Matthew the tax collector wanted to reach his peers with the gospel. How did he do it? The way business people still influence their colleagues – over a meal. At a banquet for all his tax collecting friends, Matthew introduced them to Jesus. His evangelism was one of networking, food, and friendship.

What is the best way to be a "fisher for men?" The *Four Spiritual Laws, Evangelism Explosion, Friendship Evangelism, Street Corner Preaching...?* That's tantamount to asking is one a better fisherman if he uses a standard rod and reel or prefers fly-fishing? Which is best, deep-sea fishing, or mountain streams or lakes?

Is there truly a *best* method to use? Jesus and His little band of fisherman didn't use one method, one means to fish. We don't have to either. We have been given freedom in fishing! Freedom to use your unique blend of spiritual gifts, personalities, passions, and experiences to join in on the greatest fishing expedition of all time![18]

It is no different with coaching. This is where your ability to be an artist comes into play. It's not enough to merely ask, "What needs to done to help our team become the best they can possibly be?" You need to also ask, "What is the best way to accomplish this with the individuals that I have on my team?" There are a myriad of ways to help athletes master different skills. Just because one athlete thrives and excels on certain drills doesn't mean all your athletes will respond likewise. You need to know the strengths and weaknesses of each member of your team in order to design workouts that will promote excellence in all. Don't assume an athlete is lazy, contentious, or not a good team player when they don't like some of your workouts. "One facet of leadership is the ability to recognize the special abilities and limitations of others, combined with the capacity to get each one into the job where he or she will do best."[19]

For instance, a standard workout for many distance runners who compete in the 5,000 meter race is a four-mile tempo run at around 80% of their race pace. I've had runners who could do every other type of workout well. But every time this one rolled around, dread came across their faces. They were hard workers. They raced well. But they struggled mightily with a four-mile tempo run. Rather than telling them to "suck it up," I changed workouts for them. They would run one mile four times with a minute break after each mile. That little break made all the difference for their attitude and workouts, and it segued over nicely into races. Take the time to let your athletes share what workouts energize them and which ones drain them, and why. It can be a valuable tool in learning their strengths and weaknesses as you pursue a unified goal without expecting uniformity in workouts.

Another key aspect in building unity is making sure that everyone knows that they are a vital member of the team. It's not enough to say it. They need to experience it. Your starters are going to get the exposure to kudos from the crowds. What about your non-starters? Do they truly feel that they are important in achieving the team goals? In other words, your coaching needs to build a culture where all roles have equal value. I know what you're thinking, "I can hear the scoffing from the world already." But who cares? Your ultimate goal is not the same as the world's. You are seeking to help transform the life of every athlete on your team, through the pursuit of excellence in order that Jesus may be honored above everything else.

> *There are no little people in your organization* [on your team]. Years ago, Francis Schaeffer wrote a significant book titled *no little people*. He argued that in God's view there are no little people and no little places. All have equal value to matter where they are found and what they do. I think the same principle should be practiced by every Christian leader in our attitudes about the far-flung corners of their organizations. Everyone is important.[20]

Building unity is going to mean putting your players in their place from time to time. The forward who scores a goal in soccer and runs away from her teammates to parade around in front of the fans needs to be put in her place. The basketball center who slam dunks and then proceeds to wag his head and thump his chest needs to be put in his place. The wide receiver who scores on a forty-yard pass play and walks around the end zone with his arms folded across his chest needs to be put in his place. Why? Because in each of these scenarios they have forgotten to acknowledge the team. Not one of them could have scored without the assistance of a teammate.

More importantly, however, is the fact that these attitudes do not show that Jesus is the Greatest Treasure. If you are coaching non-Christians who are behaving like this, it is a prime time to teach them about humility in the hopes that they will comprehend that their talents and abilities aren't all based on their awesomeness. And, Lord willing, it will drive the point home that the name on the front of the uniform is more important than the one on the back. And neither of those names compares in the least to the name above all names.

TOOLS

Ω Building Unity through Celebrating Diversity of Skills, Personalities, Backgrounds

Read John 4:1-30 (Jesus and the Woman of Samaria), then try to answer the following questions in light of your coaching. Are you seeking unity or uniformity?

1. "How can you learn to be flexible and deal with diversity, to see others who aren't like you in a way that allows you to meet them where they are and to help them become all they can be?
2. How can you accept people from differing backgrounds and foster their growth without abandoning your own culture and beliefs [your biblical faith]?
3. How do you value people who are different just as much as you value those who are similar to you?"[21]

Ω Building Unity through Celebrating the Less Talented

Consider implementing the following methods used by John Wooden to celebrate the athletes on your team who are rarely receive any kudos from the crowd.

"I was conscientious about making those with less significant roles feel valued and appreciated. I singled out individuals who seldom saw the limelight - the player who made an assist on an important basket, a pivotal defensive play, or a free throw at a crucial moment in the game. I was also careful to give recognition to those who did not get much playing time - the players who worked hard in practice to improve not only themselves but also their teammates who were receiving more game time… I avoided using the term *substitutes* for those who are not on the starting team. *Substitute* is a demeaning term for one who is fully executing his role on the team. A player was a starter or nonstarter, but never a substitute."[22]

Ω Building Unity through Switching Positions

If you want to help your athletes become more thankful for the roles their teammates play, have them occasionally switch positions/roles during a practice or scrimmage.

"Sometimes during practice, he [John Wooden] would have the guard switch positions with the forwards - have us do the other guy's job. He wanted everybody to understand the requirements of the player in the other positions. Coach Wooden wanted the guard to appreciate the challenges a forward faced and the forward to appreciate what a guard had to deal with. He worked very hard to figure out ways to have us think like a team, to work as a unit, not every man out for himself."[23]

Ω Building Unity through Your Home

Opening up your home not only gives your athletes an opportunity to build unity outside of practice and games, it allows them to see you in a different light also. If you seek to transform lives, pursue excellence, and honor Jesus through your coaching – you need to show them you are more than just a coach. And who doesn't desire to be part of a home where they are known and loved? "Practice hospitality." (Romans 12:13)

"To build team unity and spirit, Tracy Stevens [wife of former Butler Coach, Brad Stevens] hosts the basketball team, assistant coaches, and their families once a month. The players love to come for a home-cooked meal that she and the wives of the assistant coaches provide, and they appreciate the opportunity to get away from the pressures of college and basketball. With all the coaches' families present, they see their coaches as good husbands to their wives and fathers to their children."[24]

Ω Building Unity through Outside Activities

Athletes need to have time to interact in fun ways outside of the sports realm. For instance, the Baylor Women's Cross Country team has *Sunday Fundays* where they invite anyone who wants to come. It may be as simple as a group getting frozen yogurt together, seeing a movie, or playing volleyball. If you have a youth program, parents can plan an activity like bowling or a pizza party or a myriad of other activities. These not only help build team bonding and unity, but they also help everyone to remember life is so much more than sports.

Ω PRAYER

"Father God, I need your help in guiding our team. Do not allow me to be lazy by seeking uniformity for the sake of ease. Help me to remember that you created each athlete in a unique way to participate on this team. Please, do not allow anyone to think more highly of himself than he should. For just as the body of Christ has many members that do not all have the same function, so also each athlete on this team has a role to play. And no role is more important than another. The quarterback can't say to the center, 'I don't need you.' The wide receiver can't say to the quarterback, 'I don't need you.' And the running back can't say to the offensive lineman, 'I don't need you.' For if the entire team was comprised solely of quarterbacks, wide receivers, or running backs, the team would not function properly. Help all of us to look kindly upon those teammates who put in the effort day in and day out, with no apparent reward because they receive little playing time. Help us to celebrate their effort and input, because they help make each member of the team stronger. Let there be no division on our team. Unify us so that when one suffers, the entire team suffers. And when one rejoices, all rejoice. By the precious name of our Lord Jesus Christ, let all of us be united in the same mind because a team divided against itself cannot stand." (1 Corinthians 12:12-26; 1:10; Mark 3:24)

GOOD WORKS IN THE WORLD

"Sports have spread to every corner of the world, transcending differences between cultures and nations. Because of the global dimensions this activity has assumed, those involved in sports throughout the world have a great responsibility."[25] (Pope John Paul II)

"You are the light of the world. A city set on a hill cannot be hidden. Nor do people light a lamp and put it under a basket, but on a stand, and it gives light to all in the house. In the same way, let your light shine before others, so that they may see your good works and give glory to your Father who is in heaven." (Matthew 5:14-16)

Don't confine being a community builder to your team. In order to seek to fulfill your part of The Great Commission and The Greatest Commandment, you must search for ways to impact the world in which your team operates. The guiding principle for outward movement can be found in the words of Jesus to his disciples, immediately before he ascended back into heaven: "But you will receive power when the Holy Spirit has come upon you, and you will be my witnesses in Jerusalem and in all Judea and Samaria, and to the end of the earth."[26] Jerusalem was where the disciples were residing when they received this command from Jesus. From that home base, they were to carry the gospel in ever-widening concentric circles out into the entire world.

As a coach, you can look at Jerusalem as being your team. Judea can be the immediate community in which your team operates – a school, town, and the fans. Samaria would be those people outside this circle of 'known' people. Consider opposing teams, their fans, and local towns. The entire world means just what it says. Not many of us believe that coaching a sport can have that type of impact. But with today's social media, news can spread like a wildfire. Why not give the community beyond your team good works to cheer for; something that will point towards the glory of your Father who is in heaven?

In 2012, Meghan Vogel received more applause and attention for coming in dead last in the 3200 meter race at the Ohio State Track meet than she did for winning the 1600 meter race she ran earlier. Vogel's stellar race in the 1600 left her depleted when it came time for the longer race. She was in last place with about 100 meters to go. About 20 meters from the finish line, Arden McMath's legs began to cramp and she collapsed to the track. Instead of going by her, Meghan helped her to her feet and bolstered her up so she could make it to the finish line. When they reached the line, Meaghan made sure that Arden finished in front of her. The crowd gave them a standing ovation, breaking out in heartfelt, roaring applause.

Following the standing ovation, Vogel told the Springfield News-Sun, "Helping her across the finish line was a lot more satisfying than winning the state championship. If you work that hard to get to the state meet, you deserve to finish no matter who you are." Even though the rules state that a runner should be automatically disqualified for aiding another runner, the officials chose to ignore it. They truly understood the significance of what occurred that day. All those in attendance will long remember her act of grace exhibited in the 3200, while her 1600 meter championship will soon fade into distant memories. As McMath's coach so aptly stated, "What a selfless act. She could have just gone around Arden. But she chose to help. I've never seen that at a state meet. That's real sportsmanship." Perhaps we all could learn a lesson from the slogan that was printed on the front of Meghan's shirt, and apparently emblazoned on her soul, "Part speed. Part stamina. All heart."

Now imagine this same scenario if you, as her coach, had an opportunity to address the media. These types of selfless acts are seemingly so rare in our world today that they go viral. What a wonderful opportunity to share why you coach the way you do, and why your athletes live the way they do. These are teachable moments when you can seek to build up the greater community by helping them to see and savor who Jesus is and how he calls his children to live.

∞ How else can you use your coaching as a tool to reach the greater community beyond your team?

1. *Schools*

No matter what age group you coach, are you doing your part in making sure that your athletes are doing well in school? The tone that is set in youth sports can carry over into high school and college. Help 'student-athlete' become more than a catchy phrase that seeks to soothe our collective conscience when we are all too aware that academics regularly take a backseat to athletics. Imagine the impact on faculty and staff if you concerned yourself with your athletes' academic progress.

2. *Service*

Look for ways, as a team, to serve the community where you live. If you're too busy to have a few work days during a season, you're too busy. I'm not saying you have to devote an entire day to this, but can you spare a few hours every season? Your role as a coach is not just to aid in the pursuit of academic and athletic excellence. You also need to help your team understand their ever-increasing roles and responsibilities as citizens as they grow older. These times together will not only help the community see that your team cares about more than sports. It will also help your athletes mature as you help them see the needs of the world around them.

3. *Opposing Players and Coaches*

"Do unto others as you would have them do unto you."[27] How are you helping your athletes to treat their opponents with honor, respect, and dignity? Help your athletes be thankful for the privilege of competing against other teams. Do not allow them to vilify opponents in order to get 'fired up' to play. I've heard some Christian coaches tell their teams to "look at Jesus as your teammate or your coach." But I've yet to hear someone tell them to "look at your opponent as if he was Jesus." Ask them, "Would you treat Jesus the same way as you treat your opponents who are made in his image?" Coach, lead the way by your example interacting with opposing coaches. Communicate clearly, concisely, and effectively before the game how you seek to have your team honor and respect their opponents. After the game, take time to truly thank the opposing coach for the opportunity to compete against his team.

If you are coaching in either a Christian school, or somewhere you have the freedom to openly share your faith, here are some other ways to seek to serve opposing players and coaches:

> We constantly encourage one another to live our faith, on and off the court. We pray before every game to be Christ to our opponents and to the people who come to watch us play. We invite our opponents to pray with us after every game, taking the opportunity to forgive and seek forgiveness whenever necessary.[28]

4. *Youth Sports Parents*

By helping parents understand the culture you seek to develop through your coaching, you have a unique opportunity to counter the individualistic and narcissistic air they and their children can't help but inhale. Someone needs to counter the "It's all about me" or "It's all about my baby" mentality. Why not you? The lunacy in the stands needs to stop. You can help show them a better way. In doing so, others in the sporting community will see that your parents behave differently, and they'll want to know why.

[T]he holy father [Pope John Paul II] himself invited sportsmen "to make sports an opportunity for meeting and dialogue, over and above every barrier of language, race or culture. Sports, in fact, can make an effective contribution to peaceful understanding between peoples and to establishing the new civilization of love."[29]

TOOLS

Ω Good Works in Schools

If you coach in high school or college, consider having your athletes sit in the first three rows of all their classes. Let them know that their attendance, participation, and seating are all part of what it means to be on your team. Trust me, the teachers will be influenced by conscientious athletes in the classroom. If one of your athletes is struggling, find a way to get them extra help. Don't let them settle for the minimum standards that will allow them to participate in sports. Help them to aim higher and to pursue excellence in the classroom. If you are a youth coach, regularly sprinkle your team meetings with encouragements to be good students. Don't hesitate to ask each of your athletes individually how school is going. You don't have a lot of authority in this situation, but that doesn't mean you can't wield some healthy influence.

Ω Good Works through Service

Ask if there are volunteer opportunities at your school, or the local ball fields, gyms, or tracks where you play. Find a non-profit in your community and have your team volunteer there once a month. Find local fundraisers that need volunteers for special events. Talk to local churches to see if there are older people in their congregation who could use help with work around their house or yard. Other places to consider asking about volunteer opportunities are neighborhood associations, and local police and fire stations.

Ω Good Works among Parents - Develop a Parents' Code of Conduct

At the earliest possible time, have a parents' meeting. It is best to have a face-to-face meeting rather than rely upon written communications. Make it mandatory that at least one parent for each athlete comes to the meeting. Let the parents know that you are looking forward to coaching their kids, and it is extremely important that everyone is on the same page with behavioral expectations of athletes and parents. You may catch a little flack for this from some parents, but they need to know what culture you are trying to develop. Clear communication from the outset will help ward off additional problems in the future. Consider doing a search for "Joe Ehrmann and Parents Code of Conduct" for an example.

Ω Daily pray for the coach/coaches you will face each week.

Check the appendices for numerous example of how to pray for opposing coaches.

Ω Good Works to Parents – Playing Time

How do you handle the parents who come to you asking, pleading, or demanding more playing time for their child? Simply tell them that you are amenable to the idea on one condition. The parents have to contact all the other parents so you can have a team meeting with all parties present. At that time, the parents seeking more playing time will have the opportunity to share their request before everyone.

Ω PRAYER

"Heavenly Father, grant me wisdom how to stir up my athletes to love and good works because you said that I, as part of the body of Christ, am a light of the world. So let my light so shine before my team, that they may see my good works so that you will be glorified. Let my community-building example impact our entire team. And let all glory go to you as our team serves each other, our local community, and beyond. Fill me with your Spirit so that I have discernment where you want our team to serve so that our community is built up. There are a multitude of needs on any team, in any school or community – so show us where you want us to serve. For you said those of us who are your children will receive power through the Holy Spirit to be witnesses at home and beyond to your glory and greatness, your grace and good news. We commit our ways to you and acknowledge that you alone are the Creator, Redeemer, and Sustainer. Make our paths straight. Empower us to walk in wisdom towards those who are not your children, making the best use our time. Let your children's speech be always gracious, flowing with love, so that we will know how to answer each person in a way that will draw them nearer to you. And let each of us use the gifts we have received to serve one another in love, as good stewards of your grace. In this way we will fulfill your entire law that is summed up, 'You shall love your neighbor as yourself.'" (Hebrews 10:24; Matthew 5:14-16; Acts 1:8; Proverbs 3:6; Colossians 4:5-6; 1 Peter 4:10; Galatians 5:14)

LEARNING TO DIE TO YOURSELF

"The true meaning of life is to plant trees under whose shade you do not expect to sit." (Nelson Henderson)[30]

"Greater love has no one than this, that someone lay down his life for his friends." (John 15:13)

To End All Wars [is] the autobiographical account by Ernest Gordon, a British Army officer captured by the Japanese during World War II and assigned to the building off the Burma-Siam railway. Each day Gordon joined a work detail of prisoners to build a track bed through low-lying swampland… Gordon could feel himself gradually wasting away from a combination of beriberi, worms, malaria, dysentery, typhoid, and diphtheria. Paralyzed and unable to eat, he asked to be laid in the Death House. Gordon's friends, however, had other plans… For most of the war, the prison camp had served as a laboratory of survival of the fittest, every man for himself. Men lived like animals, and for a long time hate was the main motivation to stay alive.

Recently, though, a change had come. One event in particular shook the prisoners. A Japanese guard discovered that a shovel was missing. When no one confessed to the theft, he screamed, "All die! All die!" and raised his rifle to fire at the first man in the line. At that instant an enlisted man stepped forward and said, "I did it." Enraged, the guard lifted his weapon high in the air and brought the rifle butt down on the soldier's skull, killing him. That evening when tools were inventoried again, the work crew discovered a mistake had been made: No shovel was missing.

Gordon's book tells of a transformation within the camp so complete that when liberation finally came, the prisoners treated their sadistic guards with kindness and not revenge Attitudes in the camp began to shift. With no prompting, prisoners began looking out for each other rather than themselves… The miracle at the River Kwai was no less than the creation of an alternate community, a tiny settlement of the kingdom of God taking root in the least likely soil.[31]

Forgiveness: One of the initial ways that you can help build an "alternate community" is by modeling forgiveness. If it's true that "all have sinned and fallen short of the glory of God,"[32] why do we get so angry when we are the ones who are sinned against? Rarely does that same anger flow forth when we are the ones perpetrating ill deeds upon others. Yet frustration often boils to the surface when we believe that we have been treated unfairly, whether it was intentional or not. One of the greatest examples you can give your athletes is teaching them how to die to themselves by learning to forgive one another, because love "keeps no record of wrongs."[33] Therefore, you must pray for a forgiving heart: "Be kind to one another, tenderhearted, forgiving one another, as God in Christ forgave you."[34]

Forgiving one another can be extremely difficult, but it is commanded. One way to limit the need for having to forgive each other is by seeking the Spirit's empowering to not offend each other. The Messiah College soccer program has some wisdom to pass on in this area:

> Messiah addresses this threat through their principle of "mean no offense, take no offense." Teammates are to say nothing and do nothing that undermines one another, and on the receiving end, they're not to interpret comments or actions as personal attacks. The default assumption is that no one in this program does anything to harm or disparage anyone else – so don't do it and don't hear it that way… "[T]here's not even to be a snicker at a teammate's expense"… [I]f at practice a guy shows some body language that publicly implies frustration with a teammate, a coach pulls him aside and reminds him: "that's not how we react here."[35]

"We" Not "Me": As the penultimate leader of the team, you must help your athletes to stop thinking mainly as individuals and begin developing a "team first" mentality. It's about the name on the front of the uniform, not the one on the back. For that reason, I've always gravitated towards sports and schools that don't have players' names on their jerseys. As was discussed earlier, a primary method to teach the team concept is by showing each member of the team that they are a vital to the team's success. When each athlete is valued, it is much more likely that they will buy into the "we, not me" mantra.

Team leaders, coaches and captains, help to shape a team culture by being servants. It is imperative that you teach your athletes to be willing, if necessary, to sacrifice their personal goals for the good of the team. Team goals are more important than individual ones. Selfish athletes do not think in terms of "we." Consider how many teams have had a cadre of great players on them, but won no team titles. Why is that? Why could a group of collegiate hockey players in 1980 knock off the greatest ice hockey power in the world, yet our professional all-stars since that time have lacked the same success? Selfless versus selfish. We versus me.

If you are going to be the primary mover behind the "we, not me" movement, you must honestly question why you recruit and choose the players you do. How many times have you read about collegiate and professional coaches willingly taking an athlete with questionable character traits/issues because they can help the team become more competitive? That mentality filters all the way down to some youth teams. I'm not saying that people shouldn't be given a second chance. But be wary of the motives behind your choices. If you fail to think about how team chemistry might be disrupted by your choice, the "we" will quickly crumble.

Consider the fact that as I write this, three prominent football players are potentially wreaking havoc on their team's chemistry by their poor character exhibited through their appalling actions. Ray Rice has been indefinitely suspended by the Baltimore Ravens and the NFL because he beat his fiancé, who has since become his wife. Adrian Peterson has similarly vacated the premises of the Minnesota Vikings until the judicial system decides his case for punishing his four-year-old son with a switch that left the boy with multiple lacerations. Jameis Winston, the phenom red-shirt freshman quarterback from Florida State won the Heisman Trophy last year while being under suspicion for sexual assault charges. Since then he was in trouble for stealing crab legs, and just today is in trouble for jumping on a table in the Student Union at FSU and shouting a sexual obscenity demeaning women. You may win more games, like FSU, but at what cost? "The Messiah method rejects the assumption that we must choose between players of the highest caliber and players of the highest character."[36]

> ... [T]he practice of youth sports offers some common ground where the values of the "sports culture" and many gospel values intersect and can complement one another. For example, youth sports offer real face-to-face social interaction and team experience-something rare in an age of "virtual reality." In an age of individualism, sports still involve team play. Community sports provide places where people can work together toward a common goal such as playing a game. In an age of comfort, if not all-out hedonism, sports still speak about making sacrifices. While licentiousness is involved, sports proposed rules and restraints. Thus, we must not underestimate the opportunities sport offers the youth in today's media-dominated culture. Rather, we must capitalize on the many opportunities implicit in sport.[37]

Serve the Less Fortunate: Have you ever been the last person picked to participate in a game, the one nobody wants on their team? Or perhaps you had that queasy feeling in your stomach as you watched that person go through the angst and embarrassment of being the last one standing, again…the perpetual sports leper. The seeds of 'winning at all costs' are sown early in the lives of most kids, foundationally through parents and coaches. But how does this fit into a biblical theology that calls Christians to die to themselves and care for the weak, the neglected, the despised, and the outcasts – the "least of these"? A God-glorifying coach will consciously seek to teach her athletes to seek out and serve people like this. "We who are strong have an obligation to bear with the failings of the weak, and not to please ourselves. Let each of us please his neighbor for his good, to build him up."[38] If this isn't motivation enough for you, then may the following words of our Lord sink deep into your very soul and cause a massive transformation in your thinking and actions:

> When the Son of Man comes in his glory, and all the angels with him, then he will sit on his glorious throne. Before him will be gathered all the nations, and he will

separate people one from another as a shepherd separates the sheep from the goats. And he will place the sheep on his right, but the goats on the left. Then the King will say to those on his right, 'Come, you who are blessed by my Father, inherit the kingdom prepared for you from the foundation of the world. For I was hungry and you gave me food, I was thirsty and you gave me drink, I was a stranger and you welcomed me, I was naked and you clothed me, I was sick and you visited me, I was in prison and you came to me.' Then the righteous will answer him, saying, 'Lord, when did we see you hungry and feed you, or thirsty and give you drink? And when did we see you a stranger and welcome you, or naked and clothe you? And when did we see you sick or in prison and visit you?' And the King will answer them, 'Truly, I say to you, as you did it to one of the least of these my brothers, you did it to me.' "Then he will say to those on his left, 'Depart from me, you cursed, into the eternal fire prepared for the devil and his angels. For I was hungry and you gave me no food, I was thirsty and you gave me no drink, I was a stranger and you did not welcome me, naked and you did not clothe me, sick and in prison and you did not visit me.' Then they also will answer, saying, 'Lord, when did we see you hungry or thirsty or a stranger or naked or sick or in prison, and did not minister to you?' Then he will answer them, saying, 'Truly, I say to you, as you did not do it to one of the least of these, you did not do it to me.' And these will go away into eternal punishment, but the righteous into eternal life." (Matthew 25:31-46)

Honestly reflect on your coaching and your outreach to the community at large. How are you doing in serving the "least of these"? How are you encouraging your athletes to serve those who are less fortunate? Before you completely disregard this section because you think it is not applicable to your present coaching situation, I encourage you to continue reading. Every coach at every level of athletics can be involved in serving "the least of these" to some capacity. "For Christians, particularly, sport can also be seen as a ministry to the weak and segregated. Through sport they gain new hope and may return or be included into the community. This practical commitment to foreigners, immigrants, and the unemployed, and especially to the physically and mentally disabled, is an act of solidarity and a contribution to social integration."[39]

If you think it's tough becoming integrated into society because you're the last person picked for a team, imagine what it's like to never be picked, to never be asked to participate. For most of the history of sports, this has been the plight of those devalued because of some physical or mental issue in their lives. Consider the fact that at the 1992 Paralympics, admission was free. Why? Because the organizing committee didn't think that anyone would pay to watch "disability sport." Twenty years later, the 2012 London Paralympics were virtually sold out for every event! Yet the Christian community as a whole is still lagging behind in reaching out to these special needs individuals from youth sports and upward. If you think, like I do, that a biblical theology of coaching is hard to locate, good luck finding any Christian theological reflection on disability and sport for coaches. So how can we begin this reflection? Consider the following three stories of how athletes themselves, ages 9-17, served the "least of these" in their lives. May they motivate you to prayerfully consider how you and your team might also serve those in the special needs community:

Conner Long is the older brother who just wanted to do normal things like playing outside and biking with his younger brother, Cayden. But Cayden can't walk or speak because he has Spastic Cerebral Palsy. Somehow that didn't stop young 7-year-old Conner from dreaming. In the spring of 2011, Conner saw something in a *Nashville Parent's Magazine* that changed everything – an ad for a kid's triathlon. Conner asked his mom if he could participate with Cayden. That very day Team Long Brothers was birthed. On June 5, 2011 at the Nashville Kids Triathlon, joy knew no bounds. Conner pulled Cayden in a raft for the swim portion, had a trailer attached to his bicycle for the second leg, and finished the triathlon pushing Cayden in a trailer triumphantly through the finish line. No they didn't win the race. But that wasn't the point. It was about two brothers having fun and drawing ever-closer to each other by competing together. What motivates this young boy to exhibit such love towards his brother?

"What I like best about it is that we're together, and I don't have to do it by myself. Without Cayden it wouldn't be a team," said Conner. "I didn't want Cayden left on the sidelines because it isn't fair towards him. I don't know what I would do without Cayden. I just want him to finish," said Conner. He wants the world to see his brother through his eyes. "He still has regular feelings like we do and he understands what you say about him," Conner said when asked about his brother's physical impairment and inability to verbalize. "When I see him smiling and laughing that means he's having a good time." But it doesn't just stop with Cayden. Team Long Brothers wants to help many other people to see with clarity the potential blessings that await. According to their website, the "ultimate goal of Team Long Brothers is to form a not-for-profit organization which will provide advice, emotional, spiritual and financial support to groups and families of disabled children. We aim to help to build confidence, hope and self-esteem to the disabled by including them in family and community activities. Our mission is to provide a series of support groups for the disabled and the families of disabled individuals. We would also like to be able to provide disabled families with wheel chairs, bicycles and accessible playground equipment."

The Olivet Eagles football team at Olivet Middle School in Olivet, Michigan, decided to run a play and intentionally not score, all without their coaches knowing. The football team planned the play for weeks, all so they could set up a very special moment for a special boy. Keith Orr is a special needs child, and his buddies on the football team decided to give him the chance to run for a touchdown. Sheridan Hedrick, a player on the team, would've easily scored a touchdown, but he instead took a knee on the 1-yard line, much to the dismay of the crowd. That was until the next play happened: the "Keith Special." The ball was hiked and immediately handed to Keith, who ran forward as his teammates protected him from the oncoming defense. Keith scored without a scratch… We can all learn a lot from the boys on the Olivet Eagles, as they have shown a certain sense of humility and understanding many of us adults struggle with.[40]

…When it comes to wrestling in Georgia, next to the state championship, there is no trophy more coveted than one from the South Metro Tournament, the oldest meet in the state… During his junior year, few worked harder at McIntosh [high school] than Demetrius DeMoors who has learned to love the sport…

Meet one of the most popular kids at Georgia's Union Grove High School, Michael Lind. "Michael was born with down syndrome," says Becky Lind, Michael's mom. Like Demetrius, Michael is also a wrestler… Though he was on the team, Michael never had the chance to actually wrestle in a meet. That is until the 2012 South Metro Tournament. "I was excited, a little nervous too because I wasn't sure how it was going to be received," says Michael's mom.

The coach at Union Grove called the coach at McIntosh and asked him if they had a team member who would agree to wrestle Michael in an exhibition match. The person to step up was none other than Demetrius DeMoors… "I was thinking to myself if I could only wrestle one time, if I could only experience this one time with the crowd watching me and the cameras on me how would I want it to be," said DeMoors. "And so I tried to make it as fun and as special as possible."

Winning takes skill, what Demetrius did took character. He didn't just lie down and let Michael win, he made him earn it… And when it was over, through tears most saw that Michael Lind was the winner but Demetrius was the champion… Strength doesn't come from the gym, it comes from the soul… "To show compassion and love toward somebody else that may not be as fortunate as they are, that's a blessing," adds Demetrius' mom.[41]

May God bless you with a passion and empowering to be that type of blessing to and through your athletes. But, it's imperative that you remember that this love for God and love for your neighbor must be received from God himself. You cannot will it into happening. It is a gift of grace that will continually transform your heart to desire to shower your blessings upon those who are less fortunate. And when your team reaches out to "the least of these," be prepared for blessings to shower down upon all of you as you witness the transformation of lives. Why? Because you will watch these special needs individuals "…gain a variety of new experiences in sport and in clubs, [and] they can gain pleasure from their own activity and become better equipped for life through achieving a sense of effort and achievement. Meetings of persons with and without disabilities free them from their isolation, take them seriously and endow them with recognition as persons."[42]

A great way to view these four community pillars in action is through the understanding why geese fly in a V-formation:

- **[We are Family]** *Team-first attitude.* By flying in a V-formation, each goose creates uplift by flapping its wings and reduces resistance for the birds that follow. It's similar to a distance runner following closely behind a fellow competitor in order to conserve energy by having to deal with less wind resistance. Scientists have concluded that this formation allows the flock to fly around seventy percent further than if one goose was flying solo.

- **[Unity, not Uniformity]** *Roles.* If a goose decides to fly solo, it quickly finds out that the air resistance is significantly greater, and it quickly takes its place back in the V. By doing so, it sees that flying in unity provides much greater airlift than going it alone. Each goose plays a significant role in the V. One gap causes all to suffer, not just those who follow. Why? Because the geese rotate leadership since those flying in front bear the brunt of the workload with no one to provide lift or lessen resistance for them. So when they get tired, they drop to the rear of the flock where the resistance is the lightest. Hence, one gap affects all because each one must carry its load for the V to be successful for all.

- **[Live Such Good Lives]** *Positive attitude.* Everyone needs encouragement, even geese. Scientists postulate that the geese in the back of the V regularly honk at those in front as a means of communicating encouragement to those who are working the hardest. And, because there is a regular rotation of leadership, we can speculate that all eventually are encouraged by each other's honking.

- **[Serve the Less Fortunate]** *Perseverance and loyalty.* When a goose has special needs due to sickness or injury, it is not left alone. On the contrary, at these times, two other geese will accompany the one with special needs to the ground. They remain with the sick or injured goose until it is able to fly again or it dies. The two or three will then continue on in their journey.

Let the words of former Pope John Paul II, combined with the ultimate reason why God calls you to coach, be a potent reminder to you on the power of coaches and sports to build community:

[H]e explicitly urges all to strive together, "so that sport, without losing each true nature, can answer the needs of our time: sport that protects the weak and excludes no one, that frees young people from the snares of apathy and indifference, and arouses a healthy sense of competition in them; sport that is a factor of emancipation for poorer countries and helps to eradicate intolerance and build a more fraternal and united world; sport which contributes to the love of life, teaches sacrifice, respect and responsibility, leading to the full development of every human person."[43]

TOOLS

Ω Helping Your Athletes Solve Relational Problems on the Team

If problems arise between teammates, point them to the restoration and reconciliation principles found in Matthew 18:15-16, Romans 12:17-18, and Philippians 2:4. "If your brother sins against you, go and tell him his fault, between you and him alone. If he listens to you, you have gained your brother. But if he does not listen, take one or two others along with you, that every charge may be established by the evidence of two or three witnesses" (Matthew 18:15-16). It is important to help your athletes try to work out their differences by themselves first. If one-on-one doesn't work, then captains should get involved to try to help resolve the issue. If this also fails, then it is time for you to become directly involved. Obviously this pattern will be fluid if you are coaching young kids. Then step two will probably not be included. The key is to seek to involve as few people as possible in order to bring about forgiveness and healing. Another way to aid in this process is to remind your athletes, "If you are wronged [by a teammate], do not pay them back. Repay no one evil for evil, but give thought to do what is honorable in the sight of all. If possible, so far as it depends on you, live peaceably with all." (Romans 12:17-18). Ultimately, this process is energized by following the dictates of Philippians 2:4: "Show a sincere interest in [your teammates]. Let each of you look not only to his own interests, but also to the interests of others."

Ω Helping Those Who Fail to Make Your Team

Too many coaches of large teams do not take the time to honor the young men and women who try out but fail to make the squad. Having your name posted on a wall for all to see that you didn't measure up can be one of the most demoralizing experiences of a young person's life. Take the time to communicate with each athlete on why they didn't make the team, and what they need to do to increase their odds in the future. Make it as positive as possible so that those who failed to make the team are applauded for their efforts and honored because they are made in the image of God

Ω Helping those in the Community: Live Such Good Lives

Find local projects where your athletes can serve such as:

- Soup kitchen
- Children's Hospital
- Seasonal opportunities such as *Boxes of Love* with *CRU Inner City* at Thanksgiving time or providing backpacks and school supplies at the beginning of each school year.
- Special Olympics
- Reading/tutoring younger students in area schools

"Each year during the Christmas season, the Butler basketball team, through the Indianapolis United Christmas Service, adopts an Indianapolis area family in need... Basketball coaches' wives and family members go shopping and purchase Christmas gifts and food for each member of their adopted family. Brad and [his wife] Tracy invite all of the basketball players, the assistant coaches, and the coaches' wives to their home where the players have the assignment to wrap all the Christmas gifts for the family they have decided to serve that year. After the presents are all wrapped, the coaches and players personally deliver the gifts to the family they are serving."[44]

Ω Helping those with Special Needs: Barriers to Participation of Children with Disabilities in Youth Sports[45]

Read this entire article, which can be found in the appendices. Below is the abstract describing the article:

"Youth sports were created as opportunities for children to play, be active, and begin learning how to become better or more successful at a given sport. Unfortunately many children with disabilities may not get the same opportunities that are available to other children. There are a number of barriers that inhibit children with significant disabilities from either participating in the youth sport programming all together or have a strong impact [regarding their] level of successful participation. This article both identifies key barriers as well as provides strategies to eliminate or minimize the impact of the given barrier. This problem-solution approach is meant to help to focus our attention on the root of the problem and begin using some practical strategies that will help better serve and provide opportunities for children with disabilities to help them 'get into the game.'"

Ω PRAYER

"Heavenly Father, help me to remember that the earth belongs to you and everything in it. Every good and perfect gift I possess comes directly from you. Therefore, help me to teach my athletes about unity through sharing what they have been blessed with, so that those on the team and in the local community are built up and supplied where they are lacking. For whatever we do to 'the least of these', we do unto your Son, Jesus. It is this attitude, this mindset, that is the seedbed to help myself and my athletes to grow in the reality of seeking to daily lay down our lives for our friends, and show the world the great love you exhibit towards us by loving each other. Therefore, empower those who are strong on the team to bear with the failings of those who are weak, so that they demonstrate love towards their teammates in order to build up the weak, not to prove their own strength. So when someone on the team sins against another one, help them to show a sincere interest in their offending teammate and not seek retribution, but reconciliation and restoration. Empower them to not repay anyone evil for evil, but to give thought how to honor the offending party so that, if possible, they can live peaceably with everyone on the team. Therefore, if their teammate sins against them, remind them to go and tell him his fault, between just the two of them. If he listens to him, he has gained back his brother and strengthened the bonds of the team and given the greater community a picture of your love towards us while we were still sinners." (Psalm 24:1; James 1:17; Acts 2:44-45; Matthew 25:40; John 15:13; Romans 15:1-2; Philippians 2:4; Romans 12:17-8; Matthew 18:15; Romans 5:8)

Notes

1   C.J. Mahaney, *Living the Cross Centered Life: Keeping the Gospel the Main Thing* (Colorado Springs: Multnomah, 2006), 154.

2   1 Corinthians 14:1.

3   Ecclesiastes 4:12.

4   Victoria Osteen, "Bill Cosby Responds to Victoria Osteen," *YouTube*, 8/28/14, Accessed 8/30/14. www.youtube.com/watch?v=00-6OyXUVAOM.

5   Brad Stevens in Kent Millard & Judith Cebula, *Lead Like Butler: Six Principles for Values-Based Leaders* (Nashville: Abingdon, 2013), 40.

6   Kent Millard & Judith Cebula, *Lead Like Butler: Six Principles for Values-Based Leaders* (Nashville: Abingdon, 2013), 41.

7   Proverbs 17:17.

8   John 13:34-35.

9   Michael Zigarelli, *The Messiah Method: The Seven Disciplines of the Winningest College Soccer Program in America* (USA: Xulon, 2011), 41.

10 Galatians 5:14.

11 Romans 12:10.

12 1 John 3:16.

13 Burk Parsons, "Consider Yourself," *Ligonier Ministries*, 5/1/2012, Accessed 9/1/2014. www.ligonier.org/learn/articles/consider-yourself/.

14 Reggie McNeal, *Practicing Greatness: 7 Disciplines of Extraordinary Spiritual Leaders* (San Francisco: Jossey-Bass, 2006), 130-131.

15 Jim Thompson, *The Double-Goal Coach: Positive Coaching Tools for Honoring the Game and Developing Winners in Sports and Life* (New York: HarperCollins, 2003), 163-168.

16 Babe Ruth and Paul 'Bear' Bryant in Greg S. Smith, *Sports Theology* (Indianapolis: Dog Ear, 2010), 123-124.

17 Dave Kraft, *Leaders Who Last* (Wheaton: Crossway, 2010), 86.

18 Chris Schrader and Victor Pentz, *Catch of the Day* (Houston: Touch of Grace, 2000), 7-15.

19 J. Oswald Sanders, *Spiritual Leadership: Principle of Excellence for Every Believer* (Chicago: Moody, 2007), 137.

20 Hans Finzel, *The Top Ten Mistakes Leaders Make* (Colorado Springs: David C. Cook, 2007), 146.

21 Tony Dungy, *The Mentor Leader: Secrets to Building People and Teams that Win Consistently* (Carol Stream: Tyndale, 2010) 150.

22 John Wooden and Steve Jamison, *Wooden on Leadership* (New York: McGraw-Hill, 2005), 180.

23 Gail Goodrich in Ibid., 132.

24 Millard & Cebula, op. cit., 45.

25 Edited by Kevin Lixey, L.C., Christoph Hubenthal, Dietmar Mieth, and Norbert Muller, *Sport & Christianity: A Sign of the Times in the Light of Faith* (Washington, D.C.: The Catholic University of America Press, 2012), 128-129.

26 Acts 1:8.

27 Matthew 7:12.

28 Dale D. Brown, David Cutcliffe, Kelly Herrmann, Timothy F. Welsh, *Coach Them Well: Fostering Faith & Developing Character in Athletes* (Winona: St. Mary's, 2006), 21.

29   Lixey, Hubenthal, Mieth, and Muller, op. cit., 129.

30   Nelson Henderson, *Good Reads*, Accessed 8/24/2014. www.goodreads.com/quotes/107263-the-true-meaning-of-life-is-to-plant-trees-under.

31   Philip Yancey, "The Least Likely Soil," *Christianity Today*, August, 26, 2003.

32   Romans 3:23.

33   1 Corinthians 13:5, NIV.

34   Ephesians 4:32.

35   Zigarelli, op. cit., 126-127.

36   Zigarelli, op. cit., 25.

37   Lixey, Hubenthal, Mieth, and Muller, op. cit., 225.

38   Romans 15:1-2.

39   Lixey, Hubenthal, Mieth, and Muller, op. cit., 230.

40   Robert Gordon, "This Middle School Football Team Went Behind Their Coaches' Backs To Do Something Incredible," *Elite Daily*, 11/4/2013, Accessed 6/10/2014. http://elitedaily.com/news/world/can-learn-lot-middle-school-football-team-video.world.

41   Mike Bush, Wrestler's Amazing Act of Sportsmanship," *KSDK*, 10/20/2013, Accessed 6/10/2014. http://www.ksdk.com/story/news/local/making-a-difference/2013/10/20/3100955/.

42   Lixey, Hubenthal, Mieth, and Muller, op. cit., 230.

43   Ibid., 132.

44   Millard & Cebula, op. cit., 63.

45   Thomas E. Moran and Martin E. Block, *Barriers to Participation of Children with Disabilities in Youth Sports* (PDF of A Featured Article Published in *TEACHING Exceptional Children Plus*, February 2010), Volume 6, Issue 3.

10

LEGACY BUILDER

"It ought to be the business of everyday to prepare for our last day."[1] (Matthew Henry)

"But I do not account my life of any value nor as precious to myself, if only I may finish my course and the ministry that I received from the Lord Jesus, to testify to the gospel of the grace of God." (Acts 20:24)

What legacy will you leave behind when you are finished coaching, when you are done with life on this planet? It needs to account for so much more than wins and losses, honors and accolades. When your race is complete and you have finished your course, your coaching needs to "testify to the gospel of the grace of God." Anything less than this will leave you wondering what you were thinking, if your focus wandered from the centrality of treasuring Jesus and loving your athletes. Don't wait another day to think about your legacy. Begin seeking wisdom today on how to build it on the cornerstone that is Christ, because life is a vapor.

> Come now, you who say, "Today or tomorrow we will go into such and such a town and spend a year there and trade and make a profit"— yet you do not know what tomorrow will bring. What is your life? For you are a mist that appears for a little time and then vanishes. Instead you ought to say, "If the Lord wills, we will live and do this or that." As it is, you boast in your arrogance. All such boasting is evil. (James 4:13-16)

Always live with the last day in mind.

I do not know about the certainty of death and taxes for every person, but I do know death is inevitable. A tombstone in Devon, England sums it up succinctly:

As you pass by,
Pray cast your eye

As you are now,
So once was I.
As I am now,
So you will be
So be content to follow me.
A tombstone in Ireland had a similar inscription, except at the end of it, where someone had added,
To follow you,
I am quite content
I wish I knew
Which way you went[2]

WRITING YOUR OBITUARY

Yet it is not merely about which way you go when you die, but which way you are going while you are alive and how well you finish that will determine your legacy. Contrast the epithets written for the first two kings of Israel. Both had been tapped on the shoulder by God to lead his chosen people. Both started the race well. But the ways they finished, however, were markedly different:

So Saul died for his breach of faith. *He broke faith* with the LORD in that he did not keep the command of the LORD, and also consulted a medium, seeking guidance.[3]

When David's time to die drew near, he commanded Solomon his son, saying, "I am about to go the way of all the earth. Be strong, and show yourself a man, and *keep the charge of the LORD your God*, walking in his ways and keeping his statutes, his commandments, his rules, and his testimonies, as it is written in the Law of Moses that you may prosper in all that you do and wherever you turn, that the LORD may establish his word that he spoke concerning me, saying, 'If your sons pay close attention to their way, to walk before me in faithfulness with all their heart and with all their soul, you shall not lack a man on the throne of Israel.' "[4]

Which way are you going? How will you be remembered? It is always productive to begin with the end in mind. To aid yourself toward that goal, develop a mission statement which will help you to define in concrete terms how you desire to finish. This brings us back full circle to how we began the coaching characteristics. Your mission statement must ultimately be crafted upon the goal of Treasuring Jesus. Wherein does your treasure lie? What are you willing to give your life for? Riches, records, resumes, relatives or the redemption of the Sports Nation?

What will you be remembered for at your funeral? With your memorial service in mind, and who or what you would die for, you can begin the process of reverse engineering a purpose statement that comes from your core values – what you hold dear to your heart. A personal mission statement should be used as a silhouette against which you continually place your roles, goals, and priorities on a daily basis. In this way, you can make sure that you are coaching within the parameters of your mission statement. Any role, goal, or priority that does not fit within the boundaries of that mission statement needs to be altered or deleted so that you may stay true to your stated intentions. As a Christian, you are a steward of the time, talents, and resources God has given you. Remember the starting point - treasuring Jesus. Remember the earthly ending point – "What will your epithet read?" Remember the Judgment Day when you hope to hear, "Well done, good and faithful servant."

You are on a journey. But you are not traveling alone. Your actions will affect every athlete who comes into your sphere of influence, and many others who have a rooted interest in your team. What will you do today to make the world a better place through your coaching? You have a unique opportunity, by God's grace, to help transform athletes' lives by helping them to pursue excellence for the glory of God. Focus on how to sow seeds of salvation and sanctification today. Yesterday is gone. Tomorrow is not guaranteed. But you have today. Live passionately in the present for the glory of God and the eternal joy of your athletes!

> We must teach them [our athletes] and assist them in valuing godly character and growing in godly character as they play sports… The final day must inform our evaluation. And on that final day of divine evaluation and examination, there will not be a celebration of athletic achievement. The final day will be all about the gospel. Did you live a life worthy of the gospel? We must prepare our children [athletes] for that day.[5]

Coaching cannot be your life. It is a tool to glorify God. Your identity must be in Jesus Christ, not in being a coach. Because when the end of your season, ministry/coaching career, or life comes, you will not be in angst over games won and lost. It will be no different for you than it was for those people on board the planes hijacked on 9/11. No one was recounting great victories on the playing field, or for that matter any accolades or honors at all. Transcripts of those calls all focus on three words, "I love you." You will leave a legacy. Will it be a legacy of love through your coaching? Make it positive by considering the ultimate outcome. Someday you will be replaced. May your influence be part of the transformation of the athletes' lives that stay with them throughout their days because they knew they were loved!

> [S]uccesses are momentary. The next day you're back to work… If at the end of your career… all you can say is "I was a National Champion, and we won a lot of games," then I'd say it wasn't worth the time and energy. But if you can look back and say "I learned a lot about myself. I did things I never thought possible, both physically and psychologically. I made the most important and lasting friendships of my life. I've learned that helping others and seeing them succeed

at something is better than having it happen to me," then it is without question worth all that you do.[6]

If you live this way, you will be able to echo the words of the Apostle Paul, "I have fought the good fight, I have finished the race, I have kept the faith. Henceforth there is laid up for me the crown of righteousness, which the Lord, the righteous judge, will award to me on that Day, and not only to me but also to all who have loved his appearing."[7] The only way this will happen is by seeking to build a legacy on the rock-solid truths of God's Word. Any other paths you pursue will leave you building on shifting sand, which will end in sorrow and regret. Therefore, "Desire that your life count for something great! Long for your life to have eternal significance."[8] As a coach, the foundational part of that significance is built on your vertical relationship with God and your horizontal relationships with your athletes. "You shall love the Lord your God with all your heart and with all your soul and with all your strength and with all your mind, and your neighbor as yourself."[9]

I know this is not the foundation you were probably taught in regards to your coaching, but it is primarily about love: loving your athletes enough to shepherd them in the foundations of faith, fundamentals, family, and fun. When you're done coaching an athlete, whether because they or you move on, you want to be know that you have made their lives better through your influence. You will leave your athletes with memories that will last a lifetime. What will they remember about their time spent with you? "Some people come into our lives and quietly go. Others stay awhile, and leave footprints on our hearts, and we are never the same... 'Lord, make me a person who leaves footprints in people's lives. I don't want to be a person who comes and goes with no lasting impact. Because of contact with me, may people never be the same again. May I be a person who intentionally and lastingly influences others.'"[10]

If you coach this way, you will used to help transform your athletes in ways that will ripple through their lives into their own families, friendships, and communities throughout their time on this planet. Be a coach that sows seeds of eternal consequences into the lives of your athletes. Point them towards the Way, the Truth, and the Life by loving them enough to teach them the truth and helping them to pursue excellence in all they do. Then they, by God's grace, will become other-centered, other-focused, servant-leaders who will help shepherd the next generation.

Always live with the end in mind because a good start does not ensure a good finish. Neither does a lifetime of pursuit that ends poorly. Few will ever again hear the name Joe Paterno, and not envision his famed statue being carted away from the Penn State campus. Failure to live with the end in mind apparently caused Joe's legacy to be tarnished in a way no one would have believed possible. Wins and reputation reportedly became more important than doing what was right.

According to the 267 page Freeh report, Paterno lied – to a grand jury, no less – about his knowledge of a 1998 assault of a young boy by longtime Penn State defensive coordinator Jerry Sandusky in a football facility shower. His [Paterno's] lies, and, worse yet, his silence from the time of that first reported assault in 1998 helped empower a sexual predator for the next 13 years. Paterno did nothing to stop Sandusky. He was, said former FBI director Louis Freeh, who wrote the report, "an integral part of this active decision to conceal."[11]

And many dominoes fell from Joe's reputed silence in the face of Sandusky's criminal actions. Sin has consequences, and they were felt far beyond the Paterno family, throughout the entire Penn State community, to numerous child victims and their families. To avoid a bad finish, always remember the call: "Love your neighbor as yourself. Do this and you will honor God."[12]

> The questions you ask at the end of your life are not what material things, awards, or applause you've acquired. Certainly the question is not how many wins you've had. The questions that will matter most on your deathbed are the questions related to your relationships… [P]eople want to know…what kind of difference they made in the lives of others, their community, and their country. People want to know that they live for a reason, a cause, and a purpose that was bigger than themselves… Life, I've learned, is a team sport and ultimately is unsatisfying if it is lived solely for self.[13]

Live with the end in mind. Desire eternal significance through your coaching.

Tools

Ω Write Your Own Obituary. (What do you hope to be remembered for?)

Ask loved ones, close friends and associates what impact you are making in their lives. It's always important to be able to assess your progress towards pursuit of your personal mission/vision statement.

Ω Write Your Personal Vision/Mission Statement

If you decided to skip this tool earlier in the book, it's time to get after it. Just like you need to have markers to determine the progress of your athletes, you need similar indicators to help you to stay on the path that seeks to transform the lives of your athletes while pursuing excellence so Jesus is honored through your coaching. Consider using some of Liberty University's Track and Field objectives[14] as a template for things you'd like to accomplish through your coaching:

Liberty University Track & Field/Cross Country Mission

To develop highly competitive teams of individuals who represent Jesus Christ in athletics and in daily life.

Objectives of Liberty University Track & Field

1. To help prepare our student athletes to live lives of productive, joyous service to the Lord.
2. To help our athletes learn to apply Biblical principles to life's situations.
3. To help our athletes grow toward spiritual maturity so that they may be more effectively used by God.
4. To help our athletes reach as close as possible to their athletic potential for the glory of the Lord.
5. To assist and encourage our athletes to earn college degrees.
6. To provide opportunities for our athletes individually and as a team to represent Liberty and Christ at the highest possible competitive level.
7. To lead and encourage our athletes to serve others as representatives of Christ.
8. To lead our team to set an example to other college teams of the great superiority of a life of walking with the Lord.
9. To set an example of a Christ-centered program to other teams and students at Liberty.
10. To win conference championships.
11. To contend for ECAC and IC4A titles.
12. To develop nationally competitive, Christ-honoring teams.

Ω Daily Reminder

Put this short prayer in a place where you can regularly offer it up to the Lord as you seek to build a legacy of love:

"Lord, make me a person who leaves footprints in people's lives. I don't want to be a person who comes and goes with no lasting impact. Because of contact with me, may people never be the same again. May I be a person who intentionally and lastingly influences others."[15]

Ω Prayer

"Heavenly Father, daily remind me that my life is a mist that appears for a little while and then vanishes. So help me to always keep the end in mind and pursue my coaching in a manner that has eternal significance. Fill me to overflowing with your love so that I am empowered to love my athletes well. For you promised that if I love others, your love abides in me and will be perfected in me. Make that a reality in my life. 'Lord, make me a person who leaves footprints in people's lives. I don't want to be a person who comes and goes with no lasting impact. Because of contact with me, may people never be the same again. May I be a person who intentionally and lastingly influences others.' Therefore, empower me to display to my athletes through word and deed what is of first importance in my life, the gospel that I also received: that Christ died for our sins in accordance with the Scriptures, that he was buried, that he was raised on the third day in accordance with the Scriptures. May each athlete be transformed for eternity by these truths, by you graciously giving them eyes to see and ears to hear – just like you did for me. For from Jesus and through him and to him are all things. To him alone be glory forever and ever. Amen." (James 4:14; 1 John 4:11-12; 1 Corinthians 15:3-4; Romans 11:36)

RE-DEFINING SUCCESS

"While others will judge you strictly in relation to somebody or something else – the final score, the bottom line, or championship – that is neither the most demanding nor the most productive standard…The highest, purest, and most difficult standard of all, the one that ultimately produces one's finest performance – and the great treasure called 'peace of mind' – is that which measures the quality of your personal effort to reach Competitive Greatness." (John Wooden)

The Olympic motto is *Citius, Altius, Fortius*, which is Latin for "Faster, Higher, Stronger." It was penned by Pierre de Coubertain at the time the International Olympic Committee was formed in 1894. But, interestingly, he owes this motto to his friend, Dominican priest Henri Didon. "Didon made this formula a symbol for catholic progress as he saw in sport the possibility of preparing individuals for the requirements of a fulfilled life and the chance for an ethical understanding between different people."[16] The motto didn't mean faster, higher, stronger than someone else; rather, faster, higher, stronger than an individual was previously. John Wooden and Henri Didon were cut from a similar cloth. This was something former Oregon Track Coach Bill Bowerman didn't comprehend, by his own admission, until he coached Steve Prefontaine.

> All of my life – man and boy – I've operated under the assumption that the main idea in running was to win the…race. Actually, when I became a coach I tried to teach people how to do that. I tried to teach Pre how to do that. I tried…to teach Pre to do that… and Pre taught me – taught me I was wrong. Pre, you see, was troubled by knowing that a mediocre effort could win a race, and a magnificent effort can lose one. Winning a race wouldn't necessarily demand that he give it everything he had from start to finish. He never ran any other way. I tried to get him to. God knows I tried. But Pre was stubborn. He insisted on holding himself to a higher standard than victory.

> A race is a work of art. That's what he said. That's what he believed. And he was out to make it one every step of the way. Of course, he wanted to win. Those who saw him compete and those who competed against him were never in any doubt about how much he wanted to win. But how he won mattered to him more. Pre thought I was a hard case. But he finally got it through my head that the real purpose of

running isn't to win a race. It's to test the limits of the human heart. And that he did. Nobody did it more often. Nobody did it better.[17]

Yes, as a coach you are to help your athletes pursue winning on the scoreboard. But that is not the ultimate marker of success. It's about helping your athletes realize their fullest God-given potential on any particular day, which may mean winning on the scoreboard, and may not. Can you handle that re-definition of success? Will you pass it on to your athletes and not allow the heat of competition, your ego, or fear of someone else's opinion to sway you? If yes, you will leave a legacy of true champions on the field and in life. Any competitive goal for your athletes and yourself that is not grounded in God's truths will leave you distraught in the end. Don't waste your life!

Teach your athletes that they can be successful when they improve in their quest to master a skill set or when they reach a stepping-stone goal. Very few athletes will ever stand on the podium to be applauded by the world, but all can be, and should be, commended for their 'smaller' victories. For all success comes through the empowering of God himself, whether the athlete realizes it or not. And as we can learn from Coach Wooden, not even winning necessarily means you or your team was successful. "The fact that we were ahead was incidental. What mattered to him [Coach Wooden] was that we weren't playing to our potential. And, it worked the other way too. If the score was going against us, but we were giving it our best effort, he wouldn't get upset. Instead, coach would very calmly instruct us on changes that should be made."[18]

Becoming greater than everyone else in your sport will not ensure a legacy worth leaving. Only goals based upon glorifying God can assure that reality.

> "So I became great and surpassed all who were before me in Jerusalem. Also my wisdom remained with me. And whatever my eyes desired I did not keep from them. I kept my heart from no pleasure, for my heart found pleasure in all my toil, and this was my reward for all my toil. Then I considered all that my hands had done and the toil I had expended in doing it, and behold, all was vanity and a striving after wind, and there was nothing to be gained under the sun."
> (Ecclesiastes 2:9-11)

Look at the lives of two football 'greats,' Peyton Manning and Tom Brady. Who appears to be "striving after wind"? What will your legacy look like if you continue on your current trajectory? Will you believe the nonsense spewed forth by famed Coach Knute Rockne, "Show me a gracious loser and I'll show you a failure"? Or do you seek to coach by the rock-solid reality put forth by Martin Buber, "Success is not another name for God"?[19]

No one who has ever played for or against Peyton Manning has ever doubted his intense desire to win. Yet, in the midst of that passionate pursuit of victory, Manning seems to have a balance that is unknown to most athletes at any level. After his Broncos got shellacked by the Seahawks 43-8 in the Super Bowl, Manning did not just slump his shoulders and slink off the field. Instead, he went looking for one of his most vociferous opponents, Richard Sherman, to see how he was faring after suffering a high ankle sprain during the game. Sherman said on *Mike and Mike in the Morning* that, "He was really concerned about my well-being. After a game like that, a guy who's still classy enough to say 'How are you doing?' To show that kind of concern for an opponent shows a lot of humility and class." On Twitter, Sherman continued praising Peyton Manning, "Peyton is the Classiest person/player I have ever met! I could learn so much from him! Thank you for being a great Competitor and person." Yes, Peyton Manning lost, but is definitely not a 'loser." One can only hope the reporters interviewing him after the game learned as much about winning and losing as Richard Sherman did from Peyton. Consider this one tidbit Manning told the reporters in an effort to educate them: "It's not embarrassing at all. I would never use that word. There's a lot of professional football players in that locker room that put in a lot of work into being here, playing in that game. That word embarrassing is an insulting word, to tell you the truth." Peyton's priorities are faith, family, education, and then football. That, my friends, is balance – which Tom Brady was still searching for years ago.

> **BRADY:** Why do I have three Super Bowl rings, and still think there's something greater out there for me? I mean, maybe a lot of people would say, "Hey man, this is what is." I reached my goal, my dream, my life. Me, I think: God it's gotta be more than this. I mean this can't be what it's all cracked up to be. I mean I've done it. I'm 27. And what else is there for me?

> **KROFT:** What's the answer?

> **BRADY:** I wish I knew. I wish I knew. I mean I think that's part of me trying to go out and experience things. I love playing football, and I love being a quarterback for this team, but at the same time, I think there's a lot of other parts about me that I'm trying to find. I know what ultimately makes me happy are family and friends, and positive relationships with great people. I think I get more out of that than anything. [20]

Ten years after this interview, at the beginning of the 2014 NFL season, Tom Brady was asked when he was going to retire. His reply? "When I suck." I hope and pray Tom Brady has figured out an answer to what else there is for him to be doing in life because his time will be coming much sooner than when he did that interview. Way too many athletes hang on past their prime, past their expiration date, because their entire identity is wrapped up in being a 'winner' according to the world's standards. Just ask Chris Evert:

> "I had no idea who I was, or what I could be away from tennis. I was depressed and afraid because so much of my life had been defined by my being a tennis champion. I was completely lost. Winning made me feel like I was somebody. It made me

feel pretty. It was like being hooked on a drug. I needed the wins, the applause, in order to have an identity." (Chris Evert – best career win-loss record in professional women's tennis, as she contemplated retirement)[21]

If you are counting on your coaching accolades to carry you through life and leave a heavenly legacy, may God open your eyes to the vanity of it. This mindset is as old as humankind itself. It is a desire to leave your mark, to show you made a difference. Everyone desires a type of immortality. But the only true way to attain it is through giving your life away in serving others for the glory of Jesus. In this way, your coaching will follow the wisdom of William James, "The great use of life is to spend it for something that will outlast it."[22]

Feel free to get the tattoo G.O.A.T., *Greatest of All Time*, inked on your body like Maurice Greene did after earning the title of fastest human being when he broke the 100 meter dash world record in 1999. Three years later that tattoo was worthless – and the record has been lowered eight more times since then. Such is the vanity of a legacy built upon accolades, corruptible crowns. But you should be aiming for an immortal reward an incorruptible crown. "Do you not know that in a race all the runners run, but only one receives the prize? So run that you may obtain it. Every athlete exercises self-control in all things. They do it to receive a perishable wreath, but we an imperishable."[23] How do you run that you may obtain this imperishable wreath?

1.   Toss Every Goal that Doesn't End with its Ultimate Focus upon the Glory of Jesus.

> Therefore, since we are surrounded by so great a cloud of witnesses, let us also lay aside every weight, and sin which clings so closely, and let us run with endurance the race that is set before us, looking to Jesus, the founder and perfecter of our faith, who for the joy that was set before him endured the cross, despising the shame, and is seated at the right hand of the throne of God. (Hebrews 12:1-2)

Every coach knows that winning on the scoreboard is not guaranteed no matter how diligently they prepare their athletes. It's no different in life. Teach your team to enjoy the journey and not become overly-fixated on the destination. How many victories do coaches fail to celebrate along the way because of a skewed goal focused singularly upon some human-contrived championship? Continually help to re-orient your athletes' goals through the wins and the losses so they see the value in not only competing well, but in the people they are competing against. In this way, you are giving them pointers that direct them towards the ultimate treasure of Jesus himself.

Malik Stewart is a hardscrabble wrestler who won the hearts and minds of the crowd at the 2014 Minnesota State Championships for what he did off the mat. He came with the singular focus of winning the 120-pound title in the Class 3A tournament. His opponent, Mitchell McKee, had ideas of his own. McKee wanted to win it all for his dad, who was dying of cancer. At 1:22 into the first round, McKee's dreams came true. Stewart's ended. What Stewart did next, however, absolutely blew the crowd away. Rather than feel sorry for himself and storm off the mat, he congratulated McKee and his coaches. Then he went over to McKee's dad, shook his hand and embraced him a little bit. Stewart told him to "stay strong and everybody loves him." "When you go out there, you want to win, but if you don't win, you have got to be a good sport and you be polite. That's the biggest part," Stewart said.

Yes, the young man was upset that he lost. Yes, he shed a couple tears. But he understood the bigger picture. When Stewart was just seven-years-old, his father died of a heart attack. A loss on the mat is nothing compared to the loss of a loved one. The crowd seemed to understand as they gave both wrestlers a standing ovation. Many coaches in attendance seemed to understand: "The whole crowd gave a standing ovation, not just for [McKee] and his father, but for Stewart, who understands what true sportsmanship is. Thank you for making your athletes into what they are today. Mr. Stewart is a model wrestler that we can all use in our examples of what a true athlete is," said T.J. Anderson, Assistant Wrestling Coach, Dassel-Cokato Middle School in a letter to the Anoka Hennepin School District.

Coaches who use examples like this to teach their athletes have a much greater chance to leave the type of legacy that honors Jesus. What a golden opportunity to proclaim the reality of "loving your neighbor as yourself" through word and deed! And what a unique opportunity to teach your athletes that even 'failing' is safe in your program because it is not terminal. No one's life actually depends upon the outcome of a game. Malik Stewart did not wither up and die after the loss. Quite the contrary, later in the interview he stated his conviction to work towards two straight state titles. May your coaching help the Sports Nation to see beyond the scoreboard into the hearts of their competitors and those people they represent.

Sports ability in and of itself should never dictate a person's ultimate value. However, the outcome of a successful athletic life lived outside an intimate relationship with Jesus Christ is another matter entirely.

> Tom Lehman, 19-year PGA player and winner of the 1996 British open says it this way, "Winning the British Open was a thrill of a lifetime. But I learned a long time ago that the thrill of victory is fleeting. It's not long before you find yourself asking, what's next? As much as I longed to win a major championship, it didn't change anything. I was still the same person as before. I had the same hang-ups, the same problems - and even some new ones. The Bible says, 'All men are like grass, and their glory is like the flowers of the field. The grass withers and the flowers fall.' So what is it that lasts? The only thing that has given my life true meaning - my relationship with Jesus Christ."[24]

2. Love Your Athlete As Yourself

The only way to store up treasures in heaven through your coaching is to make sure that it is not first and foremost focused upon meeting your desires. To invest in eternity is to invest in relationships. That is what it means to be truly successful. You cannot take any of your coaching successes with you, but the treasures that your store up in heaven will never perish. "Do not lay up for yourselves treasures on earth, where moth and rust destroy and where thieves break in and steal, but lay up for yourselves treasures in heaven, where neither moth nor rust destroys and where thieves do not break in and steal. For where your treasure is, there your heart will be also."[25] The only legacy worth leaving is the one that helps your athletes become better people than when you first met them. And the only standard that will let you know they are becoming, or have become, better people is the Bible. Are you seeking to balance out the penultimate goal of developing athletes who can win with the ultimate goal of hopefully seeing young men and women who will one day call upon Jesus as their Lord and Savior?

> Basketball is just a game, but if I was doing my job as a coach that game of basketball would help our players by preparing them to do well in life, to reach their full potential as individuals. When they did that, I was very proud as a coach. That's more important to me than all the championships and titles and awards. (John Wooden, Former UCLA Men's Basketball Coach).[26]

Yet in the midst of all this talk of legacy, it can become disheartening as you look at the missteps, failures, and sins in your past coaching efforts. Do not let Satan deceive you into thinking all is hopeless. He is not called the great deceiver of the world and the accuser of the brothers for no reason.[27] However, God's grace is more formidable to forgive you and potent to empower you to move forward in your quest to leave a God-honoring and Christ-exalting legacy. For, "The steadfast love of the LORD never ceases; his mercies never come to an end; they are new every morning; great is your faithfulness."[28] So, "forgetting what lies behind and straining forward to what lies ahead, press on toward the goal for the prize of the upward call of God in Christ Jesus."[29]

If these words from God himself do not help you fully comprehend that you can still build a powerful legacy, consider the words of some mere mortals/fellow travelers that he has placed in our midst. When you stand face-to-face with the Creator, Redeemer, and Sustainer of the universe, he will not look at merely one snapshot of your coaching to determine how well you served. He will look at a lifetime lived by the empowering of the Holy Spirit, given to you through a blood-stained cross.

> The historian James Andrew Froude wrote: "The worth of a man must be measured by his life, not by his failure under a singular and peculiar trial. Peter the apostle, though forewarned, three times denied his Master on the first alarm of danger; yet that Master, who knew his nature in its strength and in its weakness, chose him."[30]

> Be more concerned with your character than your reputation, because your character is what you really are, while your reputation is merely what others think you are. Material possessions, winning scores, and great reputations are meaningless in the eyes of a Lord, because he knows what we really are, and that is all that matters. (John Wooden) [31]

Tools

Ω Peace of Mind – Legacy

When you think about the legacy you are crafting through coaching, do you have a peace of mind about the direction you are headed? Ask the Holy Spirit, and people closest to you, to help you examine your definition of coaching success. Are you more like Bill Bowerman, "The main idea in running is to win the race," or like Steve Prefontaine who ran "to test the limits of the human heart"? Consider asking your athletes how they believe you define success according to your words and actions. Regardless of where you are in this journey, meditate on Philippians 3:13-14 and ask the Holy Spirit to empower you to make it a reality in your life.

Ω Peace of Mind – Identity

Are you more like Chris Evert or Tom Lehman? Do you have a peace of mind regarding who you are in Christ, or do you allow people to manipulate your peace based upon your success in their eyes? Whenever you find yourself getting frustrated or angry this week while coaching, stop and ask the Holy Spirit to reveal why these emotions are rising in you. Is your frustration based upon God being demeaned, or on the fact that you think you are being made to look foolish by the play of your athletes? Meditate upon the awesome reality of Ephesians 1:3-10 for you. How can this passage help bring peace and clarity to your coaching, and enable you to build a Christ-exalting legacy?

> Blessed be the God and Father of our Lord Jesus Christ, who has blessed us in Christ with every spiritual blessing in the heavenly places, even as he chose us in him before the foundation of the world, that we should be holy and blameless before him. In love he predestined us for adoption as sons through Jesus Christ, according to the purpose of his will, to the praise of his glorious grace, with which he has blessed us in the Beloved. In him we have redemption through his blood, the forgiveness of our trespasses, according to the riches of his grace, which he lavished upon us, in all wisdom and insight making known to us the mystery of his will, according to his purpose, which he set forth in Christ as a plan for the fullness of time, to unite all things in him, things in heaven and things on earth. (Ephesians 3:1-10)

Ω Peace of Mind – Goal Examination

Take time this week to prayerfully examine the goals you have for your team, for this week and for the season as a whole. Toss any of the goals that do not mesh with the ultimate focus upon the glory of Jesus through the fulfillment of the Great Commandment: "And you shall love the

Lord your God with all your heart and with all your soul and with all your mind and with all your strength.' The second is this: 'You shall love your neighbor as yourself.' There is no other commandment greater than these." (Mark 12:30-31) Bottom line, are your goals designed to help your players become better athletes *and* better people by seeking godly transformation in their lives while pursuing athletic excellence in order to honor Jesus?

Ω Prayer

"Father God, do not let me be conformed to this world's definition of success, but let me be transformed by the renewal of my mind, so that by testing I may discern what your will is in regards to my coaching. I want to be in synch with your good, acceptable, and perfect will so that I bring honor to you and joy to my athletes. So do not allow your Word to depart from my mouth, but empower me to delight in meditating on it day and night so that I may be careful to coach according to all that is written in it. And when I do this, free me from being frightened or dismayed at what the world thinks. Rather, help me to be strong and courageous because you promise to be with me wherever I go. Empower me to deny myself and take up my cross and follow you…and point my athletes in that same direction. For what good will it do if they are the most successful team for a season if they lose their lives for eternity? What heart-wrenching grief would flood my heart if I failed to adequately sow seeds of salvation and sanctification through my coaching, by your Holy Spirit. Daily grant me an eternal perspective so that I do not lose sight of what is truly important. It is my eager expectation and hope that I will not be ashamed at all in how I coach, with full courage now as always Christ will be honored in my body. So help me to forget what lies behind and strain forward to what lies ahead in building a legacy that points to you. Daily empower me to press on toward the goal for the prize of the upward call of God in Christ Jesus so that I will hear, 'Well done, good and faithful servant. You have been faithful over a little; I will set you over much. Enter into the joy of your master.'" (Romans 12:2; Joshua 1:8-9; Mark 8:34-37; Philippians 1:20; 3:13-14; Matthew 25:23)

PURSUING SACRED JOY

"All men seek happiness. This is without exception. Whatever different means they employ, they all tend to this end… They will never take the least step but to this object. This is the motive of every action of every man, even of those who hang themselves."[32] (Blaise Pascal)

Herein lies a problem for all too many coaches. Yes, all men seek happiness, even coaches. Yet, there is a malaise that occurs even in the lives of many coaches who have reached the pinnacle of their sporting world. Why is that? We'll call it the "Brady Conundrum." It's the refrain that plays on an endless loop, "Is this all there is?" Pursuit of sacred joy is the only answer that will satisfy the soul. "Delight yourself in the LORD, and he will give you the desires of your heart."[33] Why is this the only way to achieve true happiness?

> Most men are not satisfied with the permanent output of their lives. Nothing can wholly satisfy the life of Christ within his followers except the adoption of Christ's purposes toward the world he came to redeem. Fame, pleasure and riches are but husks and ashes in contrast with the boundless and abiding joy of working with God for the fulfillment of his eternal plans. The men [coaches] who are putting everything into Christ's undertakings are getting out of life its sweetest and most priceless rewards.[34] (J. Campbell White)

I agree wholeheartedly that, "Nothing can wholly satisfy the life of Christ within his followers except the adoption of Christ's purposes toward the world he came to redeem." That sentence alone could sum up the underlying reason for this entire book! But the reality of the meaninglessness of multiple accolades, kudos, and championships crashes down just as hard, or maybe even harder, upon those coaches who are not followers of Jesus. What do they have to cling to when their seasons or careers are through? Where can they turn to find any truth to help them comprehend what coaching is all about if wins don't bring lasting happiness? May you help show them, and your athletes, how to pursue sacred joy. In this quest, consider the radical differences between two immensely 'successful' athletes from the past whose pursuit of joy took them in diametrically opposing directions.

The name "Ty Cobb" is synonymous with baseball royalty. Many today still consider him to be the greatest all-around player that ever took to the diamond. No one has ever matched his twelve batting titles or his career batting average of .367. His competitiveness is legendary. He played for twenty-four years and had 4,191 hits, 2,245 runs, and 892 stolen bases. When it came time to vote for the inaugural Hall of Fame class to be enshrined at Cooperstown, Cobb received more votes than Babe Ruth. Many would say that Cobb was the epitome of success on and off the field. He was a millionaire through his investments in the stock market and in the fledgling Coca-Cola Company. Yet, if he was happy or joyful, he hid it well. People detested Cobb and he, by all accounts, remained a cantankerous curmudgeon until the end of his life; a life punctuated by the sad reality that only four members of the entire baseball community attended his funeral.

Eric Liddell's time on earth told an entirely different story. From the cinder tracks of the UK to the 1924 Paris Olympics, Liddell also dominated the headlines on and off his playing field. Whereas Cobb lived a life that seemed to say, "I am the master of my fate. I am the captain of my soul," Liddell bowed at the feet of the Almighty.

> Most prospective [1924 British Olympic] team members received the schedule of events sometime in late 1923. And as soon as Eric read that the 100-meter heats were to be held on a Sunday, he knew what he must do. He would tell the committee

that he could not run in that event... Eric believed the Christian Sabbath belonged to God and was to be kept as a day of worship and rest...

After informing the Olympic authorities of his decision, he was quite willing to explore alternatives with them. The first possibility in the committee's mind was for Eric to alter his perspective. While it was true that the preliminary heats for the 100 meters were on July 6, the first Sunday of the games, they did not occur until the afternoon. There would be plenty of time for Eric to attend morning worship services, then race late in the day. But he did not see it that way. When a determined committee member reminded him that the Continental Sabbath ended at noon, Eric replied, "Mine lasts all day."

...Along with sacrificing his place in the 100 meters, Eric gave up two other races in which Britain held high hopes of winning the gold. The qualifying heats for the 4 x 100 and 4 x 400 meter relays occurred on weekdays, but the finals were scheduled for Sunday, July 13... Since neither Eric's mind nor the schedule of events could be changed, he agreed to train for the 200 and 400-meter races. He was not considered an Olympic contender at either distance... [Yet Liddell captured the bronze in the 200 and set a world record in the 400, taking the gold by five meters over his closest competitor][35]

Liddell's refusal to run on the Sabbath was just a foretaste of a life that was in pursuit of sacred joy. Rather than seeking to milk his athletic ability for all it was worth, he became a missionary to China. By all accounts, his physical ability didn't wane over the next four years. Many believe he could have competed at the same high level in the 1928 Olympics. But that was not God's call upon his life. Just as not running on the Sabbath was an easy decision based upon his love for Jesus, so, too, was the move to China.

As World War II raged on, the Japanese war machine ravaged China's landscape. In 1943 Liddell and his fellow missionaries found their village turned into a Japanese internment camp. Story after story has been told about Eric's selfless service during his entire time in China, even through the hardships of the war. He lived this way until the very end when he died in the camp at the age of forty-three on February 21, 1945. Why did he live this way? Why is his legacy so radically different from someone like Ty Cobb?

"Absolute surrender to God's Will as revealed in Jesus Christ. His was a God-controlled life and he followed his Master and Lord with a devotion that never flagged and with an intensity of purpose that made men see both the reality and the power of true religion."[36] Eric understood that giving up the potential of more medals would never compare to the ultimate treasure found in Jesus. He wholeheartedly pursued sacred joy. "The kingdom of heaven is like treasure hidden in a field, which a man found and covered up. Then *in his joy* he goes and sells all that he has and buys that field. Again, the kingdom of heaven is like a merchant in search of fine pearls, who, on finding one pearl of great value, went and sold all that he had and bought it."[37] Ty Cobb was a half-hearted creature. Eric Liddell pursued sacred joy.

> We are half hearted creatures, fooling about with drink and sex and ambition when infinite joy is offered us, like an ignorant child who wants to go on making mud pies in a slum because he cannot imagine what is meant by the offer of a holiday at the sea. We are far too easily pleased.[38] (C. S. Lewis)

∞ *What about you? How can you pursue sacred joy even in the midst of disappointing, frustrating, chaotic, or heart-wrenching events, situations, or seasons?*

Let's be honest, when you win it's easy to be thankful. And you should be fired up when your team is victorious. But what happens when you lose, or get a bad call from the referees, or a 'bad break'? How will your response to these negative situations help or hamper your legacy? Even if you receive bad press or insults for coaching snafus or losses, these are not reasons to lose hope, because this world is, at best, a shadow of the glorious things that are to come. "So we do not lose heart. Though our outer self is wasting away, our inner self is being renewed day by day. For this light momentary affliction is preparing for us an eternal weight of glory beyond all comparison, as we look not to the things that are seen but to the things that are unseen. For the things that are seen are transient, but the things that are unseen are eternal."[39]

You must spend time directing your eyes towards your final destination in order to properly deal with the inescapable setbacks of this world. Only then can your joy abound. "For now we see in a mirror dimly, but then face to face. Now I know in part; then I shall know fully, even as I have been fully known."[40] Face to face with Jesus. What trinkets that this world offers you as a coach could match that glorious truth? You are called to be a joyful coach. You are commanded to be joyful at all times. "Rejoice in the Lord *always*; again I will say, rejoice."[41] Psalm 100:2 goes even further and commands that your coaching, your service unto the Lord, be done with a joyful spirit - "Serve the Lord with gladness! Come into his presence with singing!"

Why should this be a major concern to your building of a legacy? Consider what curses fell upon God's people who didn't serve joyfully: "Because you did not serve the LORD your God *with joyfulness and gladness of heart*, because of the abundance of all things, therefore you shall serve your enemies whom the LORD will send against you, in hunger and thirst, in nakedness, and lacking everything. And he will put a yoke of iron on your neck until he has destroyed you."[42] Modeling a joy-filled attitude regardless of the circumstances will train your athletes to perform with confidence knowing that you can help them learn from whichever way the tide rolls when the final whistle blows. This will also take a lot of pressure off them, which will aid them in learning how to have joy in the journey. And the reason this is possible for those who follow Jesus, Romans 8:28-30 is true:

And we know that for those who love God all things work together for good, for those who are called according to his purpose. For those whom he foreknew he also predestined to be conformed to the image of his Son, in order that he might be the firstborn among many brothers. And those whom he predestined he also called, and those whom he called he also justified, and those whom he justified he also glorified.

Every win or loss, bad call or good call, 'bad break' or 'lucky break' for those who love God and are called according to his purpose, will be used for your good. However, because the ultimate goal is conformity to the image of Jesus, not everything will be fun – but you are still commanded to be joy-full. Only in praising God and enjoying him through the good times and the bad will you truly glorify him as loving and sovereign. No, I'm not saying that you are joyful about some situations you must endure. I'm saying that Scripture commands you to be joyful in spite of them, because God is using them to mold and shape you to be more like Jesus. And that is the only legacy worth leaving – growing in Christlikeness through the pursuit of sacred joy.

I'm persuaded that we will never be of much use in this life until we've developed a healthy obsession with the next. Our only hope for satisfaction of soul and joy of heart in this life comes from looking intently at what we can't see. Therefore, we must take steps to cultivate and intensify in our souls an ache for the beauty of the age to come... Heaven is characterized by the increase of joy. Heaven is not simply about the reality or experience of joy, but its *eternal increase*.[43]

If then you have been raised with Christ, seek the things that are above, where Christ is, seated at the right hand of God. Set your minds on things that are above, not on things that are on earth. For you have died, and your life is hidden with Christ in God. When Christ who is your life appears, then you also will appear with him in glory.[44]

Tools

Ω Develop a Heavenly Mindset

"Concerning this salvation, the prophets who prophesied about the grace that was to be yours searched and inquired carefully, inquiring what person or time the Spirit of Christ in them was indicating when he predicted the sufferings of Christ and the subsequent glories. It was revealed to them that they were serving not themselves but you, in the things that have now been announced to you through those who preached the good news to you by the Holy Spirit sent from heaven, things into which angels long to look. Therefore, preparing your minds for action, and being sober-minded, set your hope fully on the grace that will be brought to you at the revelation of Jesus Christ. As obedient children, do not be conformed to the passions of your former ignorance, but as he who called you is holy, you also be holy in all your conduct, since it is written, 'You shall be holy, for I am holy.'" (1 Peter 1:10-16)

Because you have received the salvation that the prophets spoke about long ago, you are commanded to act in specific ways:

1. "Preparing your minds for action": Be ready to see God at work and respond appropriately. God is active and calling you to join him in his Kingdom ventures.
2. "Being sober-minded": Stay mentally and spiritually alert. Don't let your mind be swayed by the world and find yourself wandering into sinful attitudes and actions. For example, don't let the idols of winning or reputation determine how you coach.
3. "Set your hope fully on the grace that will be brought to you at the revelation of Jesus Christ": Eagerly and confidently expect that even greater blessings are awaiting you when Jesus returns. This should empower you to stay on the path of righteousness when things don't go as 'planned' with your team - for your citizenship is in heaven and great rewards await you there. So let your coaching be about storing up treasures in heaven where they will never rot, rust, or fall into disrepair.

Ω Focus on Heavenly Beauty

"But our citizenship is in heaven, and from it we await a Savior, the Lord Jesus Christ, who will transform our lowly body to be like his glorious body, by the power that enables him even to subject all things to himself." (Philippians 3:20-21)

Your citizenship is in heaven 'now.' It does not say 'will be' in heaven. Are you coaching like a citizen of heaven or as if you were a citizen of earth?

"A contemplative focus on the beauty of heaven frees us from excessive dependence upon earthly wealth and comfort [wins and accolades]. If there awaits us an eternal inheritance of immeasurable glory, it is senseless to expend effort and energy here, sacrificing so much time and money, to obtain for so brief a time in corruptible form what we will enjoy forever in consummate perfection."[45]

Ω Focus on Future Justice

"Blessed are you when others revile you and persecute you and utter all kinds of evil against you falsely on my account. Rejoice and be glad, for your reward is great in heaven, for so they persecuted the prophets who were before you." (Matthew 5:11-12)

Injustices will occur in your time as a coach. They probably won't be to this extent. But if you are reviled or slandered because you seek to leave a legacy that points to the matchless beauty of Jesus, remember that "your reward is great in heaven." Justice will prevail either through the cross or through hell.

Therefore, daily meditate upon the cross. Beloved, never avenge yourselves, but leave it to the wrath of God, for it is written, "Vengeance is mine, I will repay, says the Lord." (Romans 12:19)

"A contemplative focus on heaven enables us to respond appropriately to the injustices of this life. Essential to heavenly joy is witnessing the vindication of righteousness and the judgment of evil."[46]

Ω Focus on Future Satisfaction

"For I consider that the sufferings of this present time are not worth comparing with the glory that is to be revealed to us… But if we hope for what we do not see, we wait for it with patience." (Romans 8:18, 25)

Frustration, suffering, and coming up short are part and parcel of coaching. Focusing upon and hoping for that future all-consuming satisfaction will help you to persevere in a godly manner; a legacy built upon the promises of God all being fulfilled.

"For all the promises of God find their Yes in him [Jesus]. That is why it is through him that we utter our Amen to God for his glory." (2 Corinthians 1:20)

"A contemplative focus on heaven produces the fruit of endurance and perseverance now. The strength to endure *present suffering* is the fruit of meditation on *future satisfaction!*"[47]

Ω Prayer

"Empower me to rejoice in you always, Lord, no matter what circumstances arise in my coaching. Help me to comprehend that it is how I respond to wins and losses that matters the most, not my record on the scoreboard. So let me be glad in you, rejoice, and shout for joy because I am your child. I have been made holy and righteous by the blood of Jesus. So help me to have a heavenly perspective when trials come my way in my coaching. For your word tells me that through those trials the testing of my faith will produce steadfastness and I will become more like Jesus. And we know that for those who love you all things work together for good, for those who are called according to your purpose. For those whom you foreknew you also predestined to be conformed to the image of your Son. Therefore, empower me to rejoice always, pray without ceasing, and give thanks in all circumstances; for this is your will for me in Christ Jesus. For I have been raised with Christ, so I need to seek and desire things that are above, where Christ is, seated at your right hand, Father. Help me to pursue sacred joy by setting my mind on things that are above, not on things that are on earth. Only then will I truly be satisfied." (Philippians 4:4; Psalm 32:11; James 1:2-3; Romans 8:28-29; 1 Thessalonians 5:16-18; Colossians 3:1-2)

RESTING IN GOD'S SOVEREIGNTY

Relax. God already knows the results...and he loves you.

"Therefore I tell you, do not be anxious about your life, what you will eat or what you will drink, nor about your body, what you will put on. Is not life more than food, and the body more than clothing? Look at the birds of the air: they neither sow nor reap nor gather into barns, and yet your heavenly Father feeds them. Are you not of more value than they? And which of you by being anxious can add a single hour to his span of life? And why are you anxious about clothing? Consider the lilies of the field, how they grow: they neither toil nor spin, yet I tell you, even Solomon in all his glory was not arrayed like one of these. But if God so clothes the grass of the field, which today is alive and tomorrow is thrown into the oven, will he not much more clothe you, O you of little faith? Therefore do not be anxious, saying, 'What shall we eat?' or 'What shall we drink?' or 'What shall we wear?' For the Gentiles seek after all these things, and your heavenly Father knows that you need them all. But seek first the kingdom of God and his righteousness, and all these things will be added to you. Therefore do not be anxious about tomorrow, for tomorrow will be anxious for itself. Sufficient for the day is its own trouble." (Matthew 6:25-34)

Sovereignty is about power, and, in reality, you don't have much. The majority of what occurs in your life on any given day is out of your control. This concept is the main way we tried to help our daughters grow in humility from the time they were young. For instance, if there was even a hint of superiority or smugness regarding their athletic achievements, we would remind them that they didn't choose their parents, their genetics, their geographical locale or any of a hundred other factors that play into their performances. This was not meant to downplay their efforts, just to keep them in check. Yes, it is a divine-human cooperative. But even their desire to achieve, to prepare, and to compete are all gifts from God.

He alone is the infinite Creator. We are finite, limited creatures; which means that you need to constantly keep your perspective in check when it comes to your coaching. You are dependent upon God's loving, sovereign will to do anything – so don't be anxious. And regardless of the fairy tales spawned by the media, you cannot be whatever you want. You can be what God calls and empowers you to be. Nothing more and nothing less. For no plan of God's can be stopped. And that should bring peace and a legacy that truly points to Jesus alone as the Creator, Redeemer, and Sustainer of the universe. "Then Job answered the LORD and said: 'I know that you can do all things, and that no purpose of yours can be thwarted.'[48]

Consider the life of John Wooden, one of the greatest basketball coaches that ever lived. Yet his plan was to become an English professor. God had a different career trajectory in mind.

> What I knew how to do was teach English, including Shakespeare and spelling, poetry and punctuation. As a matter of fact, just before graduation from Purdue, I was offered a fellowship with an eye toward my becoming an English professor and joining its faculty in West Lafayette, Indiana. I would have accepted the offer, except for one thing: Nellie and I were eager to get married and start a family, and the Purdue Fellowship wouldn't pay enough for us to live on. Had I intended to stay single, however, I might have taken the offer… and perhaps never becoming a full-time coach.[49]

And if that doesn't help you to comprehend what little control you truly have over much of life, ponder the reality that John Wooden wasn't 'supposed' to coach the UCLA Bruins and become the *Wizard of Westwood*. In 1947 Coach Wooden's Indiana State University basketball team came in second place at the NAIA National Championships. It didn't take long afterwards for the offers to start rolling in from schools like the University of Minnesota and UCLA. Wooden's heart leaned heavily towards Minnesota and the Big 10 Conference. He knew very little about UCLA. In fact, he only visited the school as a favor to a friend. After several weeks of negotiations with Minnesota, he felt sure that he would become their next coach. The athletic director promised he would call the following Saturday at exactly 6 p.m. regarding the school's decision. Wooden called UCLA and told them that he would most likely not be accepting their offer.

6 o'clock came and went on Saturday night with no call. The inference John Wooden drew was that Minnesota had rejected his requirements for taking the position. When the phone did finally ring, it was 7:00. The athletic director from UCLA was calling to find out what John had decided. Wooden committed to Westwood. Soon after hanging up the phone, it rang again. A blizzard had knocked out all the phone lines in Minnesota. The Gophers weren't able to get through earlier, but now they were offering Wooden everything he had requested. It was too late. He'd already given his word to UCLA. In God's sovereign will, he chose to use a low paying fellowship to get Wooden into coaching, and a blizzard to get him to the West Coast. And the rest, as they say, is history.

∞ *How should the sovereignty of God help you to build a Jesus-saturated legacy as you seek to help your athletes pursue excellence and see Jesus with greater clarity?*

As discussed previously, this should grant you a peace and remove anxiety because of the promises in Romans 8:28-29. Whether the sun is shining upon your season or you're experiencing intermittent clouds, God promises to use all of it for your good – to help you to grow in Christlikeness. When your athletes witness your even-keeled attitude, you are training them to not get too high when they experience success or too low when they hit the potholes in their pathway. Your example will become a legacy that teaches your athletes to deal with success and adversity that come with sports and life, respect authority, and follow the rules. For example:

> Perhaps you believe that the ref is unfair, the other team and their coach are cheating and the field is crummy and the wind is blowing the wrong way. Soccer is a game in which the best team does not always win, where nice kids can get hurt and flashy, selfish, ineffective players often catch the coach's eye. Some parents [coaches] simply cannot cope with the utter unfairness of it all and when they scream and yell at the ref from the sideline they are giving their child [athlete] a lifetime of free passes to blame everything in life on factors out of his control.[50]

Without faith in God's sovereign rule and reign, you either will be duped by the imposter called 'winning' or the one tabbed 'losing.' Therefore, in order to build a legacy built on faith you must teach your athletes that neither they nor you can ultimately control the scoreboard. You can train and equip your team. You can plan how you want them to execute on the day of competition. But ultimately, "Many are the plans in the mind of a man, but it is the purpose of the LORD that will stand."[51] And the truth remains that God's plans include days of jubilation and frustration for every coach that hangs a whistle around his or her neck. The key is to keep your emotions in balance because no results catch God off guard. No results prove the degree of love that God is exhibiting towards you or your team. And no results can keep you from being conformed to the image of Christ. A legacy that uses all results to draw near to Jesus is the only kind worth building.

So allow your coaching to reflect these realities, "In him we have obtained an inheritance, having been predestined according to the purpose of him who works all things according to the counsel of his will, so that we who were the first to hope in Christ might be to the praise of his glory."[52] Don't dwell on the problems you are encountering. Rather cling tightly to the promises of God. For even problems, trial, and tribulations in your coaching have a purpose in God's economy – to glorify God and refine you. So, "Count it all joy, my brothers, when you meet trials of various kinds, for you know that the testing of your faith produces steadfastness. And let steadfastness have its full effect, that you may be perfect and complete, lacking in nothing. If any of you lacks wisdom, let him ask God, who gives generously to all without reproach, and it will be given him."[53]

> Have you ever visited a pottery factory? When the pottery is placed in the kiln, its colors are dull and muted. After it has been in the fire... its colors are vivid. The fire makes it beautiful. So it is in our lives. The fires of life [coaching tribulations] bring out the beauty of the life of Christ within.[54]

In light of this, "fear not." God has a plan. "Only be strong and very courageous, being careful to do according to all the law that Moses my servant commanded you. Do not turn from it to the right hand or to the left, that you may have good success [or *may act wisely*] wherever you go."[55]

Seek to honor him in all your coaching and there is no reason to be worried about losing, what others think, or not achieving the goals you set. Any setback you encounter is temporary compared to the eternal weight of glory awaiting you. I'm not saying that makes those difficult times any easier, but they can be joy-filled. And they should be joy-filled because God is seeking to draw out the beauty of the life of Christ within you, and further define your legacy. How will you choose?

> In *Man's Search For Meaning* Frankl writes that everything can be taken from a man but one thing: the greatest of all human freedoms, the ability to choose how to respond to any given circumstance. Frankl said that we retain the freedom to choose our attitudes and actions to whatever life deals us.[56]

As you choose to rest in the loving sovereignty of Jesus, be at peace knowing that the dividends will be eternal for you – and Lord willing, for many of your athletes also. You may not see the results during a season, or multiple seasons if you coach the same athletes over time. It may be years before some of the Refiner's fire begins to bring out the beauty in the vessels you coach. Others may never respond to the call of Christ. But, you can be at peace that your legacy will be one of love, resting in God's sovereignty to not only draw some of your athletes to him, but also to purify them as they walk through this life. For God alone is the One who causes growth[57] – from alienation, to justification, to sanctification, to glorification. Build a legacy as a sower of seeds, trusting in God to cause growth where he deems.

∞ *How can keeping the Sabbath show that you have faith in God's sovereignty?*

God first instituted a day of solemn rest, a holy Sabbath, when the people of Israel were in the wilderness. After their grumbling against Moses and Aaron and saying, "Would that we had died by the hand of the LORD in the land of Egypt, when we sat by the meat pots and ate bread to the full, for you have brought us out into this wilderness to kill this whole assembly with hunger,"[58] God chose to rain down bread from heaven. Before this providential manna fell from the sky, however, "Moses said to them, 'Let no one leave any of it over till the morning.'[59] But they did not listen to Moses. Some left part of it till the morning, and it bred worms and stank. And Moses was angry with them." Why did some of them hoard the manna? Because they didn't trust God. They weren't content in receiving their daily bread from him. They believed more in their own 'sovereign' will than God's. And what did God do to show them who truly ruled and reigned? He told the people to gather twice as much as they needed on the sixth day of the week so that they would rest in him on the seventh day.

> This is what the LORD has commanded: "Tomorrow is a day of solemn rest, a holy Sabbath to the LORD; bake what you will bake and boil what you will boil, and all that is left over lay aside to be kept till the morning." So they laid it aside till the morning, as Moses commanded them, and it did not stink, and there were no

worms in it. Moses said, "Eat it today, for today is a Sabbath to the LORD; today you will not find it in the field. Six days you shall gather it, but on the seventh day, which is a Sabbath, there will be none." On the seventh day some of the people went out to gather, but they found none. And the LORD said to Moses, "How long will you refuse to keep my commandments and my laws?" (Exodus 16:23-28)

The purpose of the Sabbath was literally to force Israel to understand that they could not provide for themselves. It is no different for us today. God alone is the Provider of your daily bread. Don't delude yourself. If you are a full-time coach, working seven days a week is not the silver bullet that will propel your program to the next level. More often than not, it will slowly destroy your physical health and your closest relationships because you, like the manna, will begin to rot and stink. Therefore, "If priorities *protect* my purpose and passion, then pacing *prolongs* it… 'You chart the path ahead of me and tell me where to stop and rest. Every moment, you know where I am.'" (Psalm 139:3, TLB) [60] You must plan time into your schedule to rest and recover if you are going to build a legacy that shows by word and deed that God is sovereign. It's easy to say. Harder to do. Whether you are a full-time coach or part-time, there will always be something else to do.

> Productive work is an intoxicating thing. The temptation to base one's identity and esteem on what one produces is all but irresistible. . . The command to rest and remember God is a challenge to human productivity. It arrests and relativizes even the most demanding and consuming work, for anything which can be interrupted is not ultimate in importance. Self-important people cannot tolerate this undercutting of their significance. (Fred Sanders)[61]

Tools

Ω Memorize for Perspective

Win or lose, prosperity or adversity, moving forward or facing setbacks – you need to cling tightly to God's promises in order to build a legacy that will point your athletes to the all-sufficiency of Jesus. Put these passages in a visible place where you can regularly meditate upon them as you seek, by the power of the Holy Spirit, to memorize them and have them emblazoned upon your heart and mind – so your coaching will be transformed.

- "I know that you can do all things, and that no purpose of yours can be thwarted." (Job 42:2)
- And we know that for those who love God all things work together for good, for those who are called according to his purpose." (Romans 8:28)
- "The LORD will fulfill his purpose for me; your steadfast love, O LORD, endures forever." (Psalm 138:8)

- "Many are the plans in the mind of a man, but it is the purpose of the LORD that will stand." (Proverbs 19:21)

Ω Pray for Wisdom

"I cry out to God Most High, to God who fulfills his purpose for me" (Psalm 57:2). Pray for the Holy Spirit to reveal how he wants you to respond to the setbacks, struggles, or attacks you are presently facing – so that you may exhibit his glory, and progress in your sanctification, your growth in grace. "For it has been granted to you that for the sake of Christ you should not only believe in him but also suffer for his sake." (Philippians 1:29) "Count it all joy, my brothers, when you meet trials of various kinds, for you know that the testing of your faith produces steadfastness. And let steadfastness have its full effect, that you may be perfect and complete, lacking in nothing." (James 1:2-4)

Ω Rest for Growth

Consider implementing ideas like these from Dave Kraft in *Leaders Who Last*:

"1. Take a full day off each week, and limit my work hours.
2. Plan a full day alone for a spiritual retreat on a monthly basis.
3. Make sure I have some fun each week doing things that make me laugh.
4. Limit the number of evenings I am not at home."[62]

Ω Prayer

"Heavenly Father, remind me that I should not be surprised when persecution comes my way if I am coaching for your glory. For you said that all who desire to live a godly life in your Son will be persecuted. When this type of suffering does occur, help me to rejoice because you are calling me to share in Christ's sufferings because his glory is being revealed. So empower me to be strong and courageous because you promise to be with me always. And whether I am experiencing prosperity or adversity at any certain moment in time through my coaching, you promise to use all of it for good in order that I might be conformed to the image of Jesus. Because no plan of yours can be thwarted and you do whatever you please in heaven and on earth, let me rest in your loving sovereign rule and reign in my life. For you who did not spare your own Son but gave him up for me, will you not also with him graciously give me all things? For all your promises find their 'Yes' and 'Amen' in Jesus!" (2 Timothy 3:12; 1 Peter 4:13; Matthew 28 19-20; Romans 8:28-29: Job 42:2; Psalm 135:6; Romans 8:32; 2 Corinthians 1:20)

PURSUING SANCTIFICATION

"If successful, don't crow; if defeated don't croak." (Samuel Chadwick)[63]

"This is the great conversion in life: to recognize and believe that the many unexpected events are not just disturbing interruptions of our projects, but the way in which God molds our hearts and prepares us for his return." (Henri Nouwen)[64]

"Do you not know that in a race all the runners run, but only one receives the prize? So run that you may obtain it. Every athlete exercises self-control in all things. They do it to receive a perishable wreath, but we an imperishable. So I do not run aimlessly; I do not box as one beating the air. But I discipline my body and keep it under control, lest after preaching to others I myself should be disqualified." (1 Corinthians 9:24-27)

One of the main reasons for you to be coaching is the development of your relationships with Jesus and with others – athletes, assistant coaches, parents, administrators, and fans. And God has you in those relationships to help you grow in holiness. Sanctification is the process by which you become conformed to the image of Christ, so that what you feel, what you think, and what you do, changes. A legacy worth leaving is one where you, and others, can see evidence of a harvest of holiness over your lifetime. May the fruit of the Spirit[65] be increasingly evident in your life so that the world may know that God is at work in conforming you to the image of his Son – for his glory and your joy!

Ultimately, that's what all your life is about, including your coaching. Wins and losses will soon be like the morning dew on the grass. No one will care. Therefore, every practice, every game, every interaction with your athletes is an opportunity to worship God. He is allowing you to come alongside him in his kingdom agenda, the transformation of hearts and minds for his glory. How well you respond in love to the ups and downs that you will encounter with your athletes and all those impacted by your program will leave a greater legacy than other records kept about your coaching. "But as he who called you is holy, you also be holy in all your conduct, since it is written, 'You shall be holy, for I am holy.'"[66]

Unfortunately not all Christians understand this reality when it comes to sports. Even the famed evangelist Billy Graham at one point in his life apparently got caught up in the myth of the muscular male Christian. This is what he wrote about winning in the forward to a 1965 book authored by former Pro Bowl football player, Bill Glass:

"If you get beat, after the game is over you ought to congratulate the winner... Yes, practice good sportsmanship, but when you get in the dressing room and no one is looking, back off about ten yards and run and ram your head into the locker because you hate to lose so badly. Don't ever be a good loser. Be a bad loser. Good losers usually lose."[67]

What Billy Graham was advocating in this forward was not holiness, nor a faith in the sovereignty of God. His advice was teaching a generation of young athletes haughtiness – shake a hand in pseudo congratulations, and then go bash your head because, in reality, you should have been the winner. Have you ever behaved in a similar manner after a defeat, putting on your Sunday face then expressing your true feelings when no one was looking? I have. But thanks be to God that sanctification for Dr. Graham, for me, and for you is progressive. We can and should be growing. Just as we don't allow defeats on the field to keep us from pursuing victory, neither do we in the Christian walk! Growing in sanctification is not an option for Christians. So rejoice alongside me and continue to seek transformation by the Holy Spirit, whereby he will move you towards holiness.

"Not that I have already obtained this or am already perfect, but I press on to make it my own, because Christ Jesus has made me his own. Brothers, I do not consider that I have made it my own. But one thing I do: forgetting what lies behind and straining forward to what lies ahead, I press on toward the goal for the prize of the upward call of God in Christ Jesus."[68] Notice that not even the Apostle Paul was perfected in holiness when he walked the earth. He, like you and me, experienced progressive sanctification. Three times in this passage he uses words that show that his holiness journey was not complete: "Not that I have already obtained," "or am already perfect," so he must "press on." It is a journey. When you fail on the field, repent, then "press on toward the goal for the prize of the upward call of God in Christ Jesus." That is a primary goal of your coaching. You have been justified, you continue to be sanctified, and when you are face-to-face with Jesus, you will be glorified – for eternity. And throughout this process, "Would that God would make hell so real to us that we cannot rest; heaven so real that we must have men there."[69] Because "this gospel of the kingdom will be proclaimed throughout the whole world as a testimony to all nations [including the Sports Nation], and then the end will come."[70]

But no one said this task of bringing the gospel to the nations would be easy. In fact, quite the opposite:

"See [Jesus said], we are going up to Jerusalem, and the Son of Man will be delivered over to the chief priests and the scribes, and they will condemn him to death and deliver him over to the Gentiles. And they will mock him and spit on him, and flog him and kill him. And after three days he will rise."[71]

And Jesus said, that his disciples could expect the same kind of treatment as they proclaimed to good news. "But be on your guard. For they will deliver you over to councils, and you will be beaten in synagogues, and you will stand before governors and kings for my sake, to bear witness before them. And the gospel must first be proclaimed to all nations."[72]

Now you probably will never experience persecution or suffering anywhere near this degree because of your coaching. But if you've been at it long enough, you've probably already had your fair share of character-bashing. Expect more if you seek to show that Jesus is your ultimate treasure, when you seek to use coaching as a tool to help transform lives while pursuing excellence. But stay the course, because you can either build a legacy on the rock solid foundation of the Word that will last forever[73] or the morning dew on the grass that will quickly disappear. So seek an eternal perspective from the moment you arise until the moment your head hits the pillow. Because, "As for man, his days are like grass; he flourishes like a flower of the field; for the wind passes over it, and it is gone, and its place knows it no more. But the steadfast love of the LORD is from everlasting to everlasting on those who fear him, and his righteousness to children's children, to those who keep his covenant."[74]

I realize this is not what you usually hear in coaching classes or seminars. Those, at best, only give you part of the story. Yes, you want to help your athletes pursue excellence in the sport you coach. But if the foundational reason for pursing excellence is built upon pursuing both The Great Commission and The Greatest Commandment, the results can be glorious and eternal – a legacy worth building! So, "Have nothing to do with irreverent, silly myths. Rather train yourself for godliness; for while bodily training is of some value, godliness is of value in every way, as it holds promise for the present life and also for the life to come. The saying is trustworthy and deserving of full acceptance. For to this end we toil and strive, because we have our hope set on the living God, who is the Savior of all people, especially of those who believe. Command and teach these things."[75]

And if you want added motivation to pursue a life of holiness, a life being conformed to the image of Jesus through your coaching, consider the following. "We are given these eternal rewards for:

- Doing good works (Ephesians 6:8; Romans 2:6, 10)
- Persevering under persecution (Luke 6:22-23)
- Showing compassion to the needy (Luke 14:13-14)
- Treating our enemies kindly (Luke 6:35)
- [The] smallest acts of kindness: "If anyone gives even a cup of cold water to one of these little ones because he is my disciple, I tell you the truth, he will certainly not lose his reward." (Matthew 10:42)[76]

Who are you? What is your coaching ultimately about? May you learn from the actions of John the Baptizer when his identity was questioned. "And this is the testimony of John, when the Jews sent priests and Levites from Jerusalem to ask him, 'Who are you?' He confessed, and did not deny, but confessed, 'I am not the Christ.' And they asked him, 'What then? Are you Elijah?' He said, 'I am not.' 'Are you the Prophet?' And he answered, 'No.'" (John 1:19-21)

So what did John do when questioned about his identity? Did his pulse pound, feet shuffle, or voice stammer? No! John "confessed freely" about his identity. This word comes from the Greek *martureo* [from which we get our word, *martyr*], and it means "to be a witness, to bear witness, i.e. to affirm that one has seen or heard or experienced something, or that he knows it because taught by divine revelation or inspiration."[77] Watch John's reaction in order to keep your identity in Christ properly fixed in your head and heart – especially during the heat of coaching battles.

The first lesson you can learn from John's response is this: John wasn't trying to impress anyone. Second, his identity was not the primary issue at hand, and John refused to waste time with his opponents' errant questions. Notice how John's answers become shorter with each query, "I am not the Christ," "I am not," "No". "So they said to him, 'Who are you? We need to give an answer to those who sent us. What do you say about yourself?' He said, 'I am the voice of one crying out in the wilderness, 'Make straight the way of the Lord,' as the prophet Isaiah said.'" (Vss. 22-23)

The third lesson is this: John allows God's Word to dictate his identity and his value, not people's questions of him or possible responses to his answer. His primary role was to introduce people to Jesus – to prepare the way for the Lord. But that didn't satisfy them, so the questioning continued. "(Now they had been sent from the Pharisees.) They asked him, 'Then why are you baptizing, if you are neither the Christ, nor Elijah, nor the Prophet?' John answered them, 'I baptize with water, but among you stands one you do not know, even he who comes after me, the strap of whose sandal I am not worthy to untie.' These things took place in Bethany across the Jordan, where John was baptizing." (Vss. 24-28) The fourth lesson focuses on John's utter humility. He understood that he was nothing in comparison to the King. His value lay solely in his relationship to the Messiah – he was "the voice." Keep that in mind the next time you glance at the scoreboard. You, too, are to be a voice pointing to Jesus through your words and deeds.

"The next day he saw Jesus coming toward him, and said, 'Behold, the Lamb of God, who takes away the sin of the world! This is he of whom I said, "After me comes a man who ranks before me, because he was before me." I myself did not know him, but for this purpose I came baptizing with water, that he might be revealed to Israel.'" (Vss. 29-31) The final lesson comes when we see John immediately point to Jesus as the sacrificial lamb who would take away their sins once and for all times. Once John knew Jesus' identity, he immediately began the introductions – this is the Lamb of God, the Son of God. In fact, John's life can be summed up by verse 32, "I have seen and have borne witness that this is the Son of God."

> Sports have spread to every corner of the world, transcending differences between cultures and nations... "Because of the global dimensions this activity has assumed, those involved in sports throughout the world have a great responsibility. They are called to make sports an opportunity for meeting and dialogue, over and above every barrier of language, race or culture. Sports, in fact, can make an effective contribution to peaceful understanding between peoples and to establishing the new civilization of love."[78]

"I have seen and have borne witness that this is the Son of God." May that be your legacy through coaching so that you hear, "Well done, good and faithful coach" as you help to bring about the new civilization of love to the Sports Nation. For "God is love, and whoever abides in love abides in God, and God abides in him!"[79]

Tools

Ω Reminders - How to Pursue Sanctification

"1. *Renew your mind with prolonged Scripture reading.*
2. *Pray with an unhurried heart.*
3. *Confess the hidden sins of your heart.* [Ask] *the Spirit to bring conviction to your heart and reveal unconfessed sin.*
4. *Live in true community with others, and allow them to truly know you.*
5. *Review your calling by God.* [Why do I coach?]
6. *Review the goals and steps of action you have for your life* [for your coaching].
7. *Review the way you are managing your whole life.* [Continually place your coaching against the silhouette of Scripture]
8. *Rest in God's grace, love and acceptance of you.*"[80]

Ω Prayer

"Gracious and heavenly Father, empower me to lay aside every weight and sin which clings so closely, so that I can run with endurance the race that is set before me, looking to Jesus, the founder and perfecter of my faith, who for the joy that was set before him endured the cross, despising the shame, and is seated at your right hand. For I have been crucified with Christ. It is no longer I who live, but Christ who lives in me. And the life I now live in the flesh I live by faith in your Son, who loved me and gave himself for me. Therefore, empower me to love my athletes well so that they may be drawn ever-nearer to you. May I be sober-minded and watchful because my adversary, the devil, prowls around like a roaring lion, seeking to devour me by distracting me from the true reason that I coach – to bring glory to Jesus and joy to my athletes. So I plead with you Father, the God of peace, that you would sanctify me completely so that my whole spirit and soul and body will be kept blameless at the coming of my Lord Jesus Christ – because you who call me are faithful; you will surely do it. For this reason I bow my knees before you, Father, from whom every family in heaven and on earth is named, that according to the riches of your glory you may grant me to be strengthened with power through your Spirit in my inner being. An may Christ dwell in my heart through faith—so that I, being rooted and grounded in love, may have strength to comprehend with all the saints what is the breadth and length and height and depth, and to know the love of Christ that surpasses knowledge, that I may be filled with all the fullness of God. Now to him who is able to do far more abundantly than all that I ask or think in, with, and through my coaching, according to the power at work within me, to him be glory in the church and in Christ Jesus throughout all generations, forever and ever. Amen." (Hebrews 12:1-2; Galatians 2:20; 1 Peter 5:8; 1 Thessalonians 5:12-26; Ephesians 3:14-21)

"Friendships are borne on the field of athletic strife and are the real gold of competition. Awards become corroded, friends gather no dust." (Jesse Owens)

Notes

[1]   Matthew Henry, www.bible.org/seriespage/determining-your-destiny-genesis-491-28, Accessed 9/15/2004.

[2]   Dr. Alan J. Meenan, Sermon, *First Presbyterian Church*, Amarillo, Texas.

[3]   1 Chronicles 10:13, italics mine.

[4]   1 Kings 2:1-4, italics mine.

[5]   C.J. Mahaney, *Don't Waste Your Sports*, (Gaithersburg: Sovereign Grace Ministries, 2008), www.sovereigngraceministries.com.

[6]   Scott Frey in Michael Zigarelli, *The Messiah Method: The Seven Disciplines of the Winningest College Soccer Program in America* (USA: Xulon, 2011), 58-59.

[7]   2 Timothy 4:7-8.

[8]   John Piper, *Don't Waste Your Life* (Wheaton: Crossway, 2003), 46.

[9]   Luke 10:27.

[10] Dave Kraft, *Leaders Who Last* (Wheaton: Crossway, 2010), 40-41.

[11] Gene Wojciechowski, *Paterno Empowered a Predator*, ESPN, 7/17/2012, Accessed 9/30/2014. http://m.espn.go.con/ncf/story?storyid=8160430.

[12] Leviticus 19:18.

[13] Joe Ehrmann with Paula Ehrmann and Gregory Jordan, *Inside Out Coaching: How Sports Can Transform Lives* (New York: Simon & Schuster, 2011), 112-113.

[14] Liberty University Track and Field Team, *Mission Statement*. Accessed 6/24/2014. www.liberty.edu/Flames/index.cfm?PID=26138.

[15] Unknown Quote in Kraft, op. cit., 40-41.

[16] Edited by Kevin Lixey, L.C., Christoph Hubenthal, Dietmar Mieth, and Norbert Muller, *Sport & Christianity: A Sign of the Times in the Light of Faith* (Washington, D.C.: The Catholic University of America Press, 2012), 172.

[17] *Without Limits* – movie quotes, An Alternate Path, Accessed 9/30/2014. http://analternateroute.com/2010/bill-bowerman-quotes-without-limits-movie/.

[18] Lynn Shackelford in Wooden and Jamison, op. cit., 150-151.

[19] Lixey, Hubenthal, Mieth, Muller, op. cit., 217.

[20] Correspondent Daniel Schorn, "Tom Brady Speaks to Steve Kroft," *CBS News.* 11/4/2005, Accessed 2/6/2014. http://www.cbsnews.com/news/transcript-tom-brady-part-3/.

[21] Chris Evert in Timothy Keller, *Counterfeit Gods: The Empty Promises of Money, Sex, and Power, and the Only Hope that Matters* (New York: Dutton, 2009), 77.

[22] www.goodreads.com/author/15868.William_James.

[23] 1 Corinthians 9:24-25.

[24] Tom Lehman in Greg S. Smith, *Sports Theology* (Indianapolis: Dog Ear, 2010), 27.

[25] Matthew 6:19-21.

26 John Wooden in Jeff Janssen and Greg Dale, *The Seven Secrets of Successful Coaches: How to Unlock and Unleash Your Team's Full Potential* (Carey: Quality, 2006), 28.

27 Revelation 12:9-10.

28 Lamentations 3:22-23.

29 Philippians 3:13-14.

30 Andrew Froude in J. Oswald Sanders, *Spiritual Leadership: Principle of Excellence for Every Believer* (Chicago: Moody, 2007), 134.

31 John Wooden in Kent Millard & Judith Cebula, *Lead Like Butler: Six Principles for Values-Based Leadership* (Nashville, Abingdon, 2013), xvii.

32 Blaise Pascal in John Piper, *The Dangerous Duty of Delight* (Multnomah: Sisters, 2001), 12.

33 Psalm 37:4.

34 J. Campbell White in Piper, *Don't Waste Your Life,* op. cit., 170.

35 David McCasland, *Eric Liddell: Pure Gold* (Grand Rapids: Discovery House, 2001), 77, 80-81.

36 Dr. Arnold Bryson in Ibid., 282.

37 Matthew 13:44-46, italics mine.

38 C.S. Lewis, *The Weight of Glory* (New York, Macmillan, 1949), 3-4.

39 2 Corinthians 4:16-18.

40 1 Corinthians 13:12.

41 Philippians 4:4, italics mine.

42 Deuteronomy 28:47-48, italics mine.

43 Sam Storms, *One Thing: Developing a Passion for the Beauty of God* (Scotland: Christian Focus, 2004), 164.

44 Colossians 3:1-4.

45 Storms, op. cit., 178.

46 Ibid., 164, 166.

47 Ibid.

48 Job 42:2.

49 John Wooden and Steve Jamison, *Wooden on Leadership* (New York: McGraw-Hill, 2005), 150-151.

50 Grown and Flown, "Which Parent Are You?" *Huffington Post*, 9/12/2012, Accessed 10/26/2013. www. huffingtonpost.com/grown-and-flown/parenting-advice_b_1875280.html.

51 Proverbs 19:21.

52 Ephesians 1:11-12.

53 James 1:2-5.

54 LeRoy Eims, *Be The Leader You Were Meant To Be* (Wheaton: Victor, 1996), 113.

55 Joshua 1:7.

56 Viktor Frankl in Ehrmann, Ehrmann, Jordan, op. cit., 38.

57 1 Corinthians 3:6.

58 Exodus 16:3.

59 Exodus 16:19-20.

60 Kraft, op. cit., 69.

61 Erik Thoennes, Ph.D, "Created to Play: Thoughts on Play, Sport, and the Christian Life," *Project Hope Speaks*, Accessed 10/28/2013. http://projecthopespeaks.org/wp-content/uploads/2012/04/Created-to-Play-Chapter-Thoennes.pdf.

62 Kraft, op. cit., 74.

63 Samuel Chadwick in Sanders, op. cit., 161.

64 Henri Nouwen, *Out of Solitude,* www.tumblr.com/search/out+of+solitude.com, Accessed 9/25/2014

65 Galatians 5:22-23.

66 1 Peter 1:14-16.

67 Billy Graham in Shirl James Hoffman, *Good Game: Christianity and the Culture of Sports* (Waco: Baylor University, 2010), 132-133.

68 Philippians 3:12-14.

69 J. Hudson Taylor, vimeo.com/m/60216852, Accessed 10/6/2014.

70 Matthew 24:14.

71 Mark 10:33-34.

72 Mark 13:9-10.

73 Isaiah 40:8.

74 Psalm 103:15-18.

75 1 Timothy 4:7-11.

76 Randy Alcorn, *The Treasure Principle: Discovering the Secret of Joyful Giving* (Sisters: Multnomah, 2001), 37.

77 Strong, James: *The Exhaustive Concordance of the Bible*, S. G3140.

78 Lixey, Hubenthal, Mieth, and Muller, op. cit., 3.

79 1 John 4:16.

80 Scott Thomas and Tom Wood, *Gospel Coach: Shepherding Leaders to Glorify God* (Grand Rapids: Zondervan, 2012), 103-104.

APPENDIX #1

Basic Inductive Bible Study Steps

1. *Illumination – The Great Omission*

"And so, from the day we heard, we have not ceased to pray for you, asking that you may be filled with the knowledge of his will in all spiritual wisdom and understanding, so as to walk in a manner worthy of the Lord, fully pleasing to him, bearing fruit in every good work and increasing in the knowledge of God" (Colossians 1:9-10).

Too much study of God's Word is attempted without prayer. Pray before, during, and after your time in the Word. Allow the Holy Spirit to guide your study, and to reveal what questions are particularly relevant to help you understand and apply the text to your life. Allow the Holy Spirit to be your ultimate Guide through this sumptuous feast prepared on your behalf. It is through God's grace that you will draw near to Him.

> "The Word of God cannot be truly desired (Psalm 119:36) or spiritually comprehended (Psalm 119:18) or savingly spoken (2 Thessalonians 3:1) without the work of the Holy Spirit, whom we ask for by prayer. Being saturated with the Word of God produces an effective prayer life: "If you abide in me, and *my words abide in you*, ask whatever you wish, and it will be done for you" (John 15:7).[1]

2. *Meditation – Soaking in the Scriptures*

"This Book of the Law shall not depart from your mouth, but you shall meditate on it day and night, so that you may be careful to do according to all that is written in it. For then you will make your way prosperous, and then you will have good success" (Joshua 1:8).

> The Old Testament concept of meditation involves two things: First, a focus upon God himself (Ps. 63:6), his works (Ps. 77:12; 143:5), or his law (Josh 1:8; Ps 1:2), and second, an activity that was done aloud. This is why God told Joshua that this law book should not leave his *mouth* (as opposed to, e.g., his heart or his mind). With

233

reference to meditating upon the law, the idea is that one reads or recites the law aloud to oneself. In the ancient world, almost all reading was done aloud. Augustine remarked in a well-known passage in his *Confessions* (6.3) that he noticed St. Ambrose reading without moving his lips, a spectacle odd enough for him to comment upon. Silent reading was rare, although not unknown in the ancient world.[2]

Linger on whatever section of Scripture you are studying. Read it out loud. Carefully dwell on each word and phrase. Don't be in a hurry to get through it. Savor it. Allow it to touch all your senses. Try to visualize the stories you read. Put yourself in the story and allow the Holy Spirit to teach you.

3. *Observation – Learning to Ask Questions*

Who:

Make a list of the persons mentioned in the section being studied. Who are they?

What:

Make a list of words and/or phrases that YOU need to be explained in the section being studied. What does _____ mean?

Where:

Make a list of the places mentioned in the section being studied. Where is _____ located? Is that locale important to understanding the text?

When:

To better understand the social, political, and cultural context of the passage being studied, it is important to know when the events being studied took place.

Why:

What purpose did the author have for including the passage being studied? What is the main theme of the passage? Try to write it one sentence.

How:

How does the passage you are studying fit into the larger puzzle of the entire book? With the rest of Scripture?

4.   Interpretation - What Does it Mean?

Why did the author write this passage for the original reader(s)? What was his intent?
Your job as an interpreter is to attempt to discover that original meaning – not to discuss what it 'means to you,' but what it meant to the original author. You must enter the world of the author and the reader. Consider the following:

- You're reading someone else's mail. You have to know who wrote it and who it was written to in order to understand the content of the letter.
- "It's Greek to me." The Bible was not composed in a modern language, so you can't place 21st-century definitions on the words you read. Consider that even in our culture word meanings change over time.
- There is a cultural gap. Much of the world of the Bible was agrarian and patriarchal, with social customs that we would consider oddities, like arranged marriages.
- There is a historical gap: Scripture was written 2,000 plus years ago.
- The Bible is sacred Scripture: "God-breathed" (2 Timothy 3:16).

5.   Application – How Does the Passage Impact You?

How has the Holy Spirit spoken to you through this text? How will you use this text to bring glory to God and joy to people?

"But be doers of the word, and not hearers only, deceiving yourselves" (James 1:22).

- Each generation has a new set of questions and a unique relationship with God. He does not change, but generations and cultures do.
- Each generation has a new sense of urgency in certain areas – What are new and pressing issues in your day and age that were not important fifty years ago?
- Seek the Truth while going through different seasons of life. Don't feel threatened re-examining past 'resolved' issues as you mature. The application of God's Word to our lives is not always in black and white.

6.   Communication – Praying with God & Teaching Others

Praying G.R.A.C.E. – Praying Scripture (Found in the *Unceasing Pray-er* chapter)

Teaching Others – You must pass on what you learn in order to be obedient to the Great Commission found in Matthew 28:18-20. GO – and make disciples. Help others to cherish Jesus as their greatest treasure!

APPENDIX #2

Three Tips for Better Bible Reading[3]

You probably don't need to hear reasons that it's important to read the Bible. You know it is.

But you might need some motivation. One way to get excited about reading the Bible is to rethink your Bible-reading strategy. Here are three tips for better Bible reading:

Tip #1. Listen to audio-Bibles.

When you listen to an audio-Bible, you'll be surprised how quickly the time goes by and how much of the Bible you "read."

Sometimes I listen while doing other tasks such as driving or cleaning or running, but I've found it to be incredibly profitable to listen while following along in a different English translation… Listening to a different version than you are reading helps keep you engaged as you inquisitively consider various renderings…

Audio-Bibles work well for the Bible's many styles of literature, though they work best for stories as opposed to proverbs or letters… But it's worth remembering that the congregations whom Paul addressed in his letters typically *listened* to Paul's letters and did not own personal copies of them.

You might want to get started by downloading some free audio-Bibles from "Faith Comes by Hearing."

Tip #2. Read books of the Bible in one sitting.

There is value in Bible-reading plans that divvy up the readings so that you read one chapter from four different books of the Bible. But if that's the only way you read the Bible, it will be difficult to understand key literary features and the theological message of whole books of the Bible.

Have you ever read the Gospel according the Matthew straight through in one sitting? Or Romans? Or Job? Or Revelation? If not, you're missing out. That's the way they're meant to be read…

I understand the objection: "There's no way I could possibly find time to do this." But aren't there other activities you do in life for prolonged periods of time? Do you read other books for a few hours at a time? Do you ever spend an hour watching a TV show or two hours watching a movie or three hours watching a football game? Why not prioritize lengthy, undistracted time in the life-giving word?

Tip #3. Read without any chapter or verse references.

I am not a fan of chapter and verse references in the Bible. Bible "verses" didn't even exist until about 1550, and "chapters" go back only to the 1200s. They can obscure the text and create artificial and sometimes inaccurate divisions.

Yes, chapter and verse references help us locate specific sentences and phrases quickly. But sometimes they do more harm than good. They lead many people to think of the Bible as a reference book that collects bullet-pointed verse-nuggets — not as the literature that it really is.

So how do you read the Bible without any chapter or verse references? There are at least three options:

1. Get a Bible without them. For example, Biblica has one called *The Books of the Bible*, and Crossway is planning to release the *ESV Reader's Bible* in May.
2. Use a Bible software program like Logos to export a book or passage of Scripture to your favorite word processor without the chapter or verse numbers.
3. Manually delete the chapter and verse references in a word document on your computer. This is time-consuming, but you could copy-and-paste text from a site like Bible Gateway and then delete all the numbering. That's more feasible for shorter books. Even better, Bible Gateway has an option to hide verse numbers (click on "Page Options").

Take up and read (and listen) a lot.

APPENDIX #3

Fall Bear Prayers

Week 1 – It's all about Jesus. Pray for him to be the center of all you do as a student-athlete.

"Heavenly Father, we ask for your grace and mercy upon the Lady Bears and coaches throughout this school year. Mold and shape their hearts so that their affections for your Son grow ever deeper. Let the roots of their lives be planted deeply in the soil of Scripture, nurtured by communion with you in prayer and fellowship with each other, and empowered to grow through the indwelling of your Holy Spirit. And as they daily search your Word, please reveal more of Jesus' glory to them. 'For by him all things were created; things in heaven and earth, visible and invisible, whether thrones or powers or rulers or authorities; all things were created by him and *for him.*' Let that truth sink deeply into their hearts, minds, and souls so that their actions are in synch with your Word. They exist in order to bring glory to Jesus, not themselves. The world and their own flesh will seek to take them down another road. Help them to stay on the straight and narrow path that leads to life. May your grace flow through each of the Lady Bears so that their lives as student-athletes demonstrate that Jesus is their greatest Treasure. When they begin each practice, prepare for every meet, and reflect on how they have performed, help them to give it all over to you, Lord Jesus. For in you they 'live and move and have their very being.' You are the 'Alpha and Omega, the Beginning and the End.' May it be that, 'the things of this world will grow strangely dim in the light of His glory and grace'" (Colossians 1:16, Acts 17:28, Revelation 21:6).

Week 2 – Find a local home church where Jesus' Word is preached and lived out in community.

"Father God, we ask that you would guide each of the Lady Bears to a church home while they are at Baylor. Do not allow them to be deceived into thinking that being at a Christian university, or attending Baylor chapel services or team Bible studies is enough. You, Lord Jesus, instituted the church and 'gave yourself up for her to make her holy, cleansing her by the washing with water through the word. You did this so you could present her to yourself as a radiant church, without stain or wrinkle or any blemish, but holy and blameless.' May these young ladies gather together with the saints in corporate worship and service, and in doing so 'consider how they may spur one another on toward love and good deeds. Let them not give up meeting together, as some are in the habit of doing, but let them encourage one another – and all the more as they see the Day approaching.' Bless them with Christ-exalting, Bible-saturated congregations where the 'word is preached in season and out of season, for correction, rebuke, and encouragement – with great patience and careful instruction.' For 'all Scripture is God-breathed and is useful for teaching, rebuking, correcting and training in righteousness so that these women of God may be thoroughly equipped for every good work,' so the name of Jesus will be glorified as the gospel goes out to all the nations" (Ephesians 5:25-27; Hebrews 10:24-25; 2 Timothy 4:2; 3:16-17).

Week 3 – Have a plan how, when, and where to daily be in the Word.

"Heavenly Father, grant the Lady Bears a passion to daily drink from the well of Living Water. In the midst of their studies and training, help them to prioritize their time in your Word. May they remember that 'the grass withers and the flowers fade but the Word of God stands forever.' Bless them as they 'walk according to your law, keep your statutes and seek you with all of their hearts.' Help them to 'praise you with upright hearts as they learn your righteous laws.' 'How can a young person stay on the path of purity? By living according to your word.' Holy Spirit, help these young women to 'seek you with all of their hearts. Do not let them stray from your commands but help them to hide your Word in their hearts so that they will not sin against you. Praise be to you, Lord, teach them your decrees.' 'Cause them to understand the way of your precepts so that they may meditate on your wonderful deeds. Keep them from deceitful ways; be gracious to them and teach them your law.' Grant them a passion to 'run in the path of your commands and continually broaden their understanding.' 'Turn their eyes away from worthless things; preserve their lives according to your Word. Fulfill your promise to your servants, so that you will be feared' and your name will be glorified. 'Your word, Lord is eternal; it stands firm in the heavens. Your faithfulness continues through all generations.' Keep them daily from darkness as they follow a prescribed plan of Bible meditation, study, and memorization. For 'your Word is a lamp unto their and a light unto their paths.'" (Isaiah 40:8; Psalm 119:1-2, 7, 9-12, 18, 27, 29, 32, 80, 89-90, 97, 109)

Week 4 – Seek wisdom how to sow seeds of salvation and sanctification in the lives of those God has placed in your pathway while at Baylor.

"Gracious and heavenly Father, help the Lady Bears to understand that they have been placed by you at Baylor at this appointed time in history. You are sovereign over every student living in proximity to them. Help them to daily sow seeds of salvation and sanctification. It is not by mere chance that each of them is in Waco. Lord Jesus, open their hearts so that they pursue relationships with people who are different than them because 'by your blood you ransomed people for God from every tribe and language and people and nation.' Help the Lady Bears understand that they are members of Abraham's family who were promised that 'all nations of the earth shall be blessed through him.' The command has been placed on each of their lives to, "Go and make disciples of all the nations, baptizing them in the name of the Father and the Son and the Holy Spirit. Teach these new disciples to obey all the commands I have given you. And be sure of this: I am with you always, even to the end of the age.' Sovereign Lord, grant each of these young ladies listening ears and hearts so they will bless the nations that are living with them at Baylor. And may they lift up the needs they discern before your throne. 'Answer when they call, O God of righteousness. Give relief to those they encounter who are in distress. Be gracious to them and hear their prayers.' 'May your name endure forever, your fame continue as long as the sun! May people be blessed in you, and all nations call you blessed!' (Revelation 5:9, Genesis 18:18, Matthew 28:19-20, Psalm 4:1, Psalm 72:17)

Week 5 – "Love your neighbor as yourself."

"Heavenly Father, your Son told us that the Greatest Commandment was, 'You shall love the Lord your God with all your heart and with all your soul and with all your strength and with all your mind, and your neighbor as yourself.' Furthermore, your Apostle Paul reminded us that 'whoever sows sparingly will also reap sparingly, and whoever sows bountifully will also reap bountifully. Each one must give as he has decided in his heart, not reluctantly or under compulsion, for God loves a cheerful giver.' Let it be that the Lady Bears lavish love upon each other. Let them be known as Givers for the glory of God. For, 'just as Jesus has loved them, they should love each other. Their love for one another will prove to the world that they are your disciples.' Empower them, Holy Spirit, to daily 'think of ways to motivate one another to acts of love and good works.' 'As they live in the freedom that was purchased on the cross, let them not use their freedom to satisfy their sinful natures. Instead, may they use their freedom to serve one another in love. For the whole law can be summed up in this one command: "Love your neighbor as yourself." But if they are always biting and devouring one another, warn them to watch out! May they beware of destroying one another.' May none of them be 'be lazy and spend their time gossiping from room to room, meddling in other people's business and talking about things they shouldn't.' Rather, 'Do not let any unwholesome talk come out of their mouths, but only what is helpful for building others up according to their needs, that it may benefit those who listen.' Holy Spirit, help each of these women to 'be imitators of God, as beloved children. And walk in love, as Christ loved them and gave himself up for them, a fragrant offering and sacrifice to God' (Luke 10:27; 2 Corinthians 9:6-7; John 13:34-35; Hebrews 10:24; Galatians 5:13-15; 1 Timothy 5:13; Ephesians 4:29; Ephesians 5:1-2).

Week 6 – Allow God's Word to be the standard for your actions, not the cultural air you breathe.

"Heavenly Father, we ask for your Spirit's anointing upon all the Lady Bears and coaches. Help them to clearly see what it means to passionately pursue you through the sport of cross country.

As they deal with goals and dreams, successes and setbacks, may they look to your Word to understand how to evaluate all of it. May each of them remember that 'the LORD doesn't see things the way we see them. People judge by outward appearance, but the LORD looks at the heart.' Holy Spirit, help these young ladies and their coaches to bring every practice and meet before you, seeking your wisdom, your empowering, and your glory. In this way, they will 'work heartily, as for the Lord and not for men, knowing that from the Lord they will receive the inheritance as their reward. They are serving the Lord Jesus Christ.' Help that to be their ultimate goal, Lord Jesus, pleasing you and not people. May the words of the Apostle Paul be emblazoned upon the hearts and minds every time they lace up their shoes: 'For am I now seeking the approval of man, or of God? Or am I trying to please man? If I were still trying to please man, I would not be a servant of Christ.' Grant them a spirit of unity as they go throughout the rest of this season running side-by-side as the Body of Christ. May they 'stand firm in one spirit, with one mind striving side by side for the faith of the gospel, and not frightened in anything by their opponents.' And may they 'do nothing from rivalry or conceit, but in humility count others more significant than themselves. Let each of them look not only to their own interests, but also to the interests of others.' And through it all may they 'Rejoice always, pray without ceasing, give thanks in all circumstances; for this is the will of God in Christ Jesus for them' (1 Samuel 16:7; Colossians 3:23-24; Galatians 1:10; Philippians 1:27-28; Philippians 2:3-4; 1 Thessalonians 5:16-18).

Week 7 – Keep your eyes open for opportunities to serve.

"Father God, set your Spirit upon the Lady Bears each morning and remind them what you require of them that day – to 'fear the LORD their God, and live in a way that pleases you, and to love you and serve you with all their hearts and souls.' In the midst of their packed schedules, empower the Lady Bears to moment-by-moment seek to 'love you, walk in all your ways, obey your commands, hold firmly to you, and serve you.' They 'were called to be free, but to not use their freedom to indulge the sinful nature; rather to serve one another in love. The entire law is summed up in a single command: "Love your neighbor as yourself."' Help each of these young ladies to prayerfully search their hearts and ask how well they are serving you by serving their neighbors. For you told your disciples, 'I tell you the truth, whatever you did for one of the least of these brothers of mine, you did for me.' 'You have given each of them a gift from your great variety of spiritual gifts. May they use them well to serve one another.' In the harried world of being student-athletes, fortify their resolve - heart, mind, soul, and strength, to serve well each day. 'Let them not grow weary of doing good, for in due season they will reap, if they do not give up. So then, as they have opportunity, let them do good to everyone, and especially to those who are of the household of faith.' 'Whatever they do, help them to work at it with all their hearts, as working for the Lord, not for human masters, since they know that they will receive an inheritance from the Lord as a reward. It is the Lord Christ they are serving'" (Deuteronomy 10:12; Joshua 22:5; Galatians 5:13-14; Matthew 27:40; 1 Peter 4:10; Galatians 6:9; Colossians 3:23-24).

Week 8 – Point others to the hope found in the Good News of Jesus. We all need restoration, reconciliation, and redemption.

"Father God, fill the Lady Bears to overflowing with your Spirit 'so from now on they regard no one from a worldly point of view.' Rather, help them to point others to the hope that comes from a transformed life in, with, and through Jesus. Remind them that 'if anyone is in Christ, he is a new creation; the old has gone, the new has come! All this is from you, Father God, who reconciled the Lady Bears to yourself through Christ and gave them the ministry of reconciliation…And you have committed to them the message of reconciliation. They are therefore Christ's ambassadors.' Let them herald forth this message to their classmates: 'Be reconciled to God. For God made him who had no sin to be sin for us, so that in him we might become the righteousness of God.' May they 'devote themselves to prayer, being watchful and thankful. And help us to diligently pray for them that God may open a door for their message, so that they may proclaim the mystery of Christ… We pray that they proclaim it clearly, as they should. May they be wise in the way they act toward outsiders, making the most of every opportunity. Let their conversations be always full of grace, so that they may know how to answer everyone.' Let them not be prideful about their place in your Kingdom, which was paid for by the blood of the Lamb. Remind them that 'once they were alienated from you and were enemies in their minds because of their evil behavior. But they have been reconciled by Christ's physical body through death to be presented holy in your sight, without blemish and free from accusation— if they continue in their faith, established and firm, not moved from the hope held out in the gospel.' 'For the wages of sin is death, but the gift of God is eternal life in Christ Jesus our Lord.' Grant your compassion to the Lady Bears so that they are daily reminded that there are people all around them perishing because they have been blinded to the reality of sin; people who genuinely believe they 'have no sin, and so deceive themselves, and the truth is not in them.' Grant the Lady Bears the eternal perspective to be upon their knees seeking discernment for whom you have prepared to hear the Good News: 'If they confess their sins, Jesus is faithful and just to forgive us their sins and to cleanse them from all unrighteousness.'" (2 Corinthians 5:16-21; Colossians 4:2-6; Colossians 1:21-23; Romans 6:23; 1 John 1:9)

Week 9 – Seek opportunities outside of church and chapel to learn about the Bible from others.

"Precious Father, Giver of the written and living Word, grant the Lady Bears a passion to pursue solid biblical teaching every chance they get. As more and more papers, projects, readings, and exams get loaded upon their plates, help them to remember that none of that has eternal value like the study of your Word. Your Apostle Paul proclaimed that, 'All Scripture is God-breathed and is useful for teaching, rebuking, correcting and training in righteousness, so that the servant of God may be thoroughly equipped for every good work.' What other subject in college has such power? 'Come, let each of these young ladies worship and bow down. Let them kneel before the LORD their maker, for he is their God. They are the people he watches over, the flock under his care. If only they would listen to his voice today!' Holy Spirit, grant them discernment to understand that a weekly foray into your Word under the godly leadership of a local preacher, teacher, or chaplain is not enough. May each of them 'devote themselves to the public reading of Scripture, to preaching and to teaching.' Instill in them a passion to feast upon the Living Water and Bread of life and to desire it more than the food and drink that quenches their physical appetites. 'Let the message of Christ dwell among them richly as they teach and admonish one another with all wisdom through psalms, hymns, and songs from the Spirit, singing to God with gratitude in their hearts.' May they 'stand firm and hold fast to the teachings that we passed on to them, whether by word of mouth or by letter.' For 'each generation should set its hope anew on God, not forgetting his glorious miracles and obeying his commands.' 'Therefore let them move beyond the elementary teachings about Christ and be taken forward to maturity.' Lord, bless them with regular biblical teaching 'so that they will be presented mature in Christ.' And let us 'toil, struggling with all his energy that he powerfully works within us' to help them reach that finish line and hear, 'well done, good and faithful servant'" (2 Timothy 3:16-17; Psalm 95:6-7; 1 Timothy 4:13; Colossians 3:16; 2 Thessalonians 2:15; Psalm 78:8; Hebrews 6:1).

Week 10 – Diligently work to honor God as a student-athlete. Don't be lazy.

"Gracious and heavenly Father, we ask for your grace and mercy upon the Lady Bears as they deal with the ups and downs of life, especially when the work they put forth does not appear to bear much fruit. Help them to be 'steadfast, immovable, always abounding in the work of the Lord, knowing that in the Lord their labor is not in vain.' Sustain them in their work ethic, helping them to remember that 'whether they eat or drink, or whatever they do, to do all to the glory of God.' When they think about backing off and putting their lives on cruise control, remind them that 'the appetite of laborers works for them; their hunger drives them on', and 'one who is slack in his work is brother to one who destroys', and 'hard work brings rewards.' Holy Spirit, quicken the minds of these young ladies so they will understand the incredible privilege you have given them by allowing them to not only be in college, but to be at a university seeking to honor the name and the purpose of Jesus Christ. Grant them a passion to join in Baylor's mission so that they, too, will be a 'constant example of how others can help those in need by working hard. May they always remember the words of the Lord Jesus: 'It is more blessed to give than to receive.' And when they tire and feel they don't have any more left to give, may they cling to the Apostle Paul's promise that, 'God is able to make all grace abound to you, so that having all sufficiency in all things at all times, you may abound in every good work.' For they are 'God's handiwork, created in Christ Jesus to do good works, which you prepared in advance for them to do.' And we have the divine assurance that 'you who began a good work in them will bring it to completion at the day of Jesus Christ.' So in 'whatever they do, may they work heartily, as for the Lord and not for men, knowing that from the Lord they will receive the inheritance as their reward. They are serving the Lord Christ'" (1 Corinthians 15:58; 1 Corinthians 10:31; Proverbs 16:26, 18:9, 12:14; Acts 20:35; 2 Corinthians 9:8; Ephesians 2:10; Philippians 1:6; Colossians 3:23-24).

Week 11 – Do not go down the pathway of being unequally yoked. If you are interested in dating someone, make sure that they are also passionately pursuing Jesus as their ultimate goal.

"Heavenly Father, may we as parents continue to realize that life is but a vapor. Just yesterday we were rocking our daughters to sleep, teaching them to ride bicycles, pushing them on swings, teaching them to drive cars, watching them graduate from high school, and now marriage is t likely not that far away either. For the 'the LORD God said, "It is not good that the man should be alone; I will make him a helper fit for him."' Do not allow them to be deceived into thinking that being a 'helper' is some type of demeaning role. But remind them that you, Lord Jesus, used that exact same term in describing the Holy Spirit. Fill each of these Lady Bears to overflowing with your Spirit so that that will 'not be yoked together with unbelievers. For what do righteousness and wickedness have in common? Or what fellowship can light have with darkness?' Sear upon their minds the reality of what happens when unequal yoking in a marriage occurs. 'For when Solomon was old his [unbelieving] wives turned away his heart after other gods, and his heart was not wholly true to the LORD his God, as was the heart of David his father.' Prepare the Lady Bears for the reality that marriage is meant for a lifetime, a union that is designed to help the world understand the relationship of Christ and his church. 'Therefore a man shall leave his father and mother and hold fast to his wife, and the two shall become one flesh. This mystery is profound, and I am saying that it refers to Christ and the church.' As these young ladies prayerfully seek your guidance in regards to whom they should marry, help them to diligently prepare to be the type of women that will become godly wives. 'An excellent wife who can find? She is far more precious than jewels. The heart of her husband trusts in her, and he will have no lack of gain. She does him good, and not harm, all the days of her life.' May each husband 'rejoice in the wife of his youth' from first day of their marriage until death does them part, or you return for your children, Lord Jesus. Abba Daddy, bless each of our precious daughters with Christ-exalting, Bible-saturated husbands that will love them as Jesus loved the church, so your name will be praised in each of their households and spread from there to every tribe, tongue, people and nation" (Genesis 2:18; 2 Corinthians 6:14; Ephesians 5:31-32; 1 Kings 11:4; Proverbs 31:10-12; Psalm 5:18).

Week 12 - In the midst of constant change from one semester to the next, remember that God is the same yesterday, today, and forever. Do not fear the future – trust.

"Heavenly Father, we lift up the Lady Bears to you as they go through multitudes of changes, from being dependent upon us as parents, to growing in inter-dependence; from leaving home; from new classes every semester, to new majors as you lead them on their way. Grant them your peace as they go through these processes. Help them to remember that 'no plan of yours can be thwarted.' Holy Spirit, we ask that you will help these young ladies remember that they are never alone. For Jesus promised, 'I am with you always, even to the end of the age.' May they 'trust in you with all your heart; may they not depend on their own understanding. May they seek your will in all they do, and you promise to show them you which path to take.' Whether it is in the classroom, in the midst of their social lives, or in the middle of practice, or the heat of competition, help them to 'commit their ways to you; trust in you, and you will act.' For 'blessed are those who trust you and have made you their hope and confidence. They are like trees planted along a riverbank, with roots that reach deep into the water. Such trees are not bothered by the heat or worried by long months of drought. Their leaves stay green, and they never stop producing fruit.' And if these young ladies start feeling overwhelmed at all the decisions that need to be made, remind them that their 'lives are not their own; it is not for them to direct their steps.' Help them to 'be strong and courageous, as should all who put their hope in you!' For 'God has given both his promise and his oath. These two things are unchangeable because it is impossible for God to lie. Therefore, those who have fled to him for refuge can have great confidence as they hold to the hope that lies before them. This hope is a strong and trustworthy anchor for their souls'" (Job 41:2; Matthew 28:20; Proverbs 3:5-6; Psalm 37:4-5; Jeremiah 17:7-8, 10:23; Psalm 31:24; Hebrews 6:18-19).

Week 13 – Be an intercessory pray-er. Your family, friends, teammates need your prayers.

"Heavenly Father, help the Lady Bears to 'not turn aside from following you, but rather empower them to serve you with all their hearts. And may they not turn aside after empty things that cannot profit or deliver, for they are empty. As for the Lady Bears, far be it from them that they should sin against you by ceasing to pray for others, and may your Spirit daily instruct them in the good and the right way. May they fear the LORD and serve him faithfully with all their hearts. Let them continually consider what great things he has done for them.' Holy Spirit, grant these young ladies a sense of urgency to imitate Jesus by arising early in the morning and praying in a place where interruptions will be kept to a minimum. 'The harvest is plentiful, but the laborers are few; therefore we pray earnestly to the Lord of the harvest to send out laborers into his harvest.' And 'whenever they pray, help them to forgive, if they have anything against anyone, so that their Father also who is in heaven may forgive them their trespasses.'

Help them to 'love their enemies, do good to those who hate them, bless those who curse them, pray for those who mistreat them.' By doing so they may help sow the seeds of salvation their enemies desperately need. For 'there is salvation in no one else, for there is no other name under heaven given among men by which we must be saved', but the name of Jesus. Grant them the humility to run to you, Lord Jesus, just like the little children. For you said that 'whoever does not receive the kingdom of God like a child shall not enter it.' May they 'always pray and not lose heart.' 'Our Father in heaven, hallowed be your name. Your kingdom come, your will be done, on earth as it is in heaven. Give us this day our daily bread, and forgive us our debts, as we also have forgiven our debtors. And lead us not into temptation, but deliver us from evil. For yours is the kingdom, the power, and the glory forever. Amen'" (1 Samuel 12:20-24; Matthew 9:37-38; Mark 11:25; Luke 6:27-28; Acts 4:12; Luke 18:17, 1; Matthew 6:9-13).

Week 14 - Peace before Finals

"Father God, we come to you on behalf of the Lady Bears as they sit on the precipice of final exams. We ask that your Holy Spirit would give them the ability to rejoice in you always. Help them to remember that you are near. Help them not to be anxious about anything, but in everything, by praying to you, seeking your will and being thankful for all the blessings you have bestowed upon them – help the Lady Bears to present all their requests to you. When they do this, Lord, you promise that your peace which transcends all understanding will guard their hearts and their minds, because they are centered on you. Help them to hear that voice in their hearts that says, 'I am leaving you with a gift—peace of mind and heart. And the peace I give is a gift the world cannot give. So don't be troubled or afraid.' For 'Great is the LORD, who delights in blessing his servants with peace!'" (Philippians 4:4-6; John 14:27; Philippians 4:8-9; Psalm 35:26)

APPENDIX #4

Intercessory Prayers on Behalf of Coaches

Prayer 1

"Gracious and heavenly Father, help _____ to trust in you with all her heart and lean not on her own understanding. In all that she does in coaching her team and seeking direction for the future, help her to acknowledge that you are the Creator, Redeemer, and Sustainer of the universe. You, Lord, can do all things and no plan of yours can be thwarted. Help _____ to have your peace in knowing that you will guide her path because she acknowledges that you alone are God. When anxiety strikes at her heart and mind, help her to immediately turn to you for guidance. For you said that if anyone seeks wisdom, all they have to do is ask, and you will give it generously. Holy Spirit, guide _____ through every step, every decision as she seeks your path for her coaching" (Proverbs 3:5-6, Job 42:2; James 1:5).

Prayer 2

"Father, you said that those of us who are your children did not receive a spirit that makes us slaves again to fear, but we received the Spirit of sonship. And by that Spirit we can cry out, 'Abba, Daddy.' It is to you I bring _____, asking that the spirit of fear be broken as soon as a tinge of it strikes at his heart. Let him rest in your arms knowing that you love him greater than anyone else ever can or ever will. It is through your perfect love that fear can be cast out! For you said, 'Never will I leave you; never will I forsake you.' Let that assurance fill _____ with courage to go forth spreading seeds of salvation and sanctification, restoration and reconciliation in his team and to all others impacted through it" (Romans 8:15; I John 4:18; Deuteronomy 31:6).

Prayer 3

"Abba, Daddy, I come to you on behalf of _____ and ask that your Holy Spirit would give her the ability to rejoice in you always. Help her to remember that you are near, so she will not be anxious about anything, but in everything, by praying to you, will seek your will and be thankful for all the blessings you have bestowed upon her. Help _____ to present all her requests to you. When she does this, Lord, you promise that your peace which transcends all understanding will guard her heart and her mind because they are centered on you. Help _____ to hear that voice in her heart that says I am leaving you with a gift—peace of mind and heart. And the peace I give is a gift the world cannot give. So don't be troubled or afraid" (Philippians 4:4-6; John 14:27).

Prayer 4

"Heavenly Father, as _____ ministers in, with, and through coaching, help him to remember that 'you have given him the task of reconciling people to Jesus. For God was in Christ, reconciling the world to himself, no longer counting people's sins against them. And he gave us this wonderful message of reconciliation. So _____ is your ambassador; you will be making your appeal through _____. Help him to speak for Christ when he pleads, "Come back to God!" For you made Christ, who never sinned, to be the offering for our sin, so that we could be made right with God through Christ.' For you, Lord Jesus, told us to 'Love our enemies and pray for those who persecute us, so that we may be sons of our Father who is in heaven. For You make the sun rise on the evil and on the good, and send rain on the just and on the unjust. Help _____ to remember that, if he only loves those who love him, what reward does he have? Do not even the tax collectors do the same? And if he greets only his brothers, what more his he doing than others?' Empower _____ to show forth your love to all he coaches and others impacted by the program. Yet in the process, may he be as 'wise as a serpent and as innocent as a dove' to know how to spread that love (2 Corinthians 5:18-21; Matthew 5:43-48, 10:16).

Prayer 5

"Lord Jesus, help _____ not to be overwhelmed by all the needs she sees in the life of her team, and all the needs that people bring to her in the hopes that she can somehow resolve the problems. In the midst of all these requests, help _____ to remember that 'life is so much more than what we eat or drink; or about our bodies and what we will wear. The birds of the air do not sow or reap or store away in barns, and yet you feed them.' Help _____ to observe the birds and truly understand that she is of much greater value in your eyes than all of them. When she sees how the flowers grow all around her, help _____ to see that 'they don't labor, or spin, or work their way into a frenzy. Yet, you cause them to grow. You design their beauty. No one on this planet is clothed in such royal splendor as the flowers you have created. If you clothe these flowers with such splendor that are here today and gone tomorrow, how much more will you care for _____ and her team? Help _____ to seek first your kingdom and your righteousness, trusting that all these other things will be given to her as well.' And when that reality hits home, help her 'not to worry about tomorrow, for tomorrow will worry about itself. For nothing takes you by surprise. Not even one sparrow will fall to the ground apart from your will, Father. And even the very hairs of _____'s head are all numbered. So help her not to be afraid; for she is worth so much more than many sparrows'" (Matthew 6:25-34; Matthew 10:29-30).

Prayer 6

"Heavenly Father, as _____ ministers to his team, help him to 'fix his thoughts on what is true, and honorable, and right, and pure, and lovely, and admirable. May he continually think about things that are excellent and worthy of praise.' Help him to keep putting into practice all he has learned and received from your Word—everything he has heard from you, Lord Jesus, and saw you doing throughout Scripture. Then you promise that the God of peace will be with him. For 'Great is the LORD, who delights in blessing his servant with peace!' Help _____ to boldly proclaim what great things you have done for him, from saving his life to giving him eternal life. Let his mouth be filled be 'filled with laughter, and his tongue with shouts of joy; for 'The LORD has done great things for him. The LORD has done great things for him; we are glad.' Let _____ sing and make melody unto the Lord so that others around him are drawn to the Great Lover, the Great Reconciler, Jesus Christ" (Philippians 4:8-9; Psalm 35:26; Psalm 126:2-3).

Prayer 7

"'Oh, Sovereign Lord, you have made the heavens and the earth by your great power and outstretched arm. Nothing is too hard for you. You are the Lord, the God of all mankind. Is anything too hard for you?' Help _____ to meditate upon that reality and have it fixed firmly upon her heart when worries come dashing into her world. Help her to believe that 'what is impossible with men is possible with you.' 'You are the vine and we are the branches.' May _____ remember that 'when she obeys your commandments, she will remain in Jesus' love, just as Jesus obeyed his Father's commandments and remains in his love. Jesus told us these things so that we will be filled with his joy. Yes, _____'s joy will overflow! May that joy be exhibited by _____ loving those she encounters in the same way that she has been loved by Jesus. Help her to draw near to you, stay close to you, so that she can live a life of victory over the Great deceiver. Holy Spirit, grant _____ the ability to immediately bring any anxieties/fears unto Jesus, knowing that nothing is too hard for him. Help her to know and feel that others are praying for your perfect peace to envelop her entire being" (Jeremiah 32:17, 26-27; Luke 18:27; John 15:5, 10-12).

Prayer 8

"Have mercy on _____, O God, for in you does he seek refuge. Help him to take refuge in the shadow of your wings like the young chicks protected under the wings of the mother hen. When fear comes, help him to cry out to you, God Most High, and to wait under your wings until the anxiety passes. Let _____'s heart be steadfast, O God; let him sing and make music and praise your name among the nations. For great is your love, reaching to the heavens; your faithfulness reaches to the skies. Let him understand that you inhabit the praises of men. And where you dwell, Satan and his lies will flee. Help _____ to submit to you, Father, and resist the devil by praying your Word and singing your praises. And when he does this, you promise that Satan will flee, and you will draw near to him" (Psalm 57:7-10; James 4:7-8).

Prayer 9

"'O God, let _____'s heart be steadfast! May she sing and make melody with all her being! Let her give thanks to you, O LORD. May she sing praises to you among the nations. For your steadfast love is great above the heavens; your faithfulness reaches to the clouds.' 'For it is good to sing praises to our God; for it is pleasant, and a song of praise is fitting. The LORD heals the brokenhearted and binds up their wounds. He determines the number of the stars seen in the night sky; he gives to all of them their names. Great is our Lord, and abundant in power; his understanding is beyond measure. The LORD lifts up the humble; he casts the wicked to the ground. May _____ sing to you with thanksgiving! For you cover the heavens with clouds; you prepare rain to make the land fertile; you will make grass grow on the hills. Your delight, O Lord, is not in the strength of the horse, nor your pleasure in the legs of a man, but you take pleasure in those who fear you, in those who hope in your steadfast love'" (Psalm 108:1-4; 147:1-11).

Prayer 10

"Lord Jesus, answer _____ quickly when his spirit faints with longing, when he feels that his coaching world is caving in and he is descending into the pit of doubt. Do not hide your face from _____. Let each morning bring him word of your unfailing love, for he seeks to put his trust in you. Show _____ the way he should go, for to you we lift up his soul. Rescue him from his anxieties and fears, O Lord, let _____ hide himself in you. Teach him to do your will, for you are his God. May your good Spirit lead _____ on level ground and the straight and narrow path that leads to life everlasting. May _____ love your instructions and think about them all day long. May your commands make him wiser than any former enemies he may encounter. May your Word be his constant guide, and may he always be thinking of your laws. Let your commandments give _____ understanding so that he hates every false way of life. For your word is a lamp to guide _____'s feet, and a light for his path" (Psalm 143:7-10; 119:97-99, 104-105).

Prayer 11

"When we think of the wisdom and scope of your plan, Lord God, we fall to our knees and pray to the Father, the Creator of everything in heaven and on earth. We pray that from his glorious, unlimited resources he will give _____ mighty inner strength through his Holy Spirit. And we pray that Christ will be more and more at home in _____'s heart as she trusts in Jesus. May her roots go down deep into the soil of God's marvelous love. And may she have the power to understand, as all God's people should, how wide, how long, how high, and how deep your love really is. May _____ experience the love of Christ, though it is so great she will never fully understand it. Then she will be filled with the fullness of life and power that comes from God. Now glory be to God! By his mighty power at work within _____, he is able to accomplish infinitely more than she would ever dare to ask or hope. May the Father be given glory in _____'s life and team, forever and ever through endless ages. Amen" (Ephesians 3:14-21).

Prayer 12

"Father, we lift _____ up to you as he seeks wisdom on what needs to have priority in his life and coaching. Help him to have eyes to see, ears to hear, and a heart to obey. Help him to understand that he is an ambassador of Jesus. May 'the Spirit of the LORD be upon _____, for you have anointed him to bring Good News to the poor. You have sent him to proclaim that captives will be released, that the blind will see, that the oppressed will be set free, and that the time of the LORD's favor has come.' And so, we ask that you empower _____ to give his body to you, Lord God. Let him be a living and holy sacrifice, the kind you will accept. When _____ thinks of what you have done for him, is this too much to ask? May he not copy the behavior and customs of this world, but let your Spirit continue to transform him into a new person by changing the way he thinks. Then _____ will know what God wants him to do, and he will know how good and pleasing and perfect Your will really is" (Luke 4:18-19; Romans 12:1-2).

Prayer 13

Praise be to the God and Father of our Lord Jesus Christ, the Father of compassion and the God of all comfort, who comforts us, including _____, in all our troubles, so that we can comfort those in any trouble with the comfort we ourselves have received from God. Let _____ be convinced that neither death nor life, neither angels nor demons, neither the present nor the future, nor any powers, neither height nor depth, nor anything else in all creation, will be able to separate her from the love of God that is in Christ Jesus our Lord. Help _____ to continually cast her anxieties and fears on you, Lord, because you promise to sustain her. Place a hedge of protection around her at all times, and let her sense your very presence. Let your joy flow forth from _____'s lips as the anxieties and fears fall by the wayside. May that joy be so infectious that those she encounters want to know its sourc." (2 Corinthians 1:3-4; Romans 8:38-39; Psalm 55:2).

Prayer 14

"Lord Jesus, help _____ to operate out of a spirit of love, for you called him to love you with all of his heart, all of his mind, all of his soul, and all of his strength; and to love his neighbor as himself. Show _____, gracious Lord, how to love you with his time, talents, and treasures. Show him how to love those he coaches. As his focus moves outward from his own life, let _____'s joy increase and his fears subside. Help him to have no fear of sudden disaster or of ruin that overtakes the wicked, for you, Lord, will be his confidence and will keep him from being ensnared by the cares of this life. Help _____ to not withhold good from those who deserve it, when it is in his power to act. Let him not hold onto things in the hopes that they will provide him with comfort. Rather, empower _____ to cling to the Rock, the Fortress, the ever-present help in times of trouble. For you can meet all _____'s needs according to your glorious riches in Christ Jesus (Luke 10:27; Proverbs 3:25-27; Philippians 4:19).

Prayer 15

"Oh, most High God, let _____ sense the prayers of those interceding on her behalf – and we give thanks to you, the Father of our Lord Jesus Christ. For we have heard of _____'s faith in Christ Jesus and how she loves God's people, which comes from her confident hope of what you have reserved for her in heaven. May she know that we have not, and will not, stop praying for her and her coaching. Lord, we ask that you give _____ complete knowledge of your will, and spiritual wisdom and understanding. Then the way _____ lives will always honor and please you, and her life will produce every kind of good fruit. And all the while, may she grow as she learns to know you better and better. But help her to watch out! Help _____ to be careful never to forget what she has seen. Do not let any of _____'s memories of your goodness escape from her mind as long as she lives! Grant her an ever-growing conviction to pass your story on to those she encounters. May your praises be on her lips both now and forevermore!" (Colossians 1:3-5, 9-10; Deuteronomy 4:9)

APPENDIX #5

Barriers to Participation of Children with Disabilities in Youth Sports

Thomas E. Moran
Martin E. Block
A Feature Article Published in
TEACHING Exceptional Children Plus
Volume 6, Issue 3, February 2010

Abstract

Youth sports were created as opportunities for children to play, be active, and begin learning how to become better or more successful at a given sport. Unfortunately many children with disabilities may not get the same opportunities that are available to other children. There are a number of barriers that inhibit children with significant disabilities from either participating in the youth sport programming all together or have a strong impact their level of successful participation. This article both identifies key barriers as well as provides strategies to eliminate or minimize the impact of the given barrier. This problem-solution approach is meant to help to focus our attention on the root of the problem and begin using some practical strategies that will help better serve and provide opportunities for children with disabilities to help them "get into the game".

Keywords

Disability, youth sports, children with disabilities, disability sport, sport participation, barriers, community based sports, training, parents, coaches

SUGGESTED CITATION:

For many parents and children, Saturdays are set aside for youth soccer, baseball, football, and other youth sports. Children as young as 5-years-old proudly show off their team uniforms around the community, and new friendships between players often lead to pick-up-games in the backyard, parties, and team sleep overs. For many children the best part of the week is practice with their friends, and the best part of the weekend is getting into their uniform and competing with their teammates. For many parents, nothing is more exciting and nerve-racking than watching their child play in a game.

Research supports positive effects of youth sports on young athletes. Seefeldt, Ewing, and Walk (1992) summarized much of the research finding several benefits associated with participation in youth sports including: (a) improved sports skills such as learning how to correctly kick a soccer ball, throw a baseball, or dribble a basketball (The Tucker Center for Research on Girls & Women in Sport, 2007); (b) improved physical fitness including a greater understanding of and interest in getting into and staying in shape (Ewing & Seefeldt; 1989; US Department of Health and Human Services, 2008); (c) improved self-esteem and self-confidence (see Malina & Cumming, 2003, for a review); (d) making new friends and having a sense of belonging (see Weiss & Stuntz, 2004, for a review), (e) moral development including concepts such as fair play and sportsmanship (e.g., Bredemeier, Weiss, Shields, & Shewchuk, 1986; Gibbins, Ebbeck, & Weiss, 1995), and (f) learning how to manage one's time, how to set goals, and how stay in control (Dworkin, Larson, & Hansen, 2003).

Positive effects of participation in youth sports can be as powerful for children with disabilities as it is for children without disabilities. Unfortunately, many children with disabilities, particularly children with more significant disabilities such as physical, visual or intellectual disabilities or autism are excluded from participation in youth sports. In some cases leaders of sports programs may be concerned with the liability of having a child with a disability participate in and perhaps get hurt during a practice or game. In other cases coaches may not want a child with a disability on their team, because they feel that they lack the training in how to coach players with disabilities. In still other cases parents of children with disabilities (and children themselves) may be reluctant to sign up for youth sports fearing injury, lack of success, or being teased by peers. Finally, there may be limited sports programs (regular or special sports programs) available to serve the wide range of types and severities of disabilities. Exclusion from youth sports programs is unfortunate as the Americans with Disabilities Act (ADA) specifically forbids public and private programs (including community youth sports programs) from excluding individuals with disabilities from such programs solely on the basis of their disability (Appenzeller, 2005; Block, 1995; Stein, 2005). In addition, most youth sports programs can be adapted to accommodate the needs of children with significant disabilities through universal design (Lieberman & Houston-Wilson, 2009) and game modifications (Block, 2007; Kasser & Lytle, 2005; Lieberman & Houston-Wilson, 2009). In fact, research shows youth sports programs can be accommodated to include children with disabilities (Bernabe & Block, 1994; Nixon, 1989), and youth sports coaches are generally willing to include children with disabilities on their teams (Block & Malloy, 1999; Rizzo, Bishop, & Silva, 1999; Rizzo, Bishop, & Tobar, 1997) Regrettably, despite laws and research there continue to be many barriers that prevent youth with significant disabilities from participating in youth sports. The purpose of this article is to review some of these more common barriers to participation of children with significant disabilities in youth sports with suggestions for how to overcome these barriers.

Barrier #1: Leader of Programs Fear Liability/Do not know how to Accommodate

Problem

Perhaps the greatest barrier to the participation of children with disabilities in youth sports is the fear of liability by program leaders (Appenzeller, 2000). League administrators have two fears. First, they fear a player with a disability will get hurt and then the child's parents will sue the league. Second, they fear an athlete's adapted equipment (e.g., walker or artificial arm), would injure another player. As a result, league administrators do what they feel is the most prudent and safest thing by not allowing athletes with certain types of disabilities to participate. For example, a Ryan Taylor, 9-year-old boy with cerebral palsy who used a walker to aid his walking, was barred from playing youth soccer in his community league in Oklahoma. The commissioner of the league said Ryan's steel walker was a hazard to others, even though the walker was padded with foam and red duct tape. Ryan's parents noted the steel goalposts were more dangerous than their child's walker, and his parents eventually took the league to court to force the league to let Ryan play. The U.S. District judge agreed with the parents finding it very unlikely another player would get injured from the walker. As a result, the child was allowed to finish the season with his team (Boyd, 1999).

Solution

As in many cases where people with disabilities are summarily dismissed from participation, education is the key to changing league administrators' preconceived opinions and attitudes. Parents of a child with a disability are the best advocates for their child, and they can begin the education process with league officials. For example, Ryan's parents did try and explain to the league president how they could pad Ryan's walker to prevent others from injury (although in this case it did not work). They also could explain some simple modifications that could be implemented to allow Ryan and those around him to play safely without negatively affecting the game for peers. For example, Ryan's dad (or an extra teammate) could be on the field with Ryan to prevent other players from bumping into Ryan. Another idea is marking off a small area with cones where only Ryan could retrieve and kick the ball. Both strategies are very practical and require very little effort on the part of the league or the coach. These strategies allow Ryan to be fully included with minor modifications to the game.

Another way to educate administrators about modifications is trying out some modifications during a practice session in front of league administrators and even opposing coaches. Administrators and officials can watch the practice game with the modifications and have a better idea of the effect the modification has on the safety and flow of the game. Administrators and coaches can also "tweak" modifications and create their own modifications. By participating in the process, administrators and coaches will be more likely accept modifications. For example, Bernabe and Block (1994) included a 12-year-old girl with an intellectual disability and motor delays into a regular, fast pitch softball league. The authors went to a coaches meeting explaining the girls abilities and disabilities. They then lead a discussion with coaches and league administrators on possible modifications that would allow this girl to be successful and safe without negatively affecting the game for her teammates and other teams. The group came up with modifications including allowing the girl to hit a ball off a tee, running to a shorter first base, and then getting a pinch runner if she did make it first base. The girl was successfully included throughout the season, and no one complained about her participation. At the end of each season coaches and administrators get together to discuss any potential rule changes or safety concerns that need to be addressed to ensure safe participation for all participants for the upcoming year. We acknowledge that many of the coaches already give an enormous amount of their time and energy to coach their team and very few have time to deal with the increased demands of including a child with an intellectual disability on their team. An issue like the one described above could easily be addressed at this annual meeting and would allow coaches and administrators to be proactive in their approach. Parents could be encouraged to attend the meeting and use this platform to discuss issues with the league and assist the league in coming up with a plan that is functional and practical given the resources of the coach/league. This proactive approach increases the likelihood their child would be able to participate successfully and minimize the effort, in terms of developing appropriate strategies that would need to be put forth by the coach during the actual season.

Barrier #2: Coaches – Lack of Knowledge and Training

Problem

Gary is a volunteer little league coach who is excited about coaching his son and teaching young children how to play the game of baseball. Gary shows up on the first day of practice and sees Joey, a boy with Osteogenesis Imperfecta (brittle bone disease) rolling onto the field in his wheelchair. Coach Gary begins to panic and ask himself the following questions: "How in the world do I coach this child?" "What happens if he gets hit with the ball or gets hurt?" "Will this boy be able to learn like the other children?" Unfortunately Coach Gary is not alone, these are questions that many youth coaches are asking when a child with a disability wishes to play on their team. The coach enters the fear of the "unknown".

Many coaches agree that children with disabilities deserve "the right to participate" (Kozub & Porretta, 1998). The problem becomes that many youth coaches lack the knowledge and the training to appropriately meet the needs of children with disabilities. Many youth coaches have never received any formal training on disabilities or special education, let alone how to meet their needs. Rizzo et al. (1997) conducted a study on the attitudes of youth soccer coaches towards children with intellectual disabilities. The results of the study indicated that as coaches' perceived competence increased, there willingness to coach players with intellectual disabilities increased. Those that were less competent in their ability were less willing, again supporting the coach's fears of entering the "unknown". Many youth coaches are wonderful volunteers who are willing to give of their time but their coaching and teaching experience does not go beyond their experiences as a high school athlete, let alone trying to help a child with a given disability learn and successful.

Solution

Coaches should never feel like they are alone. Whether the coach needs assistance in developing more drills for their players at practice or needs advice on how to meet the needs of a child with a physical disability, every community has resources that would help all youth coaches feel more competent in their ability to work with a child with a disability. The problem is most organizations do not know where to go to find the support or resources. One practical solution for all youth organizations would be to establish a relationship with the local schools. Every school district has a special education teacher/coordinator that in most cases would be more than happy to provide their services or expertise to the coach, especially if they would know that it was benefitting their student. The special education teacher can work with the league and/or individual coach to identify practical strategies that will work for the specific student. The teacher can share the strategies they are using in school. In addition, the teacher may be able to willing to come and assist the child during the practices/games or potentially find a cross age peer tutor within the school that would like to get community service hours and assist the child. Communities may also have disability support groups or advocacy groups that would also be able to provide the coach with helpful resources. Most communities have a local ARC, who has staff or volunteers that may be willing to share their expertise and/or time to ensure that their clients are successful. Some communities have regional centers that employ disability specialists. For example, in Harrisonburg, VA there is an organization called the Training and Technical Assistance Center (TTAC). TTAC contracts with specialists in many different types of disabilities and provides services for educators, parents, etc. who have issues or are struggling to meet the needs of children with disabilities.

Another strategy would be to provide a clinic for coaches on how to meet needs of diverse learners. Many youth sports organizations provide clinics for their coaches at the beginning of the year to provide them with new ideas, activities, or strategies to use when they are coaching their players. A disability specialist or, if available, an adapted physical educator from the area could conduct a clinic and discuss some of the most common disabilities and provide appropriate strategies to meet their needs. Special Olympics often provides training for their coaches at local and state levels, and they would be happy to include regular youth sports coaches into their training programs. The way I would sell the thought of the training to the league is that this specialized training will not only help the one or two children with physical or intellectual disabilities who are enrolled in the league, but it will also help the coach deal with the child who appears to be a bit delayed in their motor skill development or the child that appears to have some minor processing delays or even the child that has major behavior or anger issues.

This training will help the league deliver a program of universal design where every child can grow, develop, and be successful.

Finally, a strategy to help coaches is to find additional volunteers to assist the child with a disability during practices and games. Coaching youth sports and managing a group of 15-20 players at one time can be challenging for one adult – even if there are not children with disabilities on the team. It would not be fair or appropriate for coaches to focus all their effort, attention, and energy on assisting one child with a disability, so extra help is clearly warranted. Securing volunteers is not as difficult as coaches might think. Parents or siblings of players often come and watch practices, and these parents or siblings can be recruited to provide support for the child with a disability. Outside of the team there are many community organizations that require their members to complete a given number of community service hours (Boy Scouts, Key Club, Kiwanis, etc), and many school districts now require community services hours as part of the assist your player with a disability during practices or games. By utilizing and maximizing all these resources coaches would no longer feel like they are entering the "unknown" and they will be able to work with any player, regardless of their ability or disability.

Many students who jump at this community service opportunity as they are able to see their clear purpose. This becomes quite an important leadership role as the individual realizes that the child with autism or child with cerebral palsy would not be able to participate if I did not help them.

Barrier #3: Parent and Child Fears

Problem

Bob is the father of Angie, a girl with autism. When Angie gets excited she begins flapping her arms and jumping up and down. Bob is very concerned about what other parents or players will think or how they will react when Angie begins "stimming" when she hits the ball or begins talking to herself on the volleyball court. Robbie, young boy with seizure disorders, refuses to sign up for youth basketball. Even though basketball is his favorite sport in physical education and he comes down to see Mr. McMahon (the physical educator) every day at lunchtime to shoot hoops, Robbie is so afraid of having a seizure in the middle of a practice or game and being teased by peers. Unfortunately, Robbie's answer is to not play anything, even though the thing he wants most is to play sports and be part of a "team." Just as coaches have their fear about meeting the needs of children with disabilities, children and their parents experience fears of their own when it comes to community based sports. Often parents refuse to enroll their child with a disability in community sports programs due to these fears. Parents fear for their child's safety as they are concerned that their child may get hurt or harm others. What if my child gets run over by other children while running down the basketball court or happens to accidently trip someone while running with his crutches down the soccer field? In addition, both parents as well as children with disabilities anticipate the child will not be successful in community based sports. Both parties predict that child will experience far more failure and frustration than success. As a result, a safe response becomes not to participate at all. Finally, parents are afraid of their child with a disability being ridiculed and teased by teammates or members of another team. Children are also very apprehensive of what others think or say about them. No one likes to be ridiculed or compared to others as it becomes very detrimental to their self-esteem as well as their perceived competence. As a result of these reactions parents are faced with the tough decision of *do I not let them to participate to protect them even though I want them to "belong"* or *do I take a chance and potentially subject them to negative experiences?*

Parents feel as though they are in a "No Win" situation.

Solution

One strategy is to have youth coaches talk specifically about the player with a disability who will be on the team focusing on both the child's disability but also his abilities. To begin a conversation the coach can begin by introducing the player with a disability – "Boys, we have a new player this year named Jamal, and Jamal has a disability known as Down syndrome." The coach (or perhaps Jamal's parents) can then provide brief explanation of Down syndrome and some of the specific characteristic of Down syndrome as it relates to playing the sport. For example, the coach might talk about how Jamal has a difficult time understanding directions and what exactly to do, so players can help Jamal if he seems confused. Besides the discussion on the child's differences, it is important to talk to teammates about how similar Jamal is to them. For example, Jamal's favorite baseball team is the Baltimore Orioles (the little league baseball team is in Maryland), and most of the other players on the team love the Orioles too. Jamal also loves to eat pizza and hates doing his homework, and his teammates nod their heads in agreement when the coach explains this to them.

The coach can extend this discussion by asking his players to think of at least one way everyone on the team is similar (e.g., we all love baseball, we all live in Maryland). Now think of one way we are all different, e.g., each child has slightly different hair color, each player has a different height and weight compared to teammates). Once the players respond the coach explains that each player has different strengths (abilities) and different weaknesses (disabilities) but together we work as a "team" and we use our strengths to collectively overcome or minimize our weaknesses. By shifting the focus away from what Jamal is not able to do and what he struggles with and placing the focus on what he is able to do, the coach can help the players accept each other. Players quickly realize everyone has a unique and important role on the team.

Research shows with such discussion teammates without disabilities will accept a player with a disability onto their team (Block & Malloy, 1998). For example, Mike, a youth wrestling coach in Central Virginia, had this type of discussion with his wrestlers about a teammate named Jay who was a double, above the knee amputee. The coach found that the discussion about Jay and his abilities and disabilities quickly eliminated any issues or negativity toward Jay. What Mike found out later was even more amazing; Mike learned his wrestlers went home and talked about Jay with their parents. These teammates were very actually proud to have Jay on their team, and the excitedly explained to their parents how Jay was able to wrestle. There was even one instance where the team was at a tournament and a spectator from another team yells out, "hey look at that funny kid without any legs!" Mike explained that one of his wrestlers went up in the stands and said to the fan, "His name is Jay and he is my teammate. He is one of the strongest and hardest working people you will ever meet!"

Another strategy is for the coach to talk directly with the parent of the child with a disability. The coach can even admit that they have never worked with a child with a disability and have no formal training. If the parents realize the coach is willing to learn and do whatever he can to help the child, parents will provide any and all information to the coach to help their child be successful. Many parents are true advocates for their child and will do whatever it takes to help their child be successful. By the coach admitting their limitations and asking for help the parent is able to use their resources or "go to bat" for their child and get them whatever support the coach may need so their child can participate. Most parents simply want their child to be a contributing part of the team and have fun like the rest of the players. The parents can also offer any resources and/or suggestions they may have which will help the coach meet the needs of their child. The reality is coaches should have this same talk with all of their players' parents as every child learns differently, has different abilities, and comes from different backgrounds. Once again, this proactive approach will allow the coach to be more effective in helping each member of his/her team grow and develop into the player they want to become.

Finally, it is very important for all community sports organizations to have a statement on all their programming and marketing materials indicating that they encourage participation of children with disabilities. Often, parents receive a flyer about little league or summer soccer and really wish their child could sign up, but they do not think their child is welcome. A simple statement added to the flyer such as the following can calm the fears of the parents: "Children of all abilities/disabilities are encouraged to sign up – appropriate accommodations will be made to ensure everyone can play and will be successful." Such a statement is very inviting and can help parents overcome some of their fears.

Barrier #4: Lack of Appropriate Programs

Problem

A final barrier to participation of children with disabilities in youth sports is availability of appropriate programs. Availability of program includes regular youth sports programs that offer recreational levels as well as special programs such as Special Olympics and other special sports programs. This is particularly problematic in rural and inner city communities where funding, facilities, and experienced coaches are limited (Kleinert, Miracle, & Sheppard-Jones, 2007).. For example, the suburbs surrounding Washington, DC, offer a variety of levels of regular sports programs from recreation programs for beginners and those more interested in having fun to travel programs for very skilled athletes interested in competing at the highest level. In addition, these suburban communities offer a variety of special sports programs in including an extensive Special Olympics program, Challenger Baseball (Little League Baseball for children with disabilities), and community-run therapeutic recreation programs that offer special recreation and sports programs. On the other hand, an hour or so away in rural Virginia and Maryland there are fewer (if any) introductory sports programs and few (if any) special sports programs. Similarly, the city of Washington, DC, is limited in outdoor playing fields to offer the variety of sports available in the suburbs such as soccer, lacrosse, baseball, and softball.

Even when recreation programs are available, they may only be available for younger athletes. As children get older there tends to be a drop off in recreational programs. Teenagers who are not playing for their high school teams often have competing interests (after school jobs, more homework, other interests), and as a result there are fewer recreation division for in youth sports programs for teens. For example, the Soccer Organization of Charlottesville and Albemarle (SOCA) has trouble every year fielding a girls' 16-year-old and 18-year-old recreation division. As a result SOCA often combines the 16 and 18-year-olds, and in some years they have to combine 14-year-old into the mix as well because of a limited number of recreation athletes. Even when combining these three age groups SOCA may only field 4 or 5 teams. In other cases (e.g., baseball, basketball, and lacrosse) communities may simply eliminate the older recreation age divisions focusing solely on competitive programs for more skilled athletes. Unfortunately, teens with disabilities often will not have the skill level to play on these competitive teams.

Solution

It is difficult for small rural communities and inner city communities to offer an array regular and special youth sports programs. One solution is to combine resources with other communities. For example, within a 45 minute radius five rural communities can join together to offer a Saturday morning Challenger Baseball Program. While there are not enough athletes with disabilities or qualified coaches to run a program in any one community, the combination of the 5 communities leads to the creation of 4 teams that rotate to play each other each Saturday. Special Olympics follows this model by combining several communities into one "area." For example, Area 3 Special Olympics in Virginia encompasses the city of Charlottesville and the counties of Albemarle, Greene, Louisa, and Fluvanna.

A similar solution is possible for regular recreation sports programs. Again, combining multiple community programs into one large recreation program might solve the problem.

Recreation teams could be created my community, but then they play recreation games against other communities. In essence the program is a travel team but at a recreation level. This way less skill players and players more interested in participating for fun could have a place to play.

Another possible solution is allowing older players with disabilities (who are less skilled) to play at a younger age level. As noted above, there is a greater likelihood of recreation programs available at younger ages, and it is more likely that an athlete's (with a disability) skill level and understand of the game will match younger recreation-level players. This type of accommodation would not be appropriate when an athlete with a disability has an unfair advantage due to size, strength, and/or speed or when the athlete's size poses a safety risk for other players. In addition, it would not be appropriate to have a 14-year-old play on a team with 8-10 year olds. However, in most cases a parent of a child with a disability makes a request to waive the age rule by a few years, because they know their child cannot compete physically or cognitively with same-age peers. For example, a child with Asperger's Syndrome – a high functioning form of autism – requested their 15-year-old daughter (who would have to play in a 16-year-old division) play in the 12-year-old division. The child was slightly built, very unskilled (she had not played soccer since she was 8-yers-old and just on a whim decided she wanted to play again), and had a very short attention span. Still, she wanted to try to play again (her younger sisters played soccer). The league allowed this girl to play at the younger division, and even though she was still the least skilled player on the team and perhaps in the league, she was able to play and have fun.

One final approach that would allow communities to meet the needs of all individuals in the area would be for youth sports organizations to combine their efforts and find a way to offer two participatory options: a competitive, more advanced league and a recreational, less advanced league. Each league could be considered inclusive, but it would allow appropriate accessibility by all members of the youth sports community. Any child who is more advanced in their skill development and understanding of the game should enroll in the competitive league as it would be considered that child's least restrictive environment and provide the best opportunity for success as well as growth/development. On the other hand, a child who wants to play on a team but not in a competitive environment should have the opportunity to enroll in the recreational/intramural league. This parallel-program model is perfect for children with and without disabilities who do not have the sport/physical skills or understanding of the game to be successful in the more competitive, regulation program. This recreational/intramural league also would be more flexible allowing modified equipment and rules to promote success for all athletes. Given this approach we remove the barrier of "disability" versus "non-disabled" and allow parents and children to choose a program that is most appropriate given their individual strengths and weaknesses.

Final Thoughts

Participation in youth sports offers so many benefits, and every child should have the opportunity to participate in youth sports at least once in their life. Participation in youth sports is just as important to children with disabilities as it is to children without disabilities. In some cases opportunities to participate in regular youth sports might be more important to children with disabilities who attend special classes and special schools and have limited interactions with peers without disabilities (Maryland Disability Law Center, 2009). Unfortunately, opportunities for participation in youth sports are often limited due to various social and environmental barriers. The purpose of this paper was to present these barriers along with viable solutions to these barriers so more children with disabilities can successful participate in and enjoy all the benefits of youth sports. Key strategies presented included educating and preparing league administrators as well as coaches and teammates, focusing on ability and accommodations rather than disability and obstacles, and helping communities provide new youth sports opportunities. By helping coaches and leagues understand and appreciate the uniqueness of each player we are able to create positive youth sports opportunities and successful participation for all. Practice and game days will be exciting as everyone is overcome their barriers and "get on the field". .

References

Appenzeller, T. (2005). Youth sports and the law. In H. Appenzeller (Ed.), *Risk management in sport: Issues and strategies* (2nd ed., pp. 131-142). Durham, NC: Carolina Academic Press.

Appenzeller, T. (2000). *Youth sports and the law: A guide to legal issues.* Durham, NC: Carolina Academic Press.

Bernabe, E.A., & Block, M.E. (1994). Modifying rules of a regular girls= softball league to facilitate the inclusion of a child with severe disabilities. *Journal of The Association for Persons with Severe Handicaps, 19*, 24-31.

Block, M.E. (2007). A teacher's guide to including students with disabilities in general physical education (3rd. ed.) Baltimore: Paul H. Brookes.

Block, M.E. (1995). Impact of the Americans with Disabilities Act (ADA) on Youth Sports. *Journal of Physical Education, Recreation, and Dance, 66*(1), 28-32.

Block, M.E., & Malloy, M. (1998). Attitudes of girls towards including a child with severe disabilities in a regular fast-pitch softball league. *Mental Retardation, 36*, 137-144.

Block, M.E., Zeman, R., and Henning, G.(1997). Pass the ball to Jimmy: A success story in integrated physical education. *Palaestra, 13*(3) 37-42.

Boyd, D. (1999, Nov. 14). With court assist, disabled boy gets kick out of soccer. *The Topeka Capital Journal.* Retrieved November 3, 2008, from http://findarticles.com/p/articles/mi_qn4 179/ is_19991114/ai_n11735274

Dworkin, J. B., Larson, R., & Hansen, D. (2003). Adolescents' accounts of growth experiences in youth activities. *Journal of Youth and Adolescence, 32 (1),* 17-26.

Bredemeier, B., Weiss, M.R., Shields, D.L., Shewchuk, R.M. (1986). Promoting growth in a summer sports camp: The implementation of theoretically grounded instructional strategies. *Journal of Moral Education, 15,* 212-220.

Ewing, M.E., & Seefeldt, V. (1989*). Participation and attrition patterns in American agency-sponsored and interscholastic sports: An executive summary.* Final Report.

Gibbins, S.L., Ebbeck, V., & Weiss, M.R. (1995). Fair play for kids: Effects on the moral development of children in physical education. *Research Quarterly for Exercise & Sport,* 66, 247-255.

Kasser, S.L., & Lytle, R. K. (2005). *Inclusive physical activity.* Champaign, IL: Human Kinetics.

Kleinert, H.L., Miracle, S.A., & Sheppard-Jones, K. (2007). Including students with moderate and severe disabilities in extracurricular and community recreation activities. *TEACHING Exceptional Children, 39*(6). 33-38.

Lieberman, L.J., & Houston-Wilson, C. (2009). Strategies for Inclusion: A handbook for physical educators (2nd ed.). Champaign, IL: Human Kinetics.

Malina, R.M., & Cumming, S.P. (2003). Current status and issues in youth sports. In 12

R.M. Malina & M.A. Clark (Eds.), *Youth sports: Perspectives for a new century.* (pp. 7-25). Monterey, CA: Coaches Choice.

Maryland Disability Law Center (2009). *Maryland Fitness and Athletic Equity Law for Students with Disabilities.* Retrieved from http://wwwlmdlclaw.org/chemicalcms/students_in_sports_q__a.php.

Nixon, H.L. (1989). Integration of disabled people in mainstream sports: Case study of a partially sighted child. *Adapted Physical Activity Quarterly,* 6, 17-31.

Rizzo, T.L., Bishop, P., & Silva, M. (1999). Attitudes of youth *baseball* coaches toward players with mild mental retardation. *Palaestra, 15*(3), 22-28.

Rizzo, T.L., Bishop, P., & Tobar, D. (1997). Attitudes of soccer coaches toward youth players with mild mental retardation: A pilot study. *Adapted Physical Activity Quarterly, 14*, 238-251.

Seefeldt, V., Ewing, M., & Walk, S. (1992). *Overview of youth sports programs in the United States.* Washington, DC: Carnegie Council on Adolescent Development.

Stein, J. (2005). Accommodating individuals with disabilities in regular sport programs. In H. Appenzeller (Ed.), *Risk management in sport: Issues and strategies* (2nd ed., pp. 389-398). Durham, NC: Carolina Academic Press.

The Tucker Center for Research on Girls & Women in Sport (2007). *Executive Summary. The 2007 Tucker Center Research Report, Developing physically active girls: An evidence-based multidisciplinaryapproach.* University of Minnesota, Minneapolis, MN.

U.S. Department of Health and Human Services (2008). *Physical Activity Guidelines for Americans.* Retrieved November 3, 2008, from http://www.health.gov/PAguidelines/guidelines/chapter2.aspx

Weiss, M.R., & Stuntz, C.P. (2004). A little friendly competition: Peer relationships and psychosocial development in youth sports and physical activity contexts. In M.R. Weiss (Ed.), *Developmental sport and exercise psychology: A lifespan perspective* (pp. 165-196). Morgantown, WV: Fitness Information Technology, Inc.

Notes

[1] John Piper. *www.desiringgod.org* (2007).

[2] Howard, D. M., Jr. (2001, c1998). *Vol. 5: Joshua* (electronic ed.). Logos Library System; The New American Commentary (86). Nashville: Broadman & Holman Publishers.

[3] Andy Naselli, "Three Tips for Better Bible Reading," *Desiring God*, 1/24/2014, Accessed 7/20/2014. http://www.desiringgod.org/blog/posts/three-tips-for-better-bible-reading.

Made in the USA
San Bernardino, CA
03 February 2017